ROMAN WOMEN

ROMAN WOMEN

Edited and with a New Introduction by

AUGUSTO FRASCHETTI

Translated by

LINDA LAPPIN

The University of Chicago Press
Chicago & London

AUGUSTO FRASCHETTI is professor of Roman administrative history at the University of Rome "La Sapienza." He has been director of associated studies at the École Pratique des Hautes Études in Paris. Professor Fraschetti is the author of *Rome and the Prince* (Laterza, 1990).

LINDA LAPPIN has translated more than a dozen volumes from the Italian for American university presses, including *Public Lettering: Script, Power, and Culture,* by Armando Petrucci, published by the University of Chicago Press in 1993.

The University of Chicago Press, Chicago 60637
The University of Chicago Press, Ltd., London
© 2001 by The University of Chicago
All rights reserved. Published 2001
09 08 07 06 05 04 03 02 01   1 2 3 4 5

ISBN: 0-226-26093-3 (cloth)
0-226-26094-1 (paper)

Originally published as *Roma al femminile,*
© 1994 Gius. Laterza & Figli Spa, Roma-Bari.

English language edition arranged through the
mediation of Eulama Literary Agency.

Library of Congress Cataloging-in-Publication Data

Roma al femminile. English.
    Roman women / edited and with a new introd. by Augusto
Fraschetti ; translated by Linda Lappin.
        p.   cm.
    Translation of: Roma al femminile.
    Includes bibliographical references (p.   ) and index.
    ISBN 0-226-26093-3 (cloth : alk. paper). — ISBN 0-226-26094-1 (pbk. :
alk. paper)
    1. Women—Rome—Biography.   2. Women—Rome—History.
3. Women—Biography—To 500.   4. Women—History—To 500.
HQ1136.R6613   2001
305.4'094563—dc21   98-47278
                                                               CIP

⊗ The paper used in this publication meets the minimum requirements
of the American National Standard for Information Sciences—
Permanence of Paper for Printed Library Materials,
ANSI Z39.48-1992.

CONTENTS

ACKNOWLEDGMENTS

The translator would like to thank the Università della Tuscia in Viterbo, Italy, and the American Academy in Rome for the resources they made available during the preparation of this translation. Special thanks also to Karen Wilson, Bruce Young, and Paige Kennedy-Piehl for their help in seeing the project through.

Introduction

Augusto Fraschetti

Women and Silence

If only it were possible to describe in detail the life of an ordinary Roman woman, one of those women whose names appear so often in funerary inscriptions! The biography of such a woman would give us a concrete idea of the general conditions in which women lived in ancient Rome. Unfortunately, such a biography would be quite impossible to reconstruct in any detail from beginning to end. By examining the life of a country woman, a *vilica,* the wife of the head of country slaves (*vilicus*), we may see why. The *vilica* collaborated with her husband in running the affairs of the farm, whose owner was often absent. From funerary inscriptions, we know the names of some of these women: Statia, who lived in Rome and was known by her masters as *vilica nostra;* Staccia Flora from Brindisi in Italy; Cania Urbania, from Salon in Dalmatia, who died at the age of fifty-five. Nearly always slaves, or at best, freed slaves, the *vilicae* were chosen by their masters and married without their consent to the *vilici,* who were also slaves.[1]

In their treatises on agriculture, Cato, in the first half of the second century B.C., and later Columella, in the time of Nero, described in detail the duties performed by a *vilica* during her heavy work day.[2] A typical farmer's wife spent her time almost exclusively on the farmhouse premises, while her husband kept watch over the slaves at work in the fields. In the farmhouse, the *vilica* kept the food supplies in order and saw to how they were distributed. She was in charge of the household slaves who performed such indoor tasks as the spinning of wool. She tended sick slaves—who could not be neglected because they were also the master's property. She was required to perform sacrifices to the *Lar,* the family god, but only on special days. For the rest of the time she was to refrain from making sacrifices, as it was the master of the household, the *dominus* who, when present, personally took care of all aspects of his household's religious life.

The details given here will allow us to list the activities of a day, but not to plot the course of an entire life. If, in writing the essays in this volume, we have found it difficult to reconstruct the biographies even of famous women (a noble republican matron, wife and mother of magistrates; a successful actress; a Christian saint; an intellectual who lived in the declining phase of paganism, and other women belonging to the imperial family), how can we hope to describe in detail the life of an ordinary woman from birth to death, whether a free woman, a freed slave, or a slave? We lack the documentation needed for such a task, for the Romans saw no point in recording the lives of women, because no one would be interested in reading about them. Every woman's life was surrounded by a thick silence imposed upon her by the outer world and by the woman herself. It was considered unseemly for outsiders to praise a woman's virtues, for her talents and abilities could find expression only within her home. No one but her closest relatives could know anything of her merits, and the members of her family were the only persons permitted to speak of her to others.

This was true of a certain noble matron, name unknown, whose husband, after her death, composed an extremely long eulogy, which has survived. During the civil wars following Caesar's assassination, this woman saved her husband's life after he had been proscribed by the triumvirs and was therefore destined to certain death. In this terrible emergency, she helped him escape from Rome and sacrificed her pearls and jewels to provide him with money. In his absence, she administered his property wisely. She suggested that he divorce her, as she had remained childless at his return, and take another wife who could bear him children. She also proposed that she continue to live in his house, tending the children of his new wife as if they were her own, while assuming toward him an attitude befitting a sister or a mother-in-law.

Many centuries later, the pagan senator Vettius Agorius Praetextatus praised his wife, Aconia Fabia Paulina, for similar reasons in an inscription commemorating her chastity and modesty. By then the empire had been Christianized, and Aconia Fabia Paulina's husband wished to stress not only her traditionally private virtues, but her firm faith in the gods of paganism, the faith that had led her to Greece, where she had been initiated into the mysteries of Ceres and Hecate, and to Rome, where she had been initiated into the mysteries of Mithra. The virtues of chastity, thrift, modesty, and steadfast faith were also underlined in some Christian epitaphs commemorating wives and mothers, but among those inscriptions we will find nothing resembling the long eulogy written by the unknown matron's husband in the times of Augustus, or Vettius Agorius Praetextatus's praises for his wife.[3]

These are examples of men praising the virtues of ordinary women in their families, thus allowing the world to know about them. Other women became famous because they were celebrated by their lovers— historians or poets who dedicated elegies to them. Yet, such praise was always uttered by men, and these male voices act as a dense filter certainly constraining any inquiry into the position of women in ancient Rome. The cases we have mentioned of women celebrated by their husbands—the unknown matron and Aconia Fabia Paulina—are rare. No similar examples are to be found in the readily available sources. The example we have chosen, the life of the *vilica*, illustrates how difficult it is to reconstruct a woman's life in detail.

The writers of agricultural treatises tell us clearly that these women led very hard lives, lives in which inferiority of class was joined to inferiority of gender. Using this consideration as our starting point, we could go on to study various categories of women according to their place in the social hierarchy—a free woman, a freed slave, a slave. Such an approach, however, would give us only very sketchy and stereotyped portraits, void of nuances, owing to the thinness of the existing documentation. These documents say little about women or about their social condition. In order to give a clearer picture, before introducing the individual profiles of women presented in this collection of essays, we will describe the female condition by following a Roman woman throughout the various stages of her existence, underlining the factors that determined her status in each phase of her life. We will be able to understand that status better by examining the laws presiding over her existence first as a daughter, then as a wife, and finally as a mother.

Always under the Rule of Men

The Romans believed that all women, whatever their age or status, were characterized by certain traits: a feeble intellect, weakness of character, and overall, a general incapacity innate in the female sex.[4] These weaknesses, *propter sexus infirmitatem,* indisputable and universally recognized, formed the basis of all relationships (including juridical ones) that every freeborn Roman woman established with the outer world. When a son was born, it was customary for the father to take the infant in his arms and lift it from the ground, as a sign of acceptance and recognition, but at the birth of a daughter, the father merely gave orders that the child should be fed, and not left to die of exposure, which was both lawful and possible. The possibility that some families may have allowed their infant daughters to die of exposure (just how frequently this really occurred is a matter of debate) must be considered in relationship to the social status of those families. The urban lower classes probably resorted to this practice often, as did peasant families in the countryside, where daughters could contribute little to the work in the fields. It was different for families belonging to the noble class, for their daughters could become tools of very profitable and astute marriage strategies.[5]

From the moment of her birth, a daughter was under her father's absolute authority and uncontested rule. Sons were also subject to the *patria potestas.* Not only were a man's wife and children under his control as the *paterfamilias,* but also his grandchildren—and their submission to his authority ended only when he died.[6] Patriarchal power determined all relationships within the family and was the hub around which Roman society was organized. Thus a woman's life was doubly conditioned by it. She was raised at home to be a good wife and received an education appropriate to this role. She learned how to perform household chores, such as the spinning of wool. More rarely, even in the upper classes, she might receive a liberal education, a privilege generally enjoyed only by sons destined for political careers, and trained, primarily through the study of rhetoric, to become skilled public speakers.[7]

A daughter did not stay long in her father's home. Between the ages of twelve and fourteen, she married, passing from the power (*potestas*) of one man, her father, to the hand (*manus*) of another, her husband. If the marriage occurred *cum manu,* her husband gained full authority over her. If he died, she became the ward of his closest relative on his father's side. If the marriage occurred *sine manu,* she remained under her father's control, even though her status had changed from *puella* to *uxor.* Her new status as a matron did not legally change her dependence on her own family. When the father of a woman married *sine manu* died, she could become autonomous, *sui iuris,* under no one's *potestas* or *manus.* But in such case she needed a guardian, who was chosen from among the members of her father's family, or named by a judge.[8]

The type of marriage (*cum manu* or *sine manu*) was determined by questions of patrimony. Generally, the issues of preserving and transmitting patrimony underlie the logic and functioning of the Roman family, and within this logic women also played a role. Unlike the women of ancient Greece, Roman women could inherit and bequeath their patrimony to their children or to other heirs, and were allowed (although under guardianship) to manage their own finances and property. A woman's patrimony consisted chiefly of her dowry, which she received upon marriage. In the upper classes, this could be a sizable amount. Terentia brought Cicero a dowry of four hundred thousand sesterces, corresponding to the basic census of a knight in the *equites* order. If a woman divorced, her dowry, usually entrusted to her husband's management, was returned to her. This caused Cicero serious financial problems when he divorced Terentia.[9]

At all social levels, the basic purpose of marriage was procreation. People married to "procure children for themselves" (*liberorum quaerendorum causa*): in the lower classes, to increase the work force; in the noble classes, to ensure numerous descendants. In this, the woman's role was indispensable. A matron's reputation depended not only on her modest and strict manner but also on the number of children she had. When women failed to bear children, their husbands often divorced them.

This demand for offspring could lead to paradoxical situations. A man who had no children might try to convince a close friend to divorce his fertile wife so that he could marry her and have children. Plutarch refers to this practice, which he considered typically Roman and quite peculiar, while discussing the marriage of Cato Uticensis.[10]

He married Marcia, daughter of Philippus, considered an honest woman. . . . Among Cato's many admirers, a few particularly distinguished men stood out, such as Quintus Hortensius, a highly respected man of noble character. Hortensius wanted not only to be Cato's intimate friend, but also to unite their families and their future descendants. He tried to persuade Cato to let him marry Cato's daughter Porcia (who was already married to Bibulus and who had given him two children). [Porcia was described] as a fair plot of land where he [Hortensius] might sow a new line of descendants. Some people might find this strange, but it was beautiful and politically wise that this woman at her peak should not have to remain idle and barren. [By marrying Hortensius] Porcia would spare Bibulus, who already had enough children, the ruinous financial burden of adding any more to his household. She would perform a virtuous act and by uniting herself from time to time with deserving men, virtue would be spread down through the ranks of her descendants. Through these ties of kinship the whole city would be knit into a single body. If Bibulus was determined to keep Porcia, Hortensius gladly offered to give her back once she had produced offspring. In this way, Hortensius hoped to strengthen his ties with both Bibulus and Cato by having children by the same woman. Cato replied that he loved Hortensius and appreciated the idea of their becoming relatives, but found it strange that Hortensius should talk of marrying his daughter, who was already married to someone else. Hortensius then changed his mind and boldly asked Cato to give him his own wife, who was still young and fertile. After all, Cato already had enough children. It cannot be said that Hortensius made this request because he thought Cato was not fond of Marcia. Indeed, they say that she was pregnant at the time. Cato, however, seeing how eager and determined Hortensius was, did not oppose him, but told him that they had to ask Marcia's father, Philippus, for consent. After Philippus had been consulted and had given his approval, he engaged Marcia to Hortensius in the presence of Cato, who had also given his consent.

Hortensius and Marcia had only one daughter. Following her father's illustrious example, she later became famous after making a speech in 42 B.C. against the tax policies of the triumvirs who had heavily taxed the property of the wealthier matrons.[11] When Hortensius died, Cato remarried Marcia, who in the meantime had become very rich thanks to the inheritance left by her second husband.[12] It has often been debated whether this episode reflects a customary practice or an isolated event that reflects the philosophical views of Brutus's circle.[13] Plutarch himself (our most important source) is ambiguous on this point. On one hand, in the *Life of Numa,* he suggests that it was not uncommon for a fertile woman to be circulated among a series of different husbands in order to produce offspring for childless men. On the other hand, in Brutus's case, he suggests that this was extraordinary and even slightly shocking.

This episode (no doubt the source of much gossip in Rome) was probably not an isolated case as far as the noble classes were concerned. By marrying Marcia, Hortensius not only hoped to provide descendants for himself, but also to create strong ties with Cato and Marcius Philippus, who was consul the year they married. Hortensius, with great foresight, was attempting to achieve two aims: first, the perpetuation of his name through procreation and secondly, the creation of solid alliances with Cato and Marcius Philippus for himself and his future children. The story of Hortensius and Marcia (with whom Cato willingly parted) is strikingly similar to the story of Octavian's marriage to Livia. Livia's first husband, Tiberius Claudius Nero, surrendered her to Octavian, the powerful triumvir, Caesar's adopted son, in 38 B.C. Like Hortensius, Octavian had no sons, only a daughter by Scribonia, his first wife. Livia, like

Marcia, appeared to be very fertile: early in her first marriage she had given birth to a son, Tiberius, and when Octavian suggested that she become his wife, she was pregnant again by her first husband.

Octavian made this proposal directly to Livia's husband who could not ask her father, Marcus Livius Drusus Claudianus, for consent. After the battle of Philippi (where her father had fought alongside Caesar's assassins), he had committed suicide to avoid being captured alive by Octavian and Antony. Not only did Tiberius Claudius Nero gladly agree to the marriage of Livia and Octavian, but at the wedding banquet he was treated with the honors traditionally reserved for the father of the bride. His willingness to give up his wife was no source of scandal (he was happy to make up over old quarrels with Octavian in this manner). What was slightly scandalous was the fact that she was pregnant at the time. When her son Drusus was born, Octavian, respecting both custom and law, hastily sent the infant to the home of its father, to whom it rightly belonged.[14]

Newly discovered documents as they have come to light inform us of marriages which we knew nothing about. Sometimes scholars are surprised to learn that even major historical figures, about whose lives we thought every detail was known, may have been married more than once. A passage from the commemorative speech given by Augustus after Agrippa's death in 12 B.C. tells us that P. Quintilius Varus, consul in 13 B.C., was married to one of Agrippa's daughters. This must have been before he married Claudia Pulchra, daughter of Antonia Minor and a niece of Octavia, Augustus's sister. This second marriage must have been very important for P. Quintilius Varus's political career, as it allowed him to advance himself socially—from being merely Agrippa's son-in-law to becoming part of Augustus's family.[15]

Among the Roman upper classes it was common for a person to marry several times, although Vestilia, married six times in the era of Augustus, must be considered an extreme example. As Sir Ronald Syme has observed, these plural marriages create serious embarrassment for scholars who generally suppose that both men and women were married far fewer times than they actually were.[16] With this in mind, we should note that among the upper classes, the highest praise a matron could receive was that she had preserved the lifelong status of *univira* (married only once) even after her husband died. Cornelia, mother of the Gracchi, received such praise when she rejected a marriage proposal from an Egyptian king. Another praiseworthy *univira* was Antonia, Augustus's niece. When her husband, Drusus, died, Antonia and her numerous children moved into the home of her mother-in-law, Livia, where she devoted herself to her maternal duties. By this means, Antonia managed to avoid being manipulated by her uncle into a second marriage.[17]

Noble women could choose to remain *univirae* after their husbands' deaths, but for those of humbler condition, solitary widowhood was simply the normal course of things. It was not easy for a woman of the lower classes to find a man willing to assume responsibility not only for her, no longer young, but also for her children. Such cases must have been rare. It was also unusual for a woman to be tied emotionally to two men at the same time, although when a woman had been divorced and remarried, both husbands might commemorate her after her death.[18]

The "Autonomous Woman"

In terms of freedom and autonomy, the most advantageous status for a Roman woman of the prosperous classes was that of *vidua:* a woman "without" a man. A *vidua* could be a widow, a divorced woman, or even a young girl who had become "mother of the family" when her father died. Even though the *vidua* was autonomous (*sui iuris*) she needed a guardian to assist her in any judicial proceedings involving her and to help her manage the family property and finances. In keeping with his role as guarantor of patrimony, the woman's closest relative on her father's side (*tutor legitimus*) was generally chosen as guardian, and thus he had a personal stake in making sure their property remained within the family. Sometimes a family friend (*tutor extraneus*) was named as guardian. With time, both the law and common practice rendered the guardians' authority less binding, although they were still necessary because women were considered inherently weak and incompetent. In the times of Ulpian, guardians managed all affairs regarding their *pupilli* and *pupillae* (minor children of both sexes), but were no longer directly in charge of the financial affairs of *sui iuris* women. By this time, guardians merely tried to impose their own opinions on how these matters should be handled.[19] Rich *viduae* heiresses were very much in demand, eagerly sought after by men who hoped to marry them, not to have children but to gain control of their money. When Hortensius died, some claimed that Cato had remarried Marcia not because he loved her, but because of the enormous fortune she had inherited from Hortensius.[20]

Over the long centuries of Roman history, the condition of women progressively improved, but it would be wrong to suggest, as some have done, that Roman women were ever "emancipated," from a feminist point of view. Some legislation regarding women, such as the laws of guardianship, became more lenient, or could easily be avoided.[21] The picture scholars have given us of women in ancient Rome depends greatly on how source materials have been interpreted. Historians of law have shown that women were completely under the domination of males, but that there was a very slow evolution toward a partial autonomy, never fully attained. Historians of literature and of societies, on the other hand, claim that women were relatively autonomous, and that they skirted rules and flouted traditions in a thousand ways, escaping the authority and surveillance of their husbands—sometimes following the expedients Ovid recommended during the strict moralistic climate that prevailed during the reign of Augustus.[22]

On the basis of very different sources (law codes, poetry and other literary works) scholars in general have come to very different conclusions, often diametrically opposed, concerning the position of women in Rome. Those who place legal documentation above all other forms find it easy to show—from the Twelve Tables to the Theodosian Codex— that women were undeniably subject to the absolute authority of their fathers, brothers, and husbands. This authority was so extreme that if the husband of a pregnant woman died, she did not even have control over her own womb: her unborn child belonged to her deceased husband's relatives.[23] Furthermore, women were excluded from politics and from the places where political life was conducted. They were not allowed to be seen in the forum, or even to speak out in their own defense, as they tried to do in 197 B.C., when Roman matrons gathered in the forum to demand the repeal of the Oppian law. This law, passed during the Second Punic War, had put a limit on the luxury goods a woman could own. Cato viewed that gathering of matrons (who had dared to demonstrate publicly rather than persuading their husbands at home) as a genuine female revolt (*consternatio muliebris*) equally as dangerous as the secession of the plebs.[24]

Scholars who have examined the literary evidence, including elegies and other brief references to the condition of women scattered throughout Latin literature, insist that in comparison with Greek women, Roman women were relatively independent. Attempts have been made to trace this greater independence back to the Etruscans, who held women in high esteem, and to Etruscan influence on archaic Roman society. This influence undoubtedly existed in significant proportion. It should be noted, however, that in Etruria the form for personal names included both the mother's and father's names, whereas in Rome only the father's name was used. Moreover, some Etruscan women, such as Tanaquil, the wife of King Tarquinus Priscus, appear to have been quite the opposite of the perfect matron idealized in the historical period.[25]

To judge what life was really like for women in ancient Rome, we must compare them to women in other ancient Mediterranean cultures. Although Roman women enjoyed greater freedom than Greek women, they were more dependent than Etruscan women. We cannot compare them to women in other non-Hellenic cultures of Italy because the only documentation we have of those cultures is limited to funerary artifacts. We know nothing about the women of Lucania, for example, who are often depicted alongside their warrior husbands in the tomb frescos of Posidonia/Paestum.[26]

We must also keep in mind that in Rome, in Italy generally, and in the provinces of the empire, from the period of the republic to the imperial era, the condition of women was evolving. Not only did a few laws become more lenient, such as those regarding guardianship, but a noticeable change took place in the male attitude toward marriage. In the new moral climate that prevailed after the first century A.D., friendship and solidarity in marriage became highly prized values. Seneca and Pliny the Younger testify to this change in the Roman world, Plutarch in the Greek one. The new morality altered the way husbands regarded their wives, who were now respected and treated as friends. A man's wife, a "mother of the family" was no longer seen only as a breeder of children, but like his friends (who ranked alongside her in his regard), was now worthy of his esteem. This change in attitude, often discussed in relation to the moral doctrines of the Stoics, was part of a very slow process of transformation involving the whole of Roman society during the imperial era. In this transformation, marriage, a "civic and dotal institution," as Paul Veyne has noted, became interiorized as a moral value. This new concept of marriage can be explained not only by the influence of Stoic philosophy, but also by the changes that had taken place, at least in the upper levels of society, in the daily experience of the average male citizen. He was no longer an active participant in political life, but had become a functionary of the prince.[27]

It is very difficult to evaluate how far his new value system was influenced, even subtly and indirectly, by the spread of Christianity. From the beginning, Christianity viewed women with great and undisputed dignity. St. Paul (Gal. 3:28) states that in the new faith there was no difference between the creatures of God: "neither Jew nor Greek, neither bond nor free, neither male nor female." Yet elsewhere, preaching to the gentiles, Paul underlined (1 Cor. 11:3) that "the head of the woman is the man."

Christianity showed the same double-sided attitude toward women as it showed toward slavery. The belief that all men were equal in the eyes of God did not bring about a reorganization of the foundations of Roman society, which was based on the radical difference between freemen and slaves. Equal to their masters in the eyes of God, yet other people's property, some slaves were treated more humanely by their Christian masters, and were not merely considered tools capable of speech (*instrumenta vocalia*). Although Christian slave owners did not liberate their slaves on a large scale, they did consider them as human beings. With a similar spirit, Seneca claimed that his wife was a friend and not just an indispensable component of his household.[28]

The Roman world branded women with *levitas,* frivolousness or inconstancy, and held that they were weak and incapable by nature (*infirmitas*). Christianity found in the female gender not only *infirmitas,* but also the constant inspiration of sin. Eve is the paradigm of female temptation, vulnerable to the serpent's flattery, responsible for Adam's eviction from earthly paradise. We cannot list here all the exhortations to chastity, the invitations to cover and humiliate the body, the insults and curses railed against Eve and the whole female gender by both Christian heretics and fathers of the church.[29] There was not, nor could there be, any improvement in the condition of women in the period of the Christian emperors. Social sanction had been combined with theological condemnation, which by its very nature could not be overcome.

Impossible Profiles

The silence surrounding the lives of Roman women has kept us from knowing not only about ordinary women, but also about famous ones who played an important role in the development of Roman institutions. Yet this role did not depend on any direct action taken by these women, but on the circumstances in which they found themselves involved as wives or daughters.

The Romans traced the origins of their "democracy," their republic, back to a fatal wound that a woman, Lucretia, willingly inflicted upon herself. This well-known episode is recounted by Livy (1.57–59): Sextus Tarquinius, son of Tarquin the Proud, the last king of Rome, became enamored of Lucretia, wife of his kinsman Tarquin Collatinus. Sextus had once glimpsed her while she sat spinning wool with her maids by the light of a torch, sighing for her absent husband. During the long siege of Ardea, the young Romans had assembled for a banquet, and on that occasion decided to test the virtue of their wives by visiting them unannounced. Unlike the king's daughters-in-law who were caught drinking wine at a banquet, Lucretia had appeared to Collatinus during that unexpected visit as a perfect matron, busy until late at night with household chores, in exclusively female company, thinking about her husband far away. Her chaste attitude inflamed rather than dampened Sextus's ardor. A few days later, Sextus found an excuse to call on her at her home, asked to spend the night there, and was granted his request. That night he slipped into the room where Lucretia lay sleeping and threatened to kill her if she did not accept him as her lover. Seeing the terror in her eyes, he informed her that if she refused, he would tell the world that he had caught her making adulterous love to a slave. To show that he meant what he said, he was ready to kill one of her slaves and lay his naked body at her feet. This last threat convinced her to submit in silence for he had evoked the worst shame imaginable (adultery with a slave), but immediately afterwards, she summoned her father, Lucretius, and her husband, Collatinus, home from their camp. They rushed to her aid in the company of their closest friends, Valerius and Brutus. She revealed to them Sextus's unspeakable act of violence and then before their eyes, committed suicide by drawing out a knife and stabbing herself.[30]

Brutus removed the bloody knife from the wound and swore on Lucretia's innocent blood that he would drive the Tarquin tyrants out of Rome and abolish the monarchic regime. Collatinus, Lucretius, and Valerius, the founding fathers of the republic, each touched the knife and joined him in this vow. Lucretia's body was taken to the forum and put on view. Dionysius of Halicarnassus (4.74.3 and 71.1) tells us that on Brutus's explicit suggestion, her body was displayed "just as it was, covered with blood." This treatment does not suggest that her relatives had failed to show proper respect for her remains. Her body was displayed high up in the forum, so that everyone could see it. Her funeral, which marked the end of the monarchy, may be compared with two other funerals (of men) that also took place in a rebellious city: the funerals of Clodius and of Caesar. On both these occasions, in 52 and in 44 B.C., the bodies were displayed so that the blood and wounds would be clearly visible.[31] Here again, the purpose was explicit: to stir the people to revenge, and at the sight of Lucretia's bloody corpse, the people rebelled and overthrew the Tarquin monarchy. For the Romans this change in their political system (from *regnum* to *res publica*) left its mark on their entire history.

Lucretia became part of Rome's legendary heritage, but it would be impossible to sketch even the briefest biography for her, and for this reason she will not be further mentioned in this book. We only know whose daughter and whose wife she was, that she liked to spin wool, and preferred death to dishonor. These characteristics reflect the ideal Roman matron, and as such, are to be found easily. Lucretia probably would not have been pleased by her posthumous fame, inevitably associated with an unseemly and violent incident. In Rome a woman's life was to be clothed in silence from birth to death. It would also be impossible to write a biography of Verginia, a nubile maiden, who played an equally important role in the history of Roman institutions.

Verginia was the daughter of the valiant centurion Verginius. At the time of our story, he was away fighting at the front. In approximately the second half of the fourth century B.C., Appius Claudius, head of the college of decemvirs in Rome, fell in love with her. The decemvirs were a group of ten magistrates appointed to make written records of laws. By the second year of their term, however, they had become genuine tyrants. Smitten by the beautiful Verginia, Appius Claudius, a powerful patrician, used every means to seduce the plebeian maiden. Verginia, well aware of the meaning of her name, and in any case, betrothed to someone else, put up a firm resistance. Through the intervention of one of his *clientes* who claimed that Verginia was his slave, Appius Claudius tried to gain possession of the girl and seduce her. When her father learned what was happening, he left the battlefield and rushed to Rome. In order to free her from the decemvir's clutches, he stabbed her to death. At the sight of Verginia's wounded body, the plebs rose up and rebelled against the decemvirs, and once again democracy was restored to Rome through a woman's sacrifice.

The democracy that was reestablished was an imperfect one, in which plebs and patricians struggled for equality. Nearly a century later, another woman, Fabia, criticized her father for marrying her to a plebeian, while her older sister, wife of a patrician, owned a house decorated with the symbols of her husband's rank as magistrate. Fabia's complaints moved her patrician father, Marcus Fabius Ambustus, to support the plebeian cause (championed by Licinius Stolo and Sextus Lateranus) in 367 B.C., when an important law, requiring one of the two Roman consuls to be a plebeian, was approved.[32]

Lucretia helped bring an end to the monarchy, while Verginia contributed to the overthrowing of the decemvirs. Their wounds, truly virile ones, stirred the people to revolt. Fabia's story is not a tragedy, but rather an anecdote. The legislation that helped close the gap in rank between Fabia and her sister (a gap which depended on the class difference between their husbands) laid the foundation for the political developments of the middle republic. Thus women do seem to have brought about radical political changes. Yet in the cases of Lucretia and Verginia, this occurred despite themselves, for it was men who drew the political consequences from these women's private acts of sacrifice, and we would never have heard these women's stories, had it not been for their men. If Tarquin Collatinus and the centurion Verginius are emblematic and fleeting figures, the women whose honor they defended are even vaguer ones. Even Fabia's contribution to her plebeian husband's political success depended on the intervention of a man—her patrician father.

Possible Profiles

The ancient Romans must have seen a connection between the noble Lucretia and Verginia, the daughter of a humble centurion, in that both women exemplified matchless feminine virtue.[33] Their most highly prized traits were chastity and modesty, which the Romans believed should be expressed in every moment of an honest woman's life. This is discussed by John Scheid in his essay "Claudia the Vestal Virgin," in which he illustrates a surprising ambiguity regarding the status of vestals and matrons, an ambiguity that the traditional interpretation of sources has never been able to clarify. In 204 B.C. the cult of Cybele was brought to Rome from Asia Minor. The Romans, descendants of the Trojans, considered this goddess their relative and placed her in a temple on the Palatine Hill. The Great Mother came ashore in Ostia where all the people had gathered to welcome her. The ship transporting her suddenly ran aground and was freed only after a miraculous trial of virtue, in which the leading role was played either by the vestal Claudia or by the matron Quinta Claudia, according to differing traditions. The origins of this story may lie in the powerful Claudii clan's attempt to link this important legend to a woman in their family, but we wonder how a vestal virgin, sworn to chastity, could possibly have been confused with a matron, mother of numerous children.

This confusing of Claudia the vestal virgin with the matron Quinta Claudia suggests that the vestals' sexual status was more ambiguous than it might seem.[34] Although the vestals were supposedly pure virgins (only virgins could be priestesses) their ritual vestments included some of the same garments worn by matrons to indicate their married status. Herein lies the ambiguity of the vestals: as pure virgins and chaste matrons, the vestals combine the archetypes of Verginia and Lucretia.

The status of the matron Cornelia, daughter of Scipio Africanus and mother of the Gracchi, was not ambiguous. Throughout her long life she was associated with eminent men: her father, her husband, and her unfortunate sons. Unique among women, Cornelia was well versed in the arts of literature, rhetoric, and philosophy. She was present at the philosophical disputes held in Rome by the Greek philosopher Carneades. It would seem that some of these disputes were probably held in her home, as Jerome suggests,[35] given that Cornelia, renowned for her traditional modesty, was not likely to have frequented public places in mixed company. Thanks to her influence on her children's education, her sons, Tiberius and Gaius Gracchus, studied rhetoric with excellent teachers, and became great orators. In ancient times, a collection of her letters was circulated. Yet Corrado Petrocelli, in "Cornelia the Matron," shows that the biographical data of this very famous woman cannot be reconstructed chronologically except through details connected to the careers of the men in her family.

These are the difficulties encountered in trying to write women's biographies, even for women belonging to the Roman elite. We don't even know the date of Cornelia's death. We only know that she must have died sometime after the tragic death of her son Gaius in 121 B.C. We do know that after Tiberius's death, she retired to Misenum, where she owned a villa. We would know nothing of Cornelia's life if her father, husband, and sons had not existed: she would be to us merely an emblem of virtue rather than a life, unfolding in time. Like matrons of former times, Cornelia did not care for jewelry or the display of luxury. After her husband's death, she rejected other marriage proposals, including a very flattering one from Ptolemy, king of Egypt, preferring to end her days as an *univira*. In the lower middle classes of Roman society, this must have been the common destiny of women and thus not especially praiseworthy. In the upper echelons, where wives seem to have been circulated, as the famous episode of Cato, Hortensius, and Marcia illustrates, the decision of a woman like Cornelia to remain *univira* signified that she had dedicated herself to the memory of her only husband, devoting herself to bringing up her children in a life of renunciation that would serve as a model for all future *univirae*.

Women's lives often interwove stories of political intrigue (a sphere from which they were excluded) with romantic intrigue (in which they were chief players). This was the case of Fulvia, Lycoris, and Livia, though in different ways (Livia would have been horrified by being compared to Lycoris). For a time Fulvia and Lycoris shared Antony's favor—one claiming her due as legitimate wife, the other as lover showered with his attentions. Fulvia and Livia both suffered in the civil wars, but Fulvia did not survive them, whereas Livia became a leading figure in the new regime that followed. Owing to their intimate connection with powerful men, Fulvia, Lycoris, and Livia were suspected of having too much influence on some of their men's political projects. In Rome politics was the domain of men. Women were supposed to keep a modest distance. The wounds of a Lucretia or a Verginia may have driven men to revolt (even to overturn a political regime), but both Lucretia and Verginia were involuntary victims of violent acts committed by others. If some women, such as Fulvia and Livia, seem to burst in (and they do so with force) upon this exclusively male sphere, it must be noted that their actions are described by the sources not just as acts of intrigue, but as very harmful acts as well, damaging not only the men who were involved with them, but the city as a whole.

Fulvia was married three times: to Clodius, Curio, and Antony (the only one to survive her). All three men in different capacities were principal actors in the civil wars. As Catherine Virlouvet points out in "Fulvia the Woman of Passion," it is difficult to attribute to Fulvia any direct influence on the legislation proposed by her first two husbands during their tribunates, since that legislation corresponded to the general lines of plebeian politics. Clodius was very close to Caesar, some claiming that he was Caesar's chief agent in Rome while Caesar was fighting in Gaul. Curio was also an ardent supporter of Caesar. Catherine Virlouvet suspects that Curio's marriage to Fulvia was intended to strengthen his political ties to Caesar even further. By marrying Curio's widow in 47 B.C., Antony also hoped to regain Caesar's good graces, as he had fallen out of favor with the dictator. Fulvia must have been held in high esteem by Caesar, if marrying her was a sort of guarantee, politically speaking, for her husbands. Furthermore, Fulvia's attacks on Octavian during the Perusian war stemmed from the fact that she, like her husband Antony, had never accepted Octavian as Caesar's true political heir.

During the Perusian war, Fulvia was betrayed by her husband, who was abroad in the Orient and did not see fit to intervene in the defense of his wife and his brother. It was not her husband's first act of betrayal.

Antony had betrayed her previously, although in quite a different manner, by not breaking off his affair with the actress Lycoris. In "Lycoris the Mime," Giusto Traina examines this figure within three contexts: in the social setting of her times, in the history of Roman theater during the period of the civil wars, and, more specifically, in the history of mime. Lycoris was not her real name, but a pseudonym used by the poet Cornelius Gallus to sing her praises. It is the name by which he made her famous, in the custom of Roman elegies. Originally the slave of the Roman knight Volumnius Eutrapelus, she was given her freedom and took the name of Volumnia. Through her example we may note the ambiguous status shared by all the women of her profession. As a mime, that is, someone who appeared on stage, Lycoris was officially branded with infamy, and respectable men and women were to avoid her company, at least (for men) in public. Antony, however, had her carried at his side on a litter across Italy, and she seems even to have been escorted by lictors. Terentia, Cicero's wife, did not hesitate to ask her a favor, which she granted, but it seems she treated Terentia haughtily. Cicero himself attended a banquet where Lycoris was also a guest at the home of Volumnius Eutrapelus. Lycoris rose from her original condition thanks to her undoubted talent as an artist, which won her many important admirers and companions. Among them were Mark Antony, Brutus (Caesar's murderer), and Cornelius Gallus.

Livia, younger and more fortunate, not only outlived Fulvia and Lycoris, but also survived the tumultuous years of the civil wars and later played a central role in the long decades of restoration that followed. In "Livia the Politician," we attempt to show how the noble Livia may have deeply influenced her husband at the end of the civil wars, when Octavian (later Augustus) was striving to pacify the body politic through a policy of turning his back on the past. Livia contributed to this policy on a personal level by forgetting that her own father had committed suicide after the battle of Philippi, where he had fought on Brutus and Cassius's side against Antony and Octavian, and furthermore, by forgetting that she herself had been forced, like Fulvia, to flee to Greece after the Perusian war. It is symptomatic that the records written by ancient historians, well aware of Livia's influence over Augustus, tended to draw a negative portrait of her as a fiercely ambitious woman. They insinuate that Livia first poisoned all her husband's relatives and then her own husband in order to pave the way for her son Tiberius's ascent to power. These histories, written by men, viewed the incidents of poisoning ascribed to Livia as the tools of a typically feminine political battle. These same historians later accused Agrippina of murdering Claudius by feeding him poisonous mushrooms. Livia has been treated unfairly by these sources, especially if we consider that by seeking to imitate Cornelia, she helped accomplish an almost impossible feat: the reconciliation of Augustus with the senate.

Two centuries later, Perpetua introduces us to a completely different world: the Christian communities of Africa, and specifically, of Carthage, where in these years of violent persecution, friction over doctrinal disputes had reached its peak. As Emanuela Prinzivalli points out in "Perpetua the Martyr," the *Passion of Perpetua* is an extraordinary document: a text written by a woman who describes her imprisonment and her mystical visions. Perpetua is a Christian and a woman writer. It was certainly not extraordinary for women to be Christians; we know the names of many female Christian martyrs. Interesting questions have been raised concerning the role and influence of women within the early Christian communities. What is extraordinary is that Perpetua wrote her own story. She tells us how she quarreled with her father when he attempted to convince her to abjure Christianity and describes nursing her infant son in prison. It may seem puzzling that she says nothing about her husband, but we may suppose that he was a pagan and hostile to his wife's religion.

In her last vision on the eve of her martyrdom, Perpetua imagines that she has been transformed into a man and must fight in an arena against an Egyptian gladiator. It is easy to see why she pictured her antagonist as an Egyptian, for in ancient times Egypt was considered the land of magic. What interests us is her remark "facta sum masculus," "I became a man." Perpetua is fully aware that she is a woman, she nurses her child and feels pain in her breasts. To combat her antagonist, the devil, represented by the gladiator, Perpetua must overcome her inferiority as a woman, and thus she becomes a man. Fighting like a man, she fights and wins, and also realizes that she is worthy to receive the palm of martyrdom. Only by becoming a man could she rise above the weakness of her sex.

We could search in vain in "Helena: Tavern Hostess and Empress" for any of the gaiety of Carlo Goldoni's play. Once she had left her tavern, where at best she was the proprietor and at worst, a serving maid, Helena's origins were rarely mentioned except in edifying tones to show how Christianity could change the destiny of individuals. Historians of the late-antique world marvel at her remarkable ascent up through the ranks of society: from the *stablum* where people lived with animals to the sumptuous halls of court. Yet our surprise is short-lived: Helena's success also depended upon a man. After the death of his father, Constantius I (Chlorus), Constantine, Helena's son, became emperor and was converted to Christianity. The heroic times of Perpetua and the passions of the martyrs were over, Franca Ela Consolina recounts. Christians, represented primarily by their clergy, now gained power under their emperor. Helena's social and religious origins are obscure, but it has been suggested that they might have individuated within Judaism.

The existing documents do not indicate just how much religious influence Helena and Constantine had on each other. We can only say that she had great influence—no less than Livia had in her time, on her son's political decisions. It was Helena who made sure that Constantine's half-brothers (the sons of Constantius Chlorus and Theodora) were kept in exile for many long years. It was Helena, at least according to some, who saw to it that Fausta, Constantine's wife, was eliminated through an obscure conspiracy in which Constantine's son Crispus also died. It is certain that after Helena's death, much effort was made to link her name with the legendary discovery of the True Cross, which supposedly occurred during her pilgrimage to the Holy Land, a journey uniting religious and political aims. From an episode recorded by Rufinus of Aquileia we learn that while in the Holy Land, Helena once again became a tavern maid, serving at a table of virgins consecrated to Christ.

Three religions flourished in the city of Alexandria at the beginning of the fifth century A.D. There was a powerful Christian community whose patriarch had the same rank and authority as the patriarchs in the major cities of the empire. There was a large Jewish community, the most important of the Diaspora. Numerous pagans still existed, despite the destruction of the sanctuary of Sarapis in the time of Theodosius, and a prestigious school of philosophy was still thriving, under the direction of Hypatia. After the death of her father, Theon, Hypatia had inherited his place as teacher in this illustrious school, descended from the great Neoplatonic school of Plotinus. Records were kept of the succession of professors of philosophy in the city just as they were for bishops. It was a different succession, but for those involved, no less engaging. The prefect in Egypt, Orestes, was on friendly terms with Hypatia, but despite the prefect's protection, Bishop Cyril waged war against the major representatives of Alexandrian paganism. In "Hypatia the Intellecual," Silvia Ronchey shows us that the powerful patriarch kept an armed militia of monks, who were alien and hostile to the pagan culture of the city. One day, while Hypatia was returning home, they attacked the philosopher, slaughtered her, and defiled her body.

The shock waves created by the violent murder of Hypatia (considered by some as a triumph of Christianity against declining paganism) continue to be felt today. As a woman philosopher and an intellectual, Hypatia has been treated in our culture as a sacrificial victim by authors ranging from Voltaire to Vincenzo Monti, from Leconte de Lisle to Mario Luzi. In the nineteenth century, the Italian poetess Diodata Saluzzo Roero tried unsuccessfully to make Hypatia into a Christian martyr. Despite this attempt at appropriation, Hypatia remains a pagan, and above all, a teacher of Neoplatonic philosophy, a discipline embracing mathematics and geometry. Hypatia supposedly invented various machines: a flat astrolabe, a hydroscope, and an aerometer. These activities may have aroused the suspicion, especially in Egypt, that magic was practiced. The delicate relations between pagans and Christians in this period were even further complicated by the fact that one of Hypatia's most gifted pupils was Synesius, who later became a Christian bishop at Cyrene and was himself a paradox in an era of great paradoxes.

In "Melania the Saint," Andrea Giardina introduces us to the elite of late antique Rome. Some aristocratic Roman matrons in this circle were not satisfied by their wealth and noble status: they yearned for sainthood. Among these was Melania the Younger, preceded by her grandmother, Melania the Elder. After the deaths of her husband and two of her three children, Melania the Elder abandoned Rome, visited the monks in Egypt and later founded a monastery of virgins on the Mount of Olives in Palestine. Melania the Younger firmly intended to follow in her grandmother's footsteps. It was believed that sainthood could be achieved through the practice of chastity while continuing to lead a married life. Melania was married to her cousin Pinian, a devoted and dominated husband. When their children died, first their son, born prematurely, and later their older daughter, Melania did not view these events as tragic, but rather as a further stimulus to sexual abstinence. A good pagan matron, like Cornelia, was supposed to produce as many children as possible. A Christian saint, once her wifely duties had been fulfilled, was expected to abstain from procreation.

In early childhood, Melania adopted an attitude of mortification toward her own clothing and as an adult, filled with the folly of Christ, persevered in punishing herself. Together with her husband, she carried out "subversive" acts of charity, which led to the dispersion of their enormous wealth, opposed not only by their relatives but also by the ecclesiastical authorities, for other reasons. When Melania and Pinian attempted to free their slaves en masse, the slaves rebelled, fearing they would find themselves stripped of all resources and abandoned to their fate. Given the example of her grandmother, Melania's future was clearly marked out for her. She too would go and live in Palestine, where aspiring saints went to study the scriptures and refine their knowledge. Melania dedicated herself to this task with excellent results. Though different from Perpetua (who clearly and significantly claimed in one of her visions that *facta sum masculus*), Melania also had to transform herself into a *mulier virilis,* a virile woman, in order to fulfill her spiritual longings.

ONE

CLAUDIA THE VESTAL VIRGIN

John Scheid

In his speech *Pro Caelio* Cicero contrasts Clodia, the sister of his enemy Clodius, with two great women of the Claudian family, Quinta Claudia and Claudia the Vestal virgin. In connecting these two women (whose names were also linked in later times by the poet Propertius and the biographer Suetonius) Cicero anticipates Quinta Claudia's curious replacement by Claudia the Vestal virgin in later versions of the myth recounting the arrival of the cult of Cybele in Rome. Judging from the many texts citing her as a paragon of chastity, Quinta Claudia, like the Vestal Claudia, was widely known. These two women were undoubtedly among the major female figures in the Roman imagination, yet the matron's proverbial purity and the Vestal virgin's ritual chastity were not above derogation, as we will see.

In the final years of the Second Punic War the Romans, in obedience to an oracle, decided to bring the cult of Cybele, the Great Mother of Pessinus, in Asia Minor, to Rome. The oracle of Delphi confirmed that this should be done and further stated that the goddess must be welcomed to the city by its most virtuous man (*vir optimus*). The senate chose a twenty-year-old youth, Publius Scipio, the future Nasica, who had not yet held public office. He was ordered to greet the goddess upon her arrival in Ostia, together with the matrons of the city. When the ship arrived at the mouth of the Tiber, Scipio went aboard and received from the priests the stone which represented the goddess, then disembarked and delivered it to the matrons. Among these was Quinta Claudia. (The legends, however, differ regarding her part in the return.)

The historian Diodorus records the legend in concise form, simply stating that the Romans sent their most virtuous man and their most virtuous woman (known by the name Valeria) to welcome Cybele. Other sources explain how Quinta Claudia became so famous. The earliest mention of her story is found in Cicero's *De haruspicium responsis,* in which he ironically compares Clodia to the virtuous Quinta Claudia. Other sources provide more details. According to Livy, doubts had been cast on Quinta Claudia's chastity, but she proved her innocence by performing a holy service for Cybele, which made a great impression on posterity. The most detailed account is to be found in Ovid's *Fasti,* where Quinta Claudia appears in the procession of mothers, daughters, wives, and Vestal virgins who turned out to welcome the Great Mother to Ostia. In this version, the goddess was conveyed into the city on a ship warped upriver by men, but the ship ran aground and all efforts to move it failed. At this point Quinta Claudia stepped out from the crowd. Ovid tells us that this matron had been accused of adultery by people offended by her way of dressing, or her quick tongue, but she was guiltless. After purifying herself in the Tiber, she knelt, with her hair streaming loose, before the image of the goddess and begged the Great Mother to prove her innocence by following her to Rome. When she had finished her prayer, she grasped the rope and astonished the crowd by pulling the ship along without effort. Through this miracle the goddess publicly witnessed to Claudia's innocence. During the procession, the Great Mother stopped briefly in the area marking the border of ancient Rome (*ager Romanus antiquus*) at the mouth of the Almo (just south of where the Basilica of Saint Paul now stands). Then, after a sacrifice accompanied by the frenetic music of Phrygian flutes and drums, and followed by a ritual bath, the procession entered the city through the Porta Capena, where the goddess was welcomed by the youth Scipio Nasica.

Other versions give more details. The poet Silius Italicus and the historian Appian describe the matron's test of virtue within the rational context of institutions. According to their version, when the ship ran aground, the Romans consulted their priests and seers, who replied that it could be freed only by a woman who had never committed adultery. Quinta Claudia, who had been accused of adultery but never found guilty, came forward and implored the goddess to let her prove her innocence. She tied her girdle, symbol of purity, to the ship and with it pulled the vessel upriver.

An almost identical version shows Claudia the Vestal virgin in the leading role. The first record of this is a fragment attributed to Seneca. A few decades later, this version was repeated by the poet Statius (who speaks of the *virgo* Claudia), and after the second century A.D. it became the canonical version until the time of Julian and the Fathers of the Church. In these accounts, it is the Vestal Claudia who proves her innocence by performing the miracle of pulling the ship all the way to Rome with her hair or her girdle tied to the prow.

There were also iconographic records of the legend. From Valerius

Maximus and Tacitus, we learn that in the vestibule of the temple dedicated to Cybele there once stood a statue of Claudia that survived two fires, in the years 111 B.C. and A.D. 2 (or that a statue of Claudia had been consecrated in the temple after surviving these fires). The miracle is also depicted on a medallion of the empress Faustina showing the goddess on her ship, holding a drum and sitting on a throne flanked by lions, with a group of four matrons to her right. Three matrons are turned toward the ship; the fourth figure, slightly larger, faces right and is pulling the ship along. We may identify the large figure as Quinta Claudia. An altar in the Capitoline Museum, probably dating from the second century A.D., shows a similar scene accompanied by an inscription. A Vestal virgin, recognizable by her veil, or *suffibulum,* is standing on a base representing a wharf along the Tiber. She is turned toward the ship and is pulling it along with an *infula,* a special hair ribbon worn by priestesses. The Great Mother is on the ship, sitting on her throne with her lions. The inscription tells us that the altar is dedicated to Claudia *Synthyche* (sic), to the Mother of the Gods, and to the *Navis Salvia,* the Savior Ship. A similar inscription, now in the Museum of Verona (*CIL* 6.493) was found at the foot of the Aventine on the banks of the Tiber. Another fragment (*CIL* 6.494) of a dedication made to the goddess by Quintus Nunnius Telephus most certainly came from the same area. After careful examination of the punctuation marks appearing in these inscriptions, scholars now believe that *Navis Salvia* is clearly not an epithet applied to Claudia herself, transformed into a heroine, but to the legendary ship that brought salvation to both Rome and Claudia. Judging from the site where these inscriptions were found, it is believed that a chapel dedicated to the Great Mother and the Savior Ship once stood in the area of the *emporium,* or public market, between the Aventine and the Testaccio.

Before we see how the matron Quinta Claudia could have been replaced by a Vestal virgin in the legend describing the arrival of Cybele's cult in Rome, we must clarify a few points concerning history and topography.

The first problem regards the historical truth of the anecdote. Most historians today agree that this story is an elaboration of a historical event, but the credibility of Livy's account is uncertain. F. Graf has shown that the story of Claudia's test of virtue is modeled on a legend told by Pausanias in his *Periegesis* (7.5.5–8): while a statue of Heracles was being moved from Tyre to Erythrae, the raft carrying the god's image suddenly capsized, and became trapped among the rocks. To a blind fisherman it was revealed in a dream that the only way to free the god was by means of a rope made of women's hair. The women of Erythrae refused to make this offering, but a few Thracian women living in the city offered their own hair and the raft was freed.

This model, combined with other elements (the required presence of the virtuous man) and references to the myth of Cybele and Attis (mainly the insistence on chastity) contributed to create the Roman myth of Quinta Claudia. We do not know exactly when this myth came into being. The ironic remarks made by Cicero in *De haruspicium responsis* strongly suggest that he was already familiar with it. When expressing surprise at Clodia's extraordinary resemblance to Quinta Claudia, he is hinting that all they had in common was a dubious reputation. Elsewhere Cicero contrasts the infamous Clodius-Clodia pair with the virtuous Scipio Nasica–Quinta Claudia. Nasica had been selected by the senate as Rome's purest man, and Quinta Claudia had proved her innocence beyond all doubt: thus their purity was obvious to all. The opposite was true of Clodius and Clodia, Cicero suggests, for they were abhorred by men and gods, particularly by the Great Mother, whose games Clodius had allegedly profaned. The Augustan versions of the legend, and especially Ovid's tale, allude to another woman, Augustus's daughter Julia, notorious for her flirtatiousness, sharp tongue, and uninhibited behavior, but this does not prove that the legend originated in the Augustan period. Ovid mentions a theatrical piece featuring Quinta Claudia. Perhaps the legend was first created or elaborated at some unknown time in a play presented during the Megalesia, the festival dedicated to the Great Mother. The official in charge of the festivities, the *aedile curule,* may have been a member of the *gens Claudia* and intended by means of this play not only to honor Claudia's fame but also his own. (A treasury official who issued a coin with Claudia's image on it was probably moved by similar intentions, as we will see shortly.) We know nothing more about how the story came into being.

The legend connects the Great Mother's arrival in Rome with a famous war. Ovid describes a few standard rituals of her cult: the annual procession of the image down the Almo River and its ritual bath, or *lavatio.* In the time of Claudius and later, the ritual bath took place on March 27. Ovid cites the date April 4 and is probably referring to all the festivities celebrated in the goddess's honor, taken as a whole. We may wonder why in Ovid's version Cybele enters the city through the Porta Capena, for this poses a real problem. The route of the image, whether carried by the matrons or pulled on a ship, would have had to follow the Via Ostiense, which led to the Porta Raudusculana or to the Porta Trigemina. As no direct evidence exists, we cannot retrace the goddess's very first itinerary, but we can explain the symbolism used by Ovid (or by the priests in charge of the festivities) in stressing the area of the Porta Capena. It has been suggested that metrical demands kept Ovid from using the words Raudusculana or Trigemina in composing his elegy, and while this explanation may be plausible, I suggest a symbolic one as more probable. Before the procession's original solemn entrance into Rome, it had halted at the mouth of the Almo, in a spot that marked the traditional boundary of the *ager Romanus antiquus.* (I shall not discuss the similarities between this annual ritual celebrated in Rome on the banks of the Almo and the ritual performed on the banks of the Gallos River, on the edge of the territory of Pessinus.) From the times of the Horatii and the Curiatii, of Coriolanus or Sylla, up to the siege of Rome by the Vandals and the Goths, anyone occupying this area posed a threat to the city. A network of sanctuaries and temples had been built along a line just beyond the boundaries of the *ager Romanus,* intended to safeguard Rome against invasion. By pausing briefly in this area, the Great Mother was symbolically reinforcing her connection with Mars or with Terminus, the god of boundaries. Now the Porta Capena, located at the end of the Appian way, was, like the Porta Trionfale, traditionally associated with the military: here stood the sanctuary of Mars, the temples of *Honos* and *Virtus,* and in the time of Augustus, the altar of *Fortuna Redux.* We may assume that Ovid and the priests of Cybele's cult used these symbolic references to the military to stress the protective qualities of the Great Mother. That is why, in Ovid's itinerary, the procession takes a detour. The epigraphic clues found in the area of the *emporium* (the ship's destination after being towed parallel to Via Ostiense) suggest that the route of the procession was as follows: the image was taken to a ship waiting near the temple dedicated to the Mother of the Gods and the Navis Salvia. It then left the city by means of the Porta Capena or perhaps by another one. The ship conveyed the goddess to the Almo, where the ritual was performed. Then the procession returned, entering the city through the Porta Capena.

This reconstruction and other evidence recorded by historians and poets show that the Great Mother performed the role of protector in times of war. This must not be forgotten in interpreting the myth of Claudia.

Pudicitia, or purity and modesty of manner, was the chief virtue of a matron. The term includes both the idea of conjugal faithfulness and discreet behavior, essential to a good reputation. On various occasions in the religious history of Rome, these qualities were publicly stressed. In 216 B.C. the senate chose the purest among a hundred matrons to participate in the dedication of the statue of Venus Verticordia. There were two cults of Pudicitia, one administered by patrician matrons, and the other by plebeians. For a matron, purity meant being a *univira,* married only once, and also chaste. This was, or should have been, Quinta Claudia's status.

We must ask ourselves how a matron, faithful wife and fertile mother, could have ever been confused with a Vestal virgin, sworn to chastity and prohibited from any form of sexual relationship, on pain of horrible punishment.

One element that may help explain this is the legend of Claudia the Vestal virgin whose name was often linked to Quinta Claudia. She was the daughter or sister of Appius Claudius Pulcher, the consul who won a victory over the Salassians in 143 B.C. When a tribune of the plebs tried to pull him off the triumphal chariot, Claudia protected her father (or brother) with her own body, knowing that not even a tribune of the plebs would dare harm her, and accompanied him all the way to the Capitol. Claudia was later celebrated as a model of *pietas,* especially by the members of the *gens Claudia,* and her image was depicted on the reverse side of the coins issued by Gaius Claudius Vestalis.

This superficial resemblance, based on their exemplary displays of virtue, may explain why modern historians are sometimes unsure which of the two women is portrayed in iconographic representations, such as the relief sculpture or the coin mentioned above. It does not explain how the Vestal came to replace the matron in the ancient legend. If Roman poets, historians, and philosophers made such a substitution, the structure of the myth must have allowed it. This suggests that the status of matrons (*pudica*) and that of Vestals (*casta*) were equivalent.

The Vestals' Status

The six Vestals, selected between the ages of six and ten by the Pontifex Maximus, watched over the sacred fire of Vesta in the public hearth of Rome, located, like the house of the Vestals, in the southwest corner of the forum. This fire, protected by the goddess Vesta (from whom the Vestals took their name) symbolized the origins and identity of Rome. Through their domestic duties, including the grinding and preparation of a special salted meal (*mola salsa*) used in worship, the Vestals made sure that the Romans' public sacrifices were ritually pure and effective. Vesta had no one specific image, but was represented by the flames of her fire. When she was depicted in human form it was in the guise of one of her Vestals. In these depictions, all that distinguishes the goddess from her priestesses is the larger size of her figure. The sacred fire, true talisman of Rome, was never to be extinguished. If the flame went out, from any cause whatever, it was always considered the Vestals' fault and portended imminent catastrophe. If it went out because the Vestal on duty had been careless, this was considered a forgivable offense, and the priestess was punished by flogging at the hand of the Pontifex Maximus, head of the pontifical college. If the fire went out by itself, this was a much graver matter, signifying terrible consequences both for Rome and for the Vestals. This omen revealed that one of the priestesses had committed the worst of all crimes for a Vestal: breaking her vow of chastity. The guilty priestess or priestesses were identified, judged by the Pontifex Maximus, and condemned to horrible punishment: burial alive in the Campus Sceleratus, near the Porta Collina. The purity of Vesta's sacred fire thus corresponded to the chastity of the Vestals. They were the living counterparts of Vesta, and in their service to her they rendered manifest the purity of her fire.

Through their domestic rituals, the Vestals also underlined that their hearth was the hearth of the great Roman family. Vesta's hearth was the symbol of the great Roman family and, in the words of G. Dumézil, at the same time guaranteed its continuation. Every fifteenth of June the Vestals swept the sanctuary, and several times a year they prepared the *mola salsa* (ritual flour used in public sacrifices). The Vestal virgins were always in danger of contamination by the broken vows of one of their number. Their goddess also was quite ambiguous, as she was ambivalently associated with male sexual symbols. Ovid informs us that donkeys were honored during the Vestalia on the ninth of June, in thanks for the services they performed in bakeries, where they assisted in the preparation of bread, the archetypical human food. Ovid is explicit about the sexual prowess of this animal, and he also recounts how a donkey intervened when the god Priapus attempted to rape the goddess Vesta during a feast held in Cybele's honor. Vesta was sometimes portrayed accompanied by a donkey, and her association with this animal, a symbol of sexuality, as well as myths that include the appearance of a phallus among her flames, suggest the ambiguity of fire, as both beneficial and violent.

The cruel fate that threatened the Vestals reveals the same ambiguous attitude toward sexuality, an ambiguity also expressed in the myth of Cybele and Attis.

What was the Vestals' sexual status? They were virgins and called themselves by that name. They were obliged to remain chaste for thirty years, the duration of their service. They wore the nuptial veil and head-dress, as well as the long gown and sash of a married woman; thus their virginal status was defined by the same symbolic garments as those worn by matrons. They also enjoyed a few masculine privileges. The day a Vestal was chosen by the Pontifex Maximus, she was released from her father's authority and could do as she liked with her property. She could also make a will and serve as a witness. She held high rank in the public sphere and had her own lictors. She traveled about the city in a chariot, and she was allowed to prepare the *mola salsa* and to make sacrifices for the Roman people. None of these things could matrons do. In other words, the Vestals symbolically combined typical attributes of both matrons and men, yet were obliged to remain virgins. Their sexual status was ambiguous, for they were bound by and yet free from the rules that determined the status traditionally reserved for the leading figures of Roman society: men and matrons.

The Vestals and the Matrons

This may suggest how Quinta Claudia came to be replaced by Claudia, the Vestal. Although she was sworn to chastity, a Vestal was not so different from a matron, a married woman and mother, as might appear. This does not mean that their roles were interchangeable, but that both figures shared a common relationship with sexuality: their roles were defined in part by abstinence. The matron abstained from sexual relations with any man other than her husband, the Vestal, from sexual relations with all men. Chastity and modesty were their distinguishing characteristics. The structure of the myth was not modified when the chaste matron was replaced by the Vestal, for both women had been suspected of infringing sexual rules. Quinta Claudia had offended by her way of dressing and her sharp tongue (typical of the *gens Claudia*), while the Vestal Claudia was suspected of having broken her vows of chastity. Every Vestal was potentially guilty of unchastity, especially in wartime, when even the smallest defeat could signify to the Romans that one of their Vestals had broken her sacred vows.

Livy merely mentions that it was the matrons' mission to carry the image of the goddess once it had been brought to land by Scipio Nasica, but Ovid tells us that the women's procession included "mothers, daughters, daughters-in-law, and those who with their virginity perform duties at the sacred hearth." In such a crowd, it would be easy to mistake Quinta Claudia for a Vestal, but in my view, Ovid's text deserves closer examination. All the women go to Ostia (mothers, mothers-in-law, daughters, daughters-in-law, and Vestals), so we may conclude that the story refers to Roman women in general, not just to matrons and Vestals. The point of the story may be that Roman women as a whole, whether represented by the Vestal or the matron, were suspected of impurity, for the chastity of the Vestals was complementary to the *pudicitia* of the matrons.

Matrons and Vestals were often closely associated. Many rites, such as the festival of the Bona Dea, the supplications (thanksgivings) and other sacrifices show that the Vestals represented women as a group. It is easy to see how a Vestal could have replaced a matron in performing a religious duty of importance to all Romans, such as carrying the image of the Great Mother in a religious procession. It might even seem more appropriate to entrust such a task to a Vestal, who would thereby be cast in one of her traditional roles.

Quinta Claudia and the Vestal Claudia represent two closely complementary images of female sexuality and perfection, so it is not surprising that both appear in the legend of the Great Mother's arrival in Rome. Just as young Scipio represented the most virtuous man, these women represented the most virtuous women for the Romans, and corresponded to the dictates of the oracle, which had advised that the goddess be welcomed by the best of the Romans.

Diodorus reports that the oracle demanded the collaboration of the best man and the best woman. Livy instead mentions only the man's presence, while in Ovid's and later versions, Quinta Claudia's intervention is unexpected and is connected with the divine image of the goddess. This point is particularly interesting and we will examine it in concluding.

The Romans entrusted this important task to a man *and* a woman, suggesting that the best man, the *optimus vir,* was incomplete without a woman to assist him. The more detailed versions of the myth recount that a woman succeeded in pulling the ship to Rome after the men had failed. This suggests that any act performed by a man without a woman's assistance is imperfect and incomplete, just as the flamen of Jupiter is incomplete without his wife, as Plutarch tells us. In this case we are not dealing with perfect acts performed by an individual, but an act performed by a whole people by means of its representatives. This story is similar to another famous story of female intervention: when the Roman troops (that is, the men) were unable to stop Coriolanus's attack on Rome, women, led by Coriolanus's own mother and wife, intervened and saved the city. Here too, where men failed, women succeeded. This story, together with the story of Quinta Claudia/Claudia the Vestal illustrates how vital collaboration between the sexes was for the Romans.

The men's and the women's representatives were chosen by different methods. Although we do not know how and why young Scipio was chosen (all we know is his family connection), we do know that this selection was made by the senate. Earlier, in 216 B.C. those same senators picked the most "chaste and modest" matron, Sulpicia, out of ten women chosen by lot from among a hundred matrons. In 204 B.C., the procedure was different, at least according to traditional accounts. Diodorus only gives us a general outline, simply that the best man and the best woman were chosen to welcome the goddess. In all the other versions, the selection of the best woman occurs by means of a miracle, in extraordinary circumstances. The matrons who saved their city from Coriolanus were also acting in unusual circumstances, being faced with imminent catastrophe. In both stories, the women's entrance on the scene is extraordinary and unexpected, for only male intervention would normally have been called for in such circumstances: defending a city or welcoming a goddess were traditionally tasks for men. In the former case, the army should have defended the city from the aggressor, in the latter, the role of host was assigned to a young man belonging to a politically powerful family, officially chosen by the senate. We might also note that in his purity Scipio resembles Attis, and this may be an intentional reference to the myth of Cybele.

In the myth of Quinta Claudia, the most virtuous woman, unlike young Scipio, was not selected by means of an institution (the senate), but by a miracle involving the intervention of the goddess herself. This was the most appropriate means. In the story of Coriolanus, no thanks were later offered to the gods presiding over Roman institutions, whose intervention might have been expected in normal circumstances. Instead, thanks were offered to the goddess of Fortune, *Fortuna Muliebris,* the "Fortune of Women." This goddess, notoriously fickle and ambivalent toward all those who performed official duties in Rome, traditionally protected people who had no regular place in Roman society, like slaves or women. In the case of Quinta Claudia, it was a miracle, a stroke of fortune, that allowed the most virtuous woman to be recognized.

This miracle depended upon the supreme virtue of women, *pudicitia* (or for the Vestals, chastity). The Great Mother, so cruel to Attis in the Greek myth (she forced him to castrate himself), proved the innocence of a woman accused of impurity. We might say that the Roman legend of Cybele's arrival in the city added a Roman version to the Greek myth of Cybele. At the same time, on a cultural level, the Roman priests of Cybele's cult and the festivities of the Megalesia organized by the *aediles curules* and the great patrician families, were juxtaposed to Cybele's own priests, in particular the Phrygian *Galli* (castrates), and to the rites that took place at the end of March. Ovid, in commenting on the Megalesia, establishes a parallel between the two forms of the myth and the story of the goddess's arrival embraces both aspects: after the benevolent calm of the events in Ostia, the scene of the *lavatio* in the Almo makes the *Galli* with their wild flutes and drums seem effeminate.

The story of Quinta Claudia or Claudia the Vestal illustrates different aspects of the goddess Cybele and of women's sexual status. Purity receives the major emphasis, as the goddess may be welcomed only by a pure Roman male. The senators chose a young man belonging to a great family, not yet a public figure, yet this young man's intervention had to be completed by the collaboration of an exemplary woman. The different versions of the story view this woman as both a discreet matron untainted by adultery and as a Vestal for whom purity was the *raison d'être*. It is no surprise that the woman who welcomed the Great Mother to Ostia became famous, for she manifested in a particularly evident way women's place in the Roman imagination.

Two

Cornelia the Matron

Corrado Petrocelli

"Whenever we try to picture this woman clearly in our minds, to bring her from the realm of imagination to the real world, she vanishes. She remains a dim figure, and thus we must leave her, for only in that vagueness may we recognize her." With these words, Henry Houssaye (*Aspasie, Cléopatre, Théodore* [Paris, 1890]) described the difficulties encountered in reconstructing an accurate, detailed biography of Aspasia, the most celebrated woman of classical Greece. The sources, which view her with hostility, portray her as a woman indisputably endowed with intelligence, learning, wisdom, and even political acumen, qualities rarely found in women living in Athens in the fifth century B.C. Yet she left no record of her thoughts and feelings, not a word written by her own hand. She suddenly bursts upon the scene in Plutarch's biography of Pericles when, in the midst of a discussion of the expedition against Samos, the author launches into a digression about Aspasia, underlining the remarkable intellectual abilities (*techne* and *dynamis*) with which she challenged the politicians and men of learning of her time. Nothing is known about the period prior to her relationship with Pericles (or Socrates), except that she was from Miletus and was the daughter of Axiochos. We do not know when she was born or how old she was when she arrived in Athens. An impenetrable silence also surrounds the end of her life, by which time Pericles (and shortly afterwards, Lysicles, the other politician with whom she was associated) had died.

"No Greek woman ever became famous except through men, or at least, through one man." This observation, with which Nicole Loraux (*Grecia al femminile* [Rome and Bari, 1993], 125) dutifully opens her essay on Aspasia, applies not only to the Greek world of Athens in the fifth century B.C. but to the Roman world as well. Although it is true that "in presenting a list of women famous in their times, a modern historian of ancient Rome would not find the same difficulties" as those encountered when dealing with the Greek world (ibid., xxviii), it is equally true

that the Greeks and Romans displayed a similar perspective and that the records of both cultures reveal a similar selection of information. Except for extremely rare cases, we have no direct testimony of women's voices, no direct records of their thoughts. Barred from men's duties (*virilia officia*) because of their indisputable, innate incapacity (*infirmitas, imbecillitas sexus, levitas animi, impotentia muliebris*), excluded from public life and from the rhythms of collective society, Roman women, like Greek women, were considered only in their relationship to men and in their capacity as mothers, wives, sisters, or daughters. The portrayals we have of women (mostly drawn by men) have often been inspired by stereotypes, and the examples of famous women passed down by legend or written record have systematically been reduced to models of canonical virtue or of flagrant transgression.

Plutarch, at the beginning of his treatise *Examples of Feminine Valor,* in which he attempts to show that virtue (*arete*) in a man and in a woman were substantially the same thing, mentions the Roman custom of *laudationes funebres,* eulogies delivered at the funerals of women as well as men. This contrasted with the Athenian custom of the *logos epitaphios* and the belief (which Thucydides ascribes to Pericles) that it was wise to say as little about women as possible, whether in praise or blame. Yet even when Roman women were commemorated by *laudationes funebres* (which were a late development, the first example dating from 102 B.C.: Quintus Lutatius Catulus's elegy for his mother Popilia, mentioned by Cicero in *De oratore* 2.44), they were merely *the objects* of men's judgment of their qualities. Significantly, the *laudationes funebres* had more to do with the prestige and career of the man giving the speech than with the woman being commemorated. There are no records of women delivering these commemorative speeches.

Even for someone like Cornelia, daughter of Scipio Africanus and mother of the Gracchi, a woman frequently mentioned in historical sources, it is difficult to reconstruct a biography if we wish to see her as a person rather than an idealized figure of legendary virtue. Like Aspasia, Cornelia enjoyed a fame that was unusual for the women of her time, among whom, we may reasonably conclude, she distinguished herself. This fame depended not only on her noble descent and virtuous behavior, but also and most importantly on her cultural and intellectual abilities. Aspasia, an animating force and a direct participant in Pericles' circle, was often described as the incarnation of novelty and transgression. In contrast, Cornelia was idealized by posterity as the perfect matron, the embodiment of those values that traditionally characterized the family, the underlying structural unit of Roman society. Yet in order to

describe Cornelia's life, we must resort to conjecture and refer continually to the men in her life, digging through their biographies, full of references to their careers, in search of a few scanty bits of information
about her.

An Important Marriage

The year of Cornelia's birth is unknown. Although much is known about
her life from the time of her marriage to Tiberius Sempronius Gracchus
until the death of her son Gaius, references to the other periods of her
life are few. We have no information about her adolescence and early
youth, which must have been rich in experiences, especially concerning
her education and intellectual development. The only direct record we
have (offered almost as an explanation for the tragedies in Cornelia's
life) is furnished by Pliny, who tells us that Cornelia was an example of
a very ill-omened condition for women: being born with genitals closed
(*Nat. Hist.* 7.69; see also Solinus 1.67).

It is not surprising that Cornelia makes her official appearance on
the stage of history just prior to her marriage. Marriage represented the
culminating moment in a woman's social realization. Through the abandonment and symbolic consecration of the objects of childhood, marriage marked a bride's coming of age in the same way that the donning
of the *toga virilis* symbolized the youth's break with the past and sanc-
tioned his entrance into society, with full rights and privileges.

The marriage of an eminent politician like Tiberius Sempronius Gracchus to the daughter of Publius Cornelius Scipio, Africanus Major, the
man who had defeated Hannibal, must have been a memorable event.

Livy dedicates special attention to it (38.57), while describing the final
phase of Africanus's life, specifically in his account of Sempronius Gracchus's intercession on behalf of the Scipios. During an attempt by certain
enemies to bring the Scipios to trial, Sempronius Gracchus had energeti-
cally intervened to help them, despite the deep hostility he felt for some
of the more influential members of the *gens Cornelia,* a mutual antagonism to which many authors attest (see, for example: Livy 38.52.9 and
57.4; Cicero *De provinciis consularibus* 8.18; Valerius Maximus 4.1.8;
Plutarch *Tiberius Gracchus* 1.3; and Gellius *Noctes Atticae* 12.8.1). His
intercession must have been a great surprise to the senators who later
during a solemn banquet at the Capitolium requested that Africanus
Major "promise his daughter to Gracchus." Once the engagement rites
had been concluded, Scipio returned home and informed his wife, Tertia

Aemilia. She at first resented not being consulted but then forgave her husband, for the bridegroom he had accepted was truly outstanding. Here Livy may be referring to the fact that mothers generally played a decisive role in their daughter's marriages or divorces. (In this context we might call to mind the *ius maternum* invoked by Amata against Latinus's decision in the *Aeneid* 7.402.) Livy's anecdote reflects a custom that gradually became more common: the consolidating of political alliances through marriage.

The reconciliation of these two families is recorded vividly by Valerius Maximus: those who had come to the sacred banquet as enemies, *odio dissidentes,* returned home as friends, *amicitia et adfinitate iuncti:* Scipio promised his daughter to Gracchus "right then and there" (4.2.3). And by Gellius: this all happened simply because they were sitting near each other quite by chance at a banquet at the Capitolium (12.8.4). (See also Seneca the Elder *Controversiae, exc.* 5.2.2; Dio Cassius fr. 65.1; *Latin Panegyrics* 7[6].13.4.) Another reference may be found in the rhetorical argument (about *genus argumentationis remotum*) used by Cicero to blame Scipio for the repercussions of the Gracchi's actions: "If Africanus had not married his daughter to Tiberius Gracchus, and if she had not given birth to the two Gracchi, such widespread rebellions would never have occurred" (*De inventione* 1.91).

The accuracy of records from this period, especially those regarding the "trial of the Scipios" (ca. 187–184 B.C.) has long been debated by scholars and was subject to controversy even in ancient times. More than once, Livy was forced to record discrepancies between his conflicting sources and to reveal his embarrassment at not knowing which version to follow (for example, the divergences regarding the death of Scipio, 38.56.1, for whom neither the date of death nor the place of burial is certain). One subject of conflict in the sources is whether Cornelia Minor (the older sister of Publius Cornelius Scipio Nasica Corculus) was given in marriage by Africanus himself (*haud dubie a patre collocata erat* Livy 38.57.2) or whether she married Gracchus after her father's death. Livy tends toward the former hypothesis, elaborating on it with copious detail, while treating the latter only sketchily. Plutarch, whose biographies of Tiberius and Gaius Gracchus are our main source of detailed information concerning Cornelia's life, claims, however, that the former version is untrue. According to Plutarch's account, it was Appius Claudius Pulcher who proposed during a banquet of augurs that Gracchus marry his daughter Claudia. The episode follows the same pattern of Livy's story about Scipio and Tertia Aemilia. Here too, the authoritative *princeps senatus* returned home to announce the betrothal to his wife, Antistia, who expressed surprise at such unjustified haste but forgave him because he had chosen "Tiberius Gracchus for her daughter's husband" (Plutarch *Tiberius Gracchus* 4.3). Immediately after, Plutarch states that he is aware that others have told this same story about Scipio Africanus and Sempronius Gracchus, but that more people agreed with his version. More important, he records Polybius's statement that "after Africanus died, his relatives betrothed Tiberius to Cornelia, who had been left by her father neither married nor engaged" (ibid. 4). Given this second account of the engagement, and considering the authority of Polybius, who had close ties with the Scipio family, we will take Plutarch's version as true. Moreover, the tradition that Africanus Major and Gracchus were enemies (various authors agree on this point) is puzzling and may be based, according to some modern scholars (for example Fraccaro and Carcopino), on elements that are far from cogent. Even though Plutarch confirms this supposed animosity between the two men (*Tiberius Gracchus* 1.3) by stating that Sempronius Gracchus was Scipio's enemy and not his friend, it may be that the reports of this antagonism were simply based on the conflicts that later arose between Scipio Aemilianus and Tiberius Gracchus, or were derived from the anecdote regarding their reconciliation.

Cornelia's marriage was strategically planned by a family council held by the Scipios in order to establish an alliance with the Sempronii (ties later reinforced by the marriage of Scipio Aemilianus and Sempronia, daughter of Cornelia and Sempronius Gracchus). When could this marriage have taken place? Africanus Major's death, which occurred in approximately 183 B.C., gives us a fixed point on which to base our calculations. This same date is also useful in helping us establish the year of Cornelia's birth, for at the latest, she could not have been born more than a few months after that date. Modern scholars vary in their attempts to reconstruct the chronology of her life. To calculate this chronology, we must continue to concern ourselves with the men of her family.

Only three of Cornelia's children reached adulthood: Sempronia, Tiberius, and Gaius. We will find it useful to focus on her two sons, for whom detailed records exist. From Plutarch we learn that Tiberius Gracchus was not yet thirty at the time of his assassination in 133, and that Gaius, his political heir, was nine years younger (*Gaius Gracchus* 1.2). Thus, Tiberius was born in 163 (or 162) and Gaius in 154 (or 153). Cornelia has been described by the sources as an unusually fertile example of motherhood, bearing twelve children. Pliny mentions her in his discussion of procreation: "Some people generate only daughters or only sons, whereas frequently in others we find an alternating of sons and daughters, such as in the case of the mother of the Gracchi, for twelve times, and Agrippina, the mother of Germanicus, for nine times" (*plerumque et alternant, sicut Gracchorum mater duodeciens et Agrippina Germanici noviens* [*Nat. Hist.* 7.57]).

In using this source, Mommsen interpreted *alternant* in the strictest sense. Basing his calculation on Polybius's claim (31.27.1–5) that Scipio Aemilianus generously paid the second half of the dowries of Africanus's daughters after their mother's death in 162 B.C., Mommsen postulated that Cornelia was married in 165 B.C. As it was customary to name the eldest son after the father, Mommsen also deduced that Tiberius must have been the first in a series of twelve children (or at least, second, if the eldest child had been a daughter) in which sons and daughters alternated. Carcopino and others, however, have convincingly contested such a late dating for Cornelia's marriage. Aside from the different ways this passage from Polybius may be interpreted (moreover, it is full of lacunae), the only thing it definitely proves is that by the year 162 B.C. Cornelia was already married. Forcing her to produce twelve children in less than fifteen years, and with such a rigorous alternation of sons and daughters, appears excessive, despite the attempts of scholars such as A. Guarino (who refers to these concerns as cavalier) to explain this by means of twin, premature, or multiple births. If that were the case, Pliny would probably not have described such an extraordinary example of fertility with the term *plerumque et* (a large number), which calls to mind a more common phenomenon. The other example of fecund motherhood that Pliny mentions was Agrippina Major, who gave birth nine times, bearing first six sons and then three daughters, as Mommsen himself demonstrated in 1878 (*Hermes* 13: 241ff.). On the basis of this evidence (especially Pliny *Nat. Hist.* 10.178 and Aristotle *Historia animalium* 7.6.5585B: *metabàllousin*), K. Moir interprets the words *plerumque et alternant* more loosely and suggests that Cornelia first had a series of daughters and then a series of sons. This would help clarify a problem that arises if we fix Cornelia's marriage date many years prior to 163, the year Tiberius was born, presumably her eldest son and named after his father. It has been suggested that Cornelia may have had other sons before Tiberius was born, all of whom had died in infancy and had been given their father's name. This conflicts with Plutarch's assertion that when Sempronius Gracchus died, he was survived by his wife Cornelia and their twelve children (*Tiberius Gracchus* 1.5). Tiberius and Gaius

Gracchus had at least one older sister, Sempronia, who married Scipio Aemilianus. When the young Tiberius at age sixteen accompanied Scipio Aemilianus on the African campaign, his sister was already married to Aemilianus. Plutarch (*Tiberius Gracchus* 8.7) reports that in order to encourage ambition in her children (particularly Tiberius) Cornelia complained that she was still known as Scipio's mother-in-law, rather than as the mother of the Gracchi. Scholars have dated Cornelia's marriage to a period ranging from 176 B.C. (proposed by Carcopino), to around 180 (Earl) or 181 (Moir). K. Moir has also shown how the same data may be combined to give different results and suggests 170 B.C. as an equally plausible alternative.

Two Serpents Appear

Such a late dating of Cornelia's marriage would make Sempronius Gracchus even older. Modern scholars vary in fixing the year of his birth, ranging from 220 to 208 B.C. A few important phases of his career are well documented, but it is not always easy to reconstruct the surrounding political context. He was tribune perhaps in 187, when he attempted to keep Lucius Scipio from going to prison (but some scholars date this episode to 184); aedile in 182; praetor in Spain after 180; consul in 177 and again in 163. He was a capable politician, flexible and conciliatory (as we know from his various diplomatic missions abroad and from the peace negotiations he conducted in Spain in 178), at times very rigid (as when he took repressive measures during the revolt in Sardinia), but also very generous in the financing of games, public works, and buildings. His legendary sternness as censor in 169 may have been the origin of a story claiming that when he went to bed at night the citizens put out their lights to avoid being accused of wastefulness or disorderly behavior.

By the time he married Cornelia he was a mature man, well embarked upon a successful career. The age difference between them must have been considerable. We learn this from an anecdote appearing in Cicero's *De divinatione* 2.62, which the author claims was first recorded in a letter written by Gaius Gracchus to Marcus Pomponius. The episode is described in *De divinatione* 1.36, and a rational explanation is given for the event in 2.62:

> Tiberius Gracchus, son of Publius, was twice Consul, Censor, and Augur of great authority, a wise man and exemplary citizen. One day he summoned the soothsayers because he had found a pair of serpents in his

house. His son, Gaius Gracchus, has left us the written record of this event. The soothsayers replied that if he released the male serpent, his wife would die shortly afterward. If he released the female serpent, then he would die. As he was already near the end of his life, while his wife, the daughter of Publius Scipio Africanus, was still young, he decided that he should die. He let the female serpent go and died a few days later.

In the biographies of illustrious persons, serpents often appear as portents and omens, and this is true of the traditions regarding the Scipios and the Sempronii. When a snake appeared in Pomponia's bed, this omen signified that she was no longer barren. Shortly afterwards, she became pregnant, and later Africanus Major was born. (This anecdote is similar to the story of Olympias, the mother of Alexander, told by Gellius 6.1. Another, analogous story about Atia, Augustus's mother, is told by Suetonius in *Divus Augustus* 94.) Similar premonitory apparitions of serpents also occurred in the Sempronii, foreboding unwelcome events for Tiberius Gracchus, the consul and husband of Cornelia, who fell during a skirmish with the Carthaginian, Magon (Livy 25.16 and Valerius Maximus 1.6.8), and for Tiberius, Cornelia's tribune son, shortly before his tragic end (Plutarch *Tiberius Gracchus*).

What the ancients found most striking about the story of Sempronius Gracchus and Cornelia was her longevity, for she outlived all the men in her family, and showed great ability in managing her own affairs autonomously (Plutarch *Gaius Gracchus* 19). In a society in which average life expectancy was short, especially for females (consider not only the infant mortality rate but the number of women who died in childbirth), Cornelia with her numerous pregnancies was an even more remarkable exception. When a woman had survived her husband or sons, this was mentioned in funerary inscriptions as noteworthy. Given that history is full of women who demonstrated their devotion by sacrificing their own lives after the deaths of their husbands, Gracchus, in choosing to die in Cornelia's place, was extraordinarily generous. The episode is cited by Pliny as one of various *exempla pietatis* (7.122), and Plutarch (*Tiberius Gracchus* 1.2) tells us that Gracchus's decision was motivated by love for his wife. Valerius Maximus (4.6.1) contrasts this with the story of Admetus and praises it as a remarkable illustration of conjugal love (see also *De viris illustribus* 57). He concludes by saying that he is uncertain whether we must consider Cornelia lucky for having had such a husband or pity her for having lost him. Gracchus probably died in 154 B.C. (or not long afterward), the year of Gaius's birth, most likely their last child, when Cornelia was not yet forty. Thus we may deduce that she was born around 190 B.C. or in the years just prior to that date. In fixing the year of her birth at such a late date (proposed by those scholars who also fix her marriage at a rather late date) the only point of reference we have is the year 183 B.C., the year her father died. Cornelia must have been born by that date, or it is possible she was born a few months afterward as Africanus's posthumous daughter, but there is no evidence to support this. It is much more likely that she was a small child when Africanus died (in Gellius's account—where, however, her father gives her in marriage—she is described as *virginem iam viro maturam*). Plutarch, drawing on Polybius's testimony, tells us that Cornelia had been left by her father *anèkdoton kai anèggyon,* neither married nor engaged (*Tiberius Gracchus* 4.4), hardly an appropriate description for a small child. A woman, nonetheless, could be considered *viripotens,* of marriageable age, even at the early age of twelve, and we have many records of very young brides marrying at fourteen or even earlier. The average marrying age for young girls, however, was between fifteen and twenty (here we should remember that the Augustan dispositions concerning marriage obliged women to marry between the ages of twenty and fifty). This would have been Cornelia's age if she married Gracchus between the years 176, as Carcopino believes, and 170 B.C., the late alternative proposed by Moir. This necessarily partial and approximative dating does not conflict with the main evidence we have. These sources fully agree that Cornelia lived a very long life and that when Plutarch described her in her villa at Misenum (where she retired after Gaius's tragic death in 121 B.C.), telling her guests the stories of her father and her children (*Gaius Gracchus* 19), she was quite an elderly woman. When her husband died, Cornelia rose to the occasion with the dignity required of her social position. The abilities she displayed in these circumstances suggest not only that she was a strong and spirited woman but that she was also mature enough in age to have gained much wisdom from her experiences.

In *De divinatione* 1.36, Cicero tells us that Gracchus chose to die instead of his young—the word Cicero uses is *adulescens*—wife. We would gain nothing here by discussing the heated debates of scholars who have attempted to define *adulescentia,* which may actually be interpreted rather flexibly, as the period extending from vigorous youth to the threshold of genuine *senectus,* old age. The point of the serpent episode was to emphasize the age difference between husband and wife, and the fact that Cornelia at the time of Gracchus's death (he already an old man) was still young enough to remarry and have more children. Pliny underlines this and praises Gracchus's decision, not only because it showed how much he loved his wife, but also because it displayed his concern for the good of the state. Gracchus ordered that the male serpent be killed, since "Cornelia was still young and could still have children" (*Nat. Hist.* 7.122).

Plutarch may be saying the same thing in *Life of Tiberius Gracchus* (1.5) when he states that Gracchus made his decision because "he believed that he should be the one to die, as he was older, while Cornelia was still young." Elsewhere Plutarch specifies what he means by the expression "still young" (*eti neas ouses*). In *Life of Cato the Younger* 25, Plutarch tells us that Quintus Hortensius Hortalus, wishing to provide descendants for himself and to create closer ties with Cato, asked Cato to give him his daughter, Porcia, in marriage, even though she was already married to Bibulus and had two children. When this request was denied, Hortensius changed his mind and asked Cato to give him his wife, Marcia, instead, and this time Cato agreed. What interests us here is the expression used by Plutarch in this context, almost identical to the one he uses in reference to Cornelia but with one addition which for our purposes is quite illuminating. Hortensius did not hesitate to ask Cato for his wife who was "still young enough to give birth to more children" (*nean men ousan eti pros to tiktein*).

Here Are My Jewels

Cornelia was raised not only in the stimulating and broad-minded environment of the Scipio family, but also in an era that was quite unusual, both in itself and in its attitude toward women. In this era of profound change and deep contradiction, public recognition of women (who, significantly, seem very active in this period) alternated with repression of them. Earlier, during the terrible period of the Punic wars, women, as private individuals or as groups, had received public recognition for their meritorious deeds. For example, Busa, a wealthy woman from Apulia, was honored by the senate for the assistance she gave the troops who had sought refuge in Canosa after the defeat at Cannae (Livy 22.52.7; Valerius Maximus 4.8.2). Livy also tells us of a group of matrons who were officially summoned and brought together after the appearance of an omen. Twenty-five of them were then selected and entrusted with an offering to be made to Juno, after which followed sacrifices "in purity and chastity" (Livy 27.37). The high male death rate had led to greater autonomy for women, especially in managing their patrimonies, which now frequently passed into their own control. The legislation of the time produced, aside from general provisions of a sumptuary nature, also a few restrictive measures. Later, in 169 B.C., the *lex Voconia* limited the wealth and property that matrons of the upper classes could inherit. Marriages became more unstable, while sterner attitudes prevailed in morals and behavior. Around 216/215 B.C., the cult of Venus Verticordia (she who turns her heart and soul toward Virtue) was introduced in order to encourage chastity and modesty in virgins and married women. Two vestals were accused of incest. One was buried alive, the other committed suicide (according to Livy 22.57, although the sources conflict on this point). The day after the Roman defeat at Cannae, the senate was forced to restrict the mourning period for a large number of matrons so that they could celebrate rites in honor of Ceres. Women were required to respect their religious duties, in which they performed an important role for the community, although at times this entailed setting aside their personal feelings. As Valerius Maximus (1.1.15) informs us, "as soon as the tears for their recently deceased loved ones had dried and the signs of mourning had been set aside, mothers and daughters, wives and sisters, were forced (*coactae*) to put on their white robes and make offerings of incense."

In 213 B.C. the aediles accused a number matrons of adultery and immoral behavior and several of them were convicted and sent into exile. In this same period, Rome seems to have been invaded by a wave of superstition, accompanied by an army of soothsayers and practitioners of magic. Traditional religious ceremonies fell into disuse and new cults appeared, not only within the walls of private homes, but also in public places. Livy (25.1) reports that a scandal arose because women "in the forum and the Capitolium no longer perform sacrifices and invoke the gods according to the traditional ways (*patrio more*)." The praetor intervened by banning the celebration of strange or foreign rites in public or in sacred places and ordered the confiscation of all books containing divinatory formulas, prayers, or instructions on the art of performing sacrifices. The importation of a new cult from Phrygia, the cult of Cybele, did not occur until 204 B.C., when Cybele was officially admitted to Rome and was triumphantly welcomed by Scipio Nasica and by the matrons and vestals of the city. The authorities' vigilance regarding these matters continued even after the war had ended, when new religions and mystery cults spread throughout Rome and Italy. In Rome, religion was a civic institution essentially based on ritual practices and was closely connected to politics. Women, who were excluded from politics, were also formally excluded from the sacred, collective events on which the life of the city depended. Yet they had their own religious function and space: as vestals and priestesses, in special cults where they had a specific role to perform, in rites exclusively for women (where for once they enjoyed a dominant role), and, as time passed, in the mystery cults offering personal salvation. The development of religious movements in which women could play a leading role led to the decline of women's cults. In the rites of Bacchus, women had the power to initiate men, mainly young men, thereby stealing them from both family and the city. The authorities came to view this power as subversive and cruelly suppressed the Bacchanals in 186 B.C. This was a return to darker times. Shortly afterward, the outbreak of an epidemic aroused suspicion against women in general, and many women were brought to trial for poisoning.

The case of the Bacchanals was not the only clamorous event in which women played a dominant role in the first half of the second century. In 195 B.C., they burst upon the political scene, invading the forum en masse and demonstrating before the houses of the tribunes, to show their support for the proposed repeal of the *lex Oppia*. This law had been passed twenty years earlier during the conflict with Carthage, a very crucial time in Roman history. The law limited drastically the amount of costly goods—sumptuous clothing, gold, jewelry, chariots—that a woman could own without these items being considered unnecessary, and unlawful, luxuries. Livy (34.1–8) gives an account (reflecting his own views and the temper of his own era) of the debate that took place on this question, in which the two sides were represented by Cato and by Lucius Valerius. In his speech Cato, an intransigent moralist (at the time consul), vigorously attacked these outspoken women, who, he believed, posed a serious threat to society. By violating the rules of modesty, *pudicitia,* escaping the control of their families, and assembling in public they constituted a dangerous female revolt that could have disastrous consequences. Moreover, giving in to their demands signified yielding to the greed (*avaritia*) and extravagance (*luxuria*) that had begun to spread through Roman society, destroying the roots of those wholesome practices and virtues (*mos maiorum*) on which Rome's fortune had been built. Valerius replied that there was nothing subversive about the women's demonstration. He emphasized that they could not aspire to the public, religious, political, or military honors reserved for men (*non magistratus nec sacerdotia nec triumphi nec insignia nec dona aut spolia bellica iis contingere possunt* 34.7.8) and that for them the only possible signs of distinction were beautiful clothing and jewelry (*munditiae et ornatus et cultus, haec feminarum insignia sunt,* ibid. 9). The *lex Oppia* had been passed in wartime, a period of shortages and of peril. Now that peace and prosperity had been reestablished, it was time to repeal the law and allow women to enjoy the luxuries proper to their sex. Valerius won the debate: the law was repealed and the women were allowed to keep their jewels. (Later, during his term as censor in 184 B.C., Cato limited some forms of sumptuous display and opposed fashions that had come in with the Hellenizing tendency of the time.) It is easy to imagine that a woman like Cornelia's mother, Tertia Aemilia, wife of Africanus, might have participated in the women's protest, or at least shared their views, although we have no record confirming this. Polybius informs us that when Tertia Aemilia left her home to attend official ceremonies for matrons, she cut a magnificent figure: laden with jewels, traveling about the city in her ornately decorated *pilentum,* or carriage, accompanied by an army of servants.

Jewels also play a role in Cornelia's story and in the famous anecdote concerning her (recorded by Valerius Maximus 4.4.1). One day after a matron from Campania had shown Cornelia her jewels, in reply she pointed to her two sons, just returned from school, and told the friend that these were her jewels (*haec ornamenta sunt mea*). There is no way to determine if the incident is historically true. In Plutarch's *Life of Phocion* (19), we find an almost identical story, in which Phocion's wife boasts to her friend that her most precious jewel is her husband. It would be useful to explore why this anecdote came to be associated with the legend of Cornelia. One hypothesis traces the origin of the story to Cornelia's presumed financial difficulties (Valerius Maximus refers to her as one of the famous *exempla de paupertate*). Seneca, the chief source of information about her financial problems, claimed (in *Ad Helviam matrem de consolatione* 12.6 and also in *Naturales quaestiones* 1.17.8) that Scipio's daughters received their dowries from public funds because their father had left them no money. This episode reported by Seneca actually involves another Cornelia and her father, Gnaeus Cornelius Scipio Calvus, as Valerius Maximus records (4.4.10), and occurred during the Iberian campaign. We cannot say for certain whether the decline of Africanus's family also entailed an economic crisis. Other sources agree that dowries for the two Cornelias, each fixed at fifty talents, were provided by Tertia Aemilia (for the first half of the amount) and Scipio Aemilianus (for the second half). If Africanus's son, Publius, was still alive when the first payment was made, as some scholars, such as Bandelli, have suggested, the fact that his mother paid the dowry, drawing perhaps on her own patrimony, would strongly suggest that the Scipios were in economic trouble. Trying to trace Africanus's male descendants to see if they were alive at the time would be of no help here, as it is not certain how many sons he had (theories range from three to only one). It is very likely that Aemilia (coming from a family like the Aemilii Pauli) handled her own financial affairs. Polybius tells us that she lived in luxury and that most of her wealth had been acquired in the happy days of Africanus.

We have no real proof of Cornelia's economic difficulties (except, perhaps, the fact that her dowry was only fifty talents). She continued to live in high style even after her sons died, receiving guests at her villa and "exchanging gifts with kings" (Plutarch, *Gaius Gracchus* 19.2). This would suggest that her situation was secure. As for her sons, Plutarch tells us that Tiberius Gracchus offered to pay compensation to Octavius at a moment when his own finances were far from flourishing and describes Gaius (2.4) as a man of refined tastes and a spendthrift. It is likely that the story of Cornelia's famous reply came into being at a time when the criticism of luxury and of moral decline were favorite subjects for the moralistic writers of the day. This is borne out by the stern tone used by Valerius Maximus in his treatment of the saying *maxima ornamenta esse matronis liberos*—"For married women children [are] their most precious jewels." In the Roman imagination Cornelia was pictured as an old-fashioned woman devoted to her family. She was considered to be very different from the women of her time, from the other women of the Scipios, and even from her own mother. Here we should mention another story about jewels. Cornelia's mother, Tertia Aemilia, had an adopted grandson, Scipio Aemilianus, son of Lucius Aemilius Paulus and Papiria. He had been adopted by her son, Publius. Polybius recounts that when Tertia Aemilia died, about 162 B.C., immediately after the funeral, Scipio Aemilianus collected her splendid jewels and gave them to his natural mother, Papiria. His mother was now living apart from her husband and lacked means to maintain the high standard of living that her noble rank required. Papiria did not hesitate to wear the jewels, and all the matrons (as well as Polybius) commended her son's generosity (Polybius 31.26.6ff.). Cornelia never saw her mother's jewelry again. Her famous remark may conceal a trace of bitterness about the fortune she had lost.

Legimus epistulas Corneliae

Jewels were a status symbol for matrons and also a frequent topic for public debate. Roman tradition commemorated women who had helped save Rome by donating their gold to the public coffers in the times of Camillus or during the invasions of the Gauls. We have already mentioned the provisions made during and immediately following the Second Punic War. Now times had changed and women had their own patrimonies to defend. Women like Cornelia (or her mother, Aemilia) who competently handled their own affairs and those of their families (we have no record of Cornelia being helped or hindered by a *tutor*) were no longer exceptions to the norm. When the triumvirs levied an emergency tax in 42 B.C. on the patrimonies of fourteen hundred wealthy matrons, these women (*ordo matronarum,* Valerius Maximus 8.3.3) replied with a public protest. They gathered in the forum, where they were eloquently represented by Hortensia (the daughter of the great orator Quintus Hortensius Hortalus). Their spokeswoman declared that it was wrong of men to tax the patrimonies and the dowries that allowed matrons to enjoy a manner of life befitting their social station. She reminded the men that although women were barred from the military and from politics, in the times of the Punic wars they had helped save the city, acting on their own initiative, by donating their jewels when funds were needed. Hortensia's speech convinced the men. Valerius Maximus attests to this (8.3.3), as does Appian (*Bella Civilia* 4.32–34) who records her entire speech.

Quintilian praises Hortensia's speech and mentions it in connection with the education of children and the need for parents to pass on to their children a rich cultural heritage (1.1.6). Hortensia and Lelia (daughter of Gaius Lelius) were praised as examples of women who carried on the illustrious examples of their fathers, while Cornelia was remembered for her contribution to her sons' education and to their development as great orators. Evidence of her influence may be found in the letters Cornelia passed down to later generations. Cicero states that he had read those letters (*Brutus* 211), *"legimus epistulas Corneliae matris Gracchorum,"* and that he understood why it was said that her sons "had been raised in eloquence rather than in their mother's womb" (*apparet filios non tam in gremio educatos quam in sermone matris*). The letters attributed to Cornelia are the earliest examples of private correspondence in Latin, with very few exceptions (we have record of a few individual letters from the legendary royal period and a few references to Cato's epistles) prior to Cicero's own letters.

Cicero's praise for the letters is remarkable, because they were written by a woman. His praise for her sons, however, is not surprising. Despite the hostile attitude toward them evinced in the sources, Tiberius and Gaius were universally known as eloquent men. Records exist which mention writings by Gaius Gracchus (for example the anecdote of Sempronius Gracchus and the snakes), including a *biblìon* about his brother (mentioned by Plutarch in *Tiberius Gracchus* 8.9). The Gracchi's speeches were certainly recorded and read in later times (this is proved by numerous references to them in the sources). Cicero describes the oratorical skills of the two brothers in *Brutus* 104: "the speeches of Carbo and Gracchus in our possession (*Carbonis et Gracchi habemus orationes*), not yet splendid in style, expressed extremely intelligent and deeply pondered ideas." Pliny gives us the surprising news (it matters little whether it is true) that he had seen at the home of his friend Pomponius Secundus original manuscripts by Tiberius and Gaius Gracchus, nearly two hundred years old (*Nat. Hist.* 13.83: *"Tiberi Gaique Gracchorum manus apud Pomponium Secundum vatem civemque clarissimum vidi annos fere post ducentos"*). Thus it is plausible that a collection of Cornelia's letters was also preserved. Plutarch also refers to letters written by Cornelia to Gaius (*Gaius Gracchus* 13.2), but there is debate over this, given the obscure wording of the passage.

Cornelia's letters must surely have been a rich mine of information about the events of her era. Another similar testimony by a woman was the autobiography supposedly written by Nero's mother, Agrippina, in which she told the story of her family. Both Tacitus (*Annales* 4.53: *"id ego [. . .] repperi in commentariis Agrippinae filiae, quae Neronis principis mater vitam suam et casus suorum posteris memoravit"*) and Pliny (*Nat. Hist.* 7.46, in discussing Nero's birth: *"scribit parens eius Agrippina"*) refer to this autobiography, stating that they used it as a source. Their use of it indicates that it was in regular circulation at the time. No trace of Agrippina's autobiography has survived, and later historians remembered her only for her immoral behavior, which they described in detail. To the two much-discussed fragments of letters written by Cornelia, however, and to Plutarch's mention of *epistolia* we will return presently.

Cornelia, with her learning and keen mind, was an exceptional woman. In early childhood she had been exposed to the fervid intellectual climate of her family, the broad-minded Scipios, who were receptive to Greek influences and who had a deep impact on the second century B.C. Among the Scipios, according to R. A. Bauman, women seem to have been held in high esteem. Most certainly, Cornelia personally selected the tutors entrusted with her sons' moral and intellectual development. These men, Blossius of Cuma and Diophanes of Mytilene, not only played a crucial role in Tiberius's education, but also in his political career. In *Brutus* (104), Cicero stresses that Tiberius Gracchus owed his excellent education in early childhood and his knowledge of Greek letters mainly to his mother, for thanks to her *diligentia,* he was instructed by some of the most brilliant scholars of the time.

Moreover, the sources also tell us that Cornelia could hold her own in the company of famous people. Jerome (*Commentarii in Sophoniam prophetam, Prologus* 655 Adriaen = *PL* 25, 1337C), after mentioning famous Greek women intellectuals such as Aspasia, Sappho, and Themisto, says that Cornelia was so renowned for her knowledge of philosophy that Carneades found nothing unseemly about participating in philosophical disputes in her presence. Plutarch, in describing the last years of Cornelia's life after the death of her youngest son, Gaius, portrays her in her villa in Misenum, surrounded by guests, mostly Greeks and men of letters, whom she entertained with impeccable hospitality and pleasant conversation (*Gaius Gracchus* 19.2–3).

Women who excelled in intellectual pursuits, or who merely cultivated real interest in such pursuits, were extremely rare in Cornelia's day. She remains unique for her era. If we comb through the sources we may find traces of such women a century later. We have record of another Cornelia, the daughter of Metellus Scipio, first married to Crassus's son and later to Pompey. Plutarch praises her for her learning, which ranged from philosophy to geometry, and for her skill in playing the lyre (*Pompeius* 55, 66, and 74, 76, 78–80). Octavia, Augustus's sister and Marcus Antonius's wife, was also known as an erudite woman. She participated in readings of the *Aeneid,* and Athenodorus, son of Sandon, dedicated his works to her, as Plutarch tells us in *Life of Publicola,* 17.5. The appreciable talents of women in these circles appear to have been stifled by their personalities, which supposedly tended toward licentious conduct, as legend often claims. This is the case of Sempronia (later involved in the Catilinian conspiracy), a noble woman who had excelled in her studies of Greek, music, and dancing, and was famous for her poetry and witty conversation (Sallust *De coniuratione Catilinae* 25). Another poet was Cornificia (sister of the poet Quintus Cornificius), who must have distinguished herself with some skill, considering that centuries afterward her *insignia epigrammata* were still remembered. The *corpus Tibullianum* (3.13–18) contains a few elegies written by the young poetess Sulpicia, daughter of Servius Sulpicius Rufus and pupil of Valerius Messalla. Martial (10.35) sang the praises of another poet by this same name, wife of his friend Calenus, comparing her to Sappho. Ovid affectionately celebrates young Perilla (*Tristia* 3.7), for her unusual learning and fertile poetic gift.

Caerellia played a complex role in Cicero's life (as we learn from his epistles), thanks to her age, position, and status, and also to her connections. She was an unusual woman, despite the malicious portrayal of her found in some sources (for example, Dio Cassius 46.18.6), and was so deeply interested in Cicero's philosophy that she once secretly obtained a copy of *De finibus* from Atticus's workshop before it was published. Philosophy had begun to interest women, occasionally for very specific reasons: in one of the memorable sayings attributed to Epictetus, the women of Rome were ridiculed for reading Plato's *Republic* and were described as being shocked by Plato's remark that "women must be common," being unable to grasp the philosophical meaning. Stoic philosophy had many women followers. Horace criticized a matron who had grown too old and unattractive to seduce men, and claimed that not even the volumes of the Stoics, which she kept wrapped in silk, would have been of any help to her (*"Quid? Quod libelli Stoici inter Sericos / iacere pulvillos amant . . . ," Epodi* 8.15–16).

Later, Musonius Rufus recommended that the same education be given to young people of both sexes, who were to study philosophy (see especially *Diatribae* 3, "Let women philosophize," and 4, "Should the same education be given to sons and daughters?"). These were praiseworthy intentions. Seneca believed that intellectual activities could help women overcome the flaws in their characters and their natural inferiority: "Women are irrational creatures, and if lacking in culture or good manners, they are instinctive and prey to passion" (*De constantia sapientis* 14.1). Yet in Cornelia's time women were not allowed to translate these ideas into daily practice. In *To Helvia on Consolation,* Seneca encourages his mother to bury herself in her studies to find comfort for the pain of recent loss. Yet he is forced to admit that she had to limit those studies, owing to the disapproval of her old-fashioned husband (17.3–5).

The Education of Her Sons

We have explained why Cornelia was so remarkable for her times and also why the sources are so frugal in describing her intellectual interests and abilities. She is most often remembered for her role in her children's education and her skill in running her household. Plutarch portrays her after her husband's death: "She took upon herself the burden of her children and the managing of her patrimony and proved to be so wise, so full of motherly love and so noble of character that it would seem that Tiberius had made no mistake when he chose to die in place of such a woman" (*Tiberius Gracchus* 1.6). Concerning her sons' education Plutarch says: "though they were without dispute in natural endowments and dispositions the first among the Romans of their time, yet they seemed to owe their virtues even more to their education than their birth" (Dryden translation of Plutarch's *Life of Tiberius Gracchus* 7). All the other testimonies evince this same tone, insisting mainly (as we have seen in Cicero and Quintilian) on her sons' indisputable oratorical skills: Tiberius with his softer style, Gaius, the more passionate speaker (*Tiberius Gracchus* 2.3). Such skills could have only come from the education they received from their mother, as their father had died before having a chance to contribute to their intellectual development. Furthermore (as Cicero tells us in *De Oratore* 1.38) Sempronius Gracchus, a serious and cautious man, was no great orator (*"homo prudens et gravis haudquaquam eloquens"*). The example of Cornelia shows that Roman women played an important role in society, not only as breeders of children, but as transmitters of cultural values, which was not true among the Greeks. By nursing their children at their own breasts and overseeing their education, Roman women performed a task useful not only to the family but to society, for they helped transmit the fathers' cultural heritage and were instrumental in the development of great men. When in Tacitus's *Dialogue on Oratory* (28.4–6) Messalla bitterly laments the corruption of morals and the laxity rampant in the education of children, he cites a triad of exemplary mothers who by wisely dispensing *disciplina ac severitas* influenced their sons' education and destiny. Cornelia comes first in this list, followed by Aurelia, Caesar's mother, and Atia, Augustus's mother:

> Each of these three women of antiquity raised their sons, born of chaste motherhood, not in the chamber of a hired nurse, but at their own breasts and in their own laps. A mother's chief praise lay in governing her house and caring for her children. An elderly relative was chosen, a woman of esteemed reputation, and was entrusted with the care of all the children in the same family. In her presence children could not say anything foul or do anything dishonest. With a sacred reserve and modesty, she directed, with the mother's assistance, the children's studies and games. Thus did

Cornelia, mother of the Gracchi; Aurelia, mother of Caesar; and Atia, mother of Augustus, preside over the education of their sons and prepare them for their destiny as princes.

Plutarch tells us (*Tiberius Gracchus* 1.7) that Cornelia rejected an offer of marriage (and thus a kingdom) from King Ptolemy, probably Ptolemy VIII Euergetes II, named Physkon (certainly no handsome fellow, to judge from his nickname "big belly"—Polybius considered him one of the most repulsive of kings). This story, for which there is no independent evidence, reinforced Cornelia's public image as an ideal matron. The anecdote may be a propagandistic fabrication, intending to stress the good relations between Rome and Ptolemaic Egypt, or it may reflect Cornelia's social connections with foreign kings and celebrities. In moving in such high circles, Cornelia could rely on her prestigious status as a member of the Scipio family and on the influence and reputation of her husband, who had conducted many successful diplomatic missions abroad. It was primarily thanks to her choice to remain *univira,* faithful forever to one man, that Cornelia was elevated to mythic stature. It was believed that her decision not to remarry had been made entirely for her sons' benefit. Dionysius of Halicarnassus (8.48) records an illustrious precedent: Veturia, reproaching her son, Coriolanus, underlined the sacrifices she made for his education and claimed that after his father died, she had been for him mother, father, nurse, sister, and had chosen not to remarry or have other children for his sake.

Roman history is full of famous men influenced by their mothers (a genuine form of *materna auctoritas*), and when those mothers were widows, their influence was even stronger. Often the sons of widows were destined to become leaders of great upheavals or to turn against their own country. Thus runs the tradition for Coriolanus, Sertorius, Marcus Antonius (this is stressed in Plutarch's *Lives;* see Le Corsu, Salvioni).

It is beyond our scope here to discuss the political turmoil that led Tiberius and Gaius to their tragic ends, or to analyze the judgments of ancient historians concerning the brothers Gracchus. We may legitimately ask, however, what influence Cornelia had on her sons' political careers. Here we must repeat that women were expected to keep their distance from politics and public life. Their participation in such matters could never be direct, although they often found themselves used as tools in the designs of others. Hallett has noted that Roman matrons tended to focus their ambition on their children rather than on their husbands, and the sources record many examples of women who did so (according to Polybius, Pomponia, Africanus's mother, also took a very active interest in the careers of her sons, Lucius and Publius). This phenomenon became more pronounced as time passed. Seneca in his *To Helvia on Consolation* expresses gratitude to Helvia's sister (his aunt) for helping him obtain his quaestorship (19.2) and complains about those mothers who, excluded from public affairs because they are women, exploit their sons' influence and use them to satisfy their own ambitions (14.2 *"per illos ambitiosae sunt"*). Cornelia's influence on her sons' political views is open to debate (although there is a tendency to see her as generally agreeing with them). Plutarch records conflicting information on this point. Some evidence suggests that she tended toward more moderate views. For instance, in *Life of Gaius Gracchus* (4.2), Plutarch tells us that Gaius first proposed and then withdrew a law that would have directly affected Marcus Octavius (the proposed law prevented anyone who had been dismissed from public office from ever holding any other office again). Gaius later explained that he had withdrawn the law at his mother's request (a more hostile version of this story appears in Diodorus 34/35.25.2; see Botteri [1992], 85–86).

This may have been a strategic move on the part of young Gaius to gain political consensus and enhance his personal prestige, or perhaps it was the first sign of tension in his relationship with his mother, which grew more troubled as things came to a head. Traces of Cornelia's disapproval of Gaius's politics appear in two fragments preserved in the conclusion of *Lives* by Cornelius Nepos (fr. 59 Marshall; *Epistolographi Latini Minores* 124.3–4 Cugusi). The *inscriptio* describes these fragments as sections of Cornelia's letters, extracted from a book by Nepos, *On the Latin Historian*. The longer fragment (dating from 124 B.C., judging from its mention of Gaius's position as tribune, to which he was elected in that same year) is extremely interesting:

> I would even say that, excluding those people who killed Tiberius Gracchus, no enemy has caused me such embarrassment and pain as you have. Why could you not have behaved as all my other children have done till now to ensure that in my old age I should have a minimum of distress, obeying me in all circumstances and considering it impious to do anything against my will, especially as I have not long to live? Not even this, not even the fact that I have not much time left, is enough to keep you from disobeying me and plotting to bring about the ruin of the republic. When will all this stop? When will our family stop committing such madness? When will it be possible to put an end to all this? When will we stop in-

flicting suffering and then having to suffer ourselves? When will we feel shame for bringing disorder and trouble to the state? However, if this cannot be, then at least wait until I am dead before presenting yourself to the tribunate. You may do as you please after I am no longer able to see and feel. When I am dead you must make the proper sacrifices and invoke our family god.

For years scholars have discussed the authenticity of these fragments (some scholars, such as Ed. Meyer or E. Malcovati, have modified their ideas on this), along with the question of how Cornelia's letters came to be preserved and circulated (Cicero knew of the letters and was a friend of Nepos). The fragments may have been taken from the same original text, but a few variations in tone and style have led some scholars to believe that they come from two different letters (in the first fragment some scholars have seen an obscure reference to Cornelia's intercession on behalf of Marcus Octavius). The stylistic and linguistic features, the use of archaic expressions, the familiar tone, have convinced many that this was a private letter (though others think it may have been a public communication), closely resembling other Latin prose of the era, and similar in style to the writings of Cato and Plautus (Horsfall). Cornelia did have the ability to write such elegant prose. Moreover, according to some scholars, the presence of a few repetitions and incongruities in the fragments demonstrates their authenticity (Cugusi), since a forger would no doubt have been careful to avoid any inconsistencies (we must also consider that Nepos himself may have done some editing). Yet there are other possible explanations for the incongruities. Let us suppose that the forger was not a student of rhetoric performing a neat exercise at his desk, but someone in later times, deliberately searching for effects that might make his forgery seem more authentic (anacoluthons, repetitions, redundancies appropriate to a woman feeling the pressure of events around her, in a state of agitation and worry about what will happen to her son). In that case those incongruities may merely reflect unsuccessful attempts at this. In fact, many different scholars have concluded that the letter was not really written by Cornelia, although they approach the question from different directions. Some express surprise that the anti-Gracchian party did not make use of the letter as propaganda against the Gracchi, which they surely would have done if it had been genuine. Others suggest that the letter was fabricated in order to discredit the Gracchi by showing them in conflict with their mother. Still others think the letter was intended to explain a sort of ideological gap between Cornelia and her sons. Some skeptics have pointed out the striking contrast between these fragments and the traditional view of Cornelia as an uncritical mother who actively supported her sons' politics. Lastly, some scholars, for this very same reason, have attempted to soften the accusatory tone of the letter and have suggested that it merely reflects the chiding of a worried mother. These are the main arguments concerning the letter's authenticity.

It is difficult to answer to all the questions raised by such conflicting points of view. If Cornelia was not the author of these fragments (although a collection of her letters did once exist, and she was known to be capable of writing such prose) who could have written them? After analyzing the stylistic and linguistic features of the fragments some scholars have concluded that they were written shortly after the period to which they refer (and as S. Barnard has suggested) by Cornelia's daughter, Sempronia. It cannot be denied that they express strong disapproval of Gaius's political views. Though not so much in the first fragment, where we find further evidence of the well-documented Roman concept that *inimicitiae,* like family interests, must take second place to the good of the state. Right from the beginning, the second fragment has a tone which, far from being calm and reflective, is critical and provocative: as well as displaying an open aversion for Gaius's politics, their mother demonstrates disapproval of Tiberius, notably in the relentless series of rhetorical questions and in the expression: *"ecquando desinet familia nostra insanire?"* Phrases such as *"rem publicam profliges,"* and especially *"miscenda atque perturbanda re publica,"* voice the very criticisms uttered by the Gracchi's enemies (Instinsky) and seem excessive (and therefore suspect). It is no coincidence that in Cicero, for example, the Gracchi are more than once defined as *perturbatores rei publicae* and similar expressions are also found in Velleius and Tacitus. Cassius Dio, probably quoting exactly the Latin source used for accounts of the feats of the Gracchi, says (fr. 83.7) *phyrōn kai tarassōn.* Cornelia's rhetorical outburst against her son's political actions, her valiant defense of the state, and her insistence on her own authority as his mother sound all too familiar. In fact, they echo the words spoken by Coriolanus's mother while defending the supreme interests of the state against her own son in Livy, and especially in Dionysius of Halicarnassus.

The perfect harmony existing between Cornelia and her sons, as they are traditionally portrayed, may have been flawed, yet her deep love and respect for them may not necessarily have led her to endorse their political views. She may have supported Tiberius's views: after all, young Tiberius's political ideas had been inspired by his teachers Blossius and Dio-phanes, whom she had personally chosen as his tutors. Sources tell us that her sons sometimes evoked her image in order to manipulate the public conscience. (See Plutarch *Tiberius Gracchus* 13.6 and Dio Cassius fr. 83.8).

After Tiberius's death, Cornelia withdrew to Misenum (Orosius 5.12.9), fleeing from the political turmoil of the times. Her previous pres-tige was not impaired, and even after the death of Gaius she continued her former way of life to the very end. There is no record of her being penalized as a consequence of her sons' misfortunes (by contrast, Li-cinia, Gaius's widow, was not allowed to dress in mourning and her dowry was confiscated; *Gaius Gracchus* 17.6). Plutarch portrays Cornelia as an elderly woman surrounded by guests, telling the stories of her sons' tragic lives as if they were heroes from an archaic era (no doubt her way of honoring their memory) and contrasts this with another, very pleas-ant (*hedìste*) conversation in which she regaled her listeners with stories about her father, Africanus. Plutarch emphasizes that Cornelia's guests were astonished by the detachment and self-control she displayed in talking about her sons, for she never showed any signs of sorrow. Even when speaking of the holy places where they were slain (claiming that "their dead bodies were worthy of such sepulchers") she manifested her maternal *pietas* in the most dignified way. For Cornelia, who had always been *philòteknos,* loving her sons meant preserving their memory, and at that time, according to Plutarch (*Gaius Gracchus* 18.3), the people honored and made sacrifices to the memory of the brothers Gracchus, as if they were gods.

Gaius was devoted to his mother and cites her as an example of fecun-dity and chastity. He reacted vehemently whenever anyone criticized her, as shown by some of his remarks about her that have become almost proverbial (see, for example, Plutarch *Gaius Gracchus* 4). Plutarch fur-nishes other information about their relationship (13.2) which gives a slightly different picture of Cornelia's attitude toward her son's politics. According to Plutarch, some sources claim that Cornelia assisted Gaius in the crisis of 121 B.C. by secretly hiring men outside Rome and sending them to the city disguised as reapers to participate in the protest. Proof of this was supposedly to be found in an obscure reference (*tauta* [. . .] *e(i)nigmèna gegràphthai*) in one of Cornelia's letters to Gaius. This is yet another reference to her letters (even if the term used, *epistolia,* and its ambiguous contents suggest something very different from the letters that for Cicero and Quintilian were a model of style and rhetoric), this time suggesting that she did support her sons' ideas. Plutarch seems to doubt this: he introduces this information generically ("they say") and hastens afterward to add a disclaimer: "Others, however, say that Cornelia firmly (*pany*) disapproved of what had been done."

This mention of Cornelia's alleged assistance to Gaius is the only explicit information in Plutarch's biography touching on her intervention in her sons' political activities—with the exception of her request that Gaius withdraw the law that would penalize Marcus Octavius. The story may be one of the few traces left of a slanderous attempt by the Gracchi's enemies to cast both mother and sons in a dubious light. As the myth of Cornelia took shape in the public imagination, those negative traces were swept away, and Africanus's daughter came to be esteemed universally as a symbol of maternal devotion. She had indeed performed her duties well, for the Gracchi's virtues were indisputably recognized even by their political opponents, and the credit for those talents and gifts was traced back to Cornelia. Their political ideas were considered by their adversaries as deviating from the great tradition of their forefathers (they were frequently compared unfavorably with their father, Sempronius Gracchus, and grandfather, Africanus, shining examples of loyalty to the state), but Cornelia could not be blamed for that. Women, after all, had no authority in the field of politics, the domain of men.

There may be a few oblique references in the sources to Cornelia's alleged involvement in her sons' political careers. Plutarch describes her impatiently spurring Tiberius on to greatness because she was tired of being known as "the daughter of Scipio rather than the mother of the Gracchi." This may be an allusion to her own responsibilities in encouraging her recently elected son to take prompt political action, motivated only by her personal ambitions. Perhaps these ambitions and her lavish life style helped create the proverbially haughty image of her, described by Juvenal (6.166) and later by Claudian (*Laus Serenae* 42–43).

In this chorus of praise, one voice can be heard singing out of tune, accusing Cornelia of a serious crime: the mysterious death of her son-in-law, Scipio Aemilianus.

Misunderstandings between Aemilianus and Tiberius increased as time passed. After Tiberius was killed, Scipio harshly criticized his brother-in-law's politics (Plutarch *Tiberius Gracchus* 21.7–8). In the following years Scipio used his influence to hinder the plans of Gaius and his circle (who supported the cause of the Italians). Then in 129, the night before he was to address an important assembly, Scipio was found dead in his chamber. Gaius and his followers, Fulvius Flaccus and Valerius Carbo, were suspected of having murdered him, but were not brought to trial. Different rumors circulated about the condition in which Scipio's body had been found, along with conflicting theories concerning the cause of death (natural, murder, or suicide) that have intrigued both ancients and moderns. Plutarch tells us (*Tiberius Gracchus* 21.9) that he also wrote a biography of Scipio Aemilianus, which would doubtless help clarify the mystery of his death, but no trace of this text has survived. Appian gives an account of Scipio's death (*Bella Civilia* 1.20), and is unsure if it was by murder or suicide. If it was murder, he suggests that Cornelia and her daughter, Sempronia, may have been responsible:

> The night he died Scipio had placed beside him a tablet on which he in- tended to write down his speech. He was later found dead, with no wounds. Some say that Cornelia, mother of Gracchus, had him killed be- cause she did not want her son's law to be abolished. She was supposedly helped by her daughter Sempronia, who was married to Scipio, but who was not loved by him because she was ugly and barren. Nor did she love him. Others think he killed himself because he could not deliver what he had promised.

Appian is the only source to accuse Cornelia even though he does give her the benefit of the doubt by suggesting suicide as an equally plausible alternative. In hinting that Scipio was poisoned (for poison leaves no visible traces) and by depicting Sempronia as ugly and barren, Appian is repeating the traditionally misogynous view of women as po- tential conspirators and poisoners. No other sources blame Cornelia, and Plutarch does not mention this suspicion when he discusses the mystery of Aemilianus's death. Other sources accuse only Sempronia. Livy, in *Periocha* 59, tells us that Sempronia was suspected of poisoning her hus- band, and *Scholia Bobiensia* in *Pro Mil.* (118 Stangl) lay the blame on Gaius Gracchus and his sister. Orosius also accuses Sempronia (5.10.10: *uxoris suae . . . dolo necatum*) and does not even mention Cornelia. It is particularly significant that in these latter versions, Sempronia's motive was not rancor toward husband (stressed in Appian's version) but family loyalty to her brother. In *Periocha* 59 Livy says: "His wife, Sempronia, was accused of poisoning him, especially because she was the sister of the Gracchi, with whom Africanus had disagreed." Orosius in recording his version (which he attributes generically to "some"—*quidam . . . fer- unt*) claims that through this crime, a family which "was already so ruin- ous to the state because of the impious sedition of its men, became even more heinous through the villainous actions of its women (*facinoribus mulierum*)," but no mention is given here of Cornelia's involvement. Such suspicions arose and spread most likely in environments hostile to the Gracchi, and later sources surely embellished the story with more details. According to Valerius Maximus, Sempronia continued to enjoy respect, if we are to believe his account (2.8.6) that she testified, in 101 B.C., in public proceedings involving a man (Equitius) who claimed to be Tiberius's son. Sempronia (*Ti. et C. Gracchorum soror, uxor Scipionis Aemiliani*), ignoring the noisy incitements of the crowd, did not betray the nobility of her paternal heritage and scornfully refused to recognize the claimant. During these proceedings, Sempronia was called on as the only witness who could furnish any proof regarding this controversial question of identification. This suggests that she was the only member of Cornelia's family still alive, keeper of its secrets and perhaps of its documents. By that date the mother of the Gracchi was no more, and this episode is the only evidence the sources give us concerning her demise.

Daughter of Africanus, Mother of the Gracchi

Sempronia had a curious destiny. Perhaps if Plutarch's biography of Aemilianus had survived, we might have had a more complete picture of her, rather than Appian's sketch of a harpy and murderess. Some sources ignore her completely and bring Cornelias's descendants to an end after the deaths of Tiberius and Gaius. Seneca, in his *To Helvia on Consolation* says that destiny had reduced Cornelia's twelve children to two (16.6), and in his *To Marcia on Consolation,* he specifies that Cornelia "had twelve children and an equal number of funerals. She waited patiently for the others, whom the city never noticed, living or dead. But Tiberius and Gaius, whose virtue may be denied but not their greatness, she lived to see murdered and buried" (16.3).

In both passages Seneca praises Cornelia for her dignity and strength of character in mourning her dead and bearing her losses. Plutarch tells us that Cornelia's astonishing self-control when talking of her sons' deaths caused some to believe that she was no longer in her right mind: "her age and the great burden of her afflictions had caused her to lose her reason. She no longer understood her own misfortunes" (*Gaius Gracchus* 19.4). There may have been mental instability in the Gracchi family (as Cornelia may be suggesting in the second letter fragment when she mentions the family's tendency to "run mad": *"ecquando desinet familia nostra insanire?"*). Diodorus (34/35.28a) describes Gaius as furious and psychologically disturbed.

Seneca's mention of Cornelia in *To Helvia on Consolation* bears examining. In this same context, Seneca urges Helvia to immerse herself in her studies to distract herself from her sorrows, yet he makes no mention of Cornelia's learning and intellectual abilities. By that time Cornelia had been idealized by the public imagination as a model of old-fashioned, womanly virtue, a piece of Roman history, a source of inspiration for posterity. Her name was linked to the mothers of great men and she was compared to figures of legend. While Seneca evoked her alongside Lucretia, Cloelia, Rutilia (mother of Cotta), and Tacitus compared her to the mothers of Caesar and Augustus, Martial ridiculed her in an obscene epigram (11.104), picturing her in the company of Julia (Pompey's wife), Porcia (daughter of Cato and wife of Brutus), Lucretia, Andromache, and Penelope. Aelian praised her as the Roman Penelope, paragon of matronly virtue (*Varia Historia* 14.45). In the introduction to *Mulierum Virtutes* (*Moralia* 243d), Plutarch presents a gathering of women of former times who were celebrated for their virtues just as men were and compares Cornelia's lofty and noble character (*megalòphron*) to that of Olympias, mother of Alexander. Among the Christian writers, Jerome (in *Adversus Iovinianum* 1.49 [320]), ranks her between Lucretia and Porcia as examples of women who were equal to men in virtue, while in *Epistula* (54 par.4) he defines her as chaste and fruitful, *"pudicitiae simul et fecunditatis exemplar."* These were the same qualities for which Gaius had once praised her: defending her against an effeminate detractor, her son said: "How dare you compare Cornelia to yourself? Have you brought forth children as she has done? And yet all Rome knows that she has refrained from the company of men longer than you have" (Plutarch *Gaius Gracchus* 4.6). Juvenal refers to this proverbial image of Cornelia in his famous sixth satire when he claims that he prefers a simple woman from Venosa to such a proud and noble model of virtue (6.166 ff.)

A statue was raised to Cornelia's honor. This was exceptional, considering that until the second century B.C., public recognition of women by means of statues was limited to the archaic period or connected with legendary events. Pliny discusses this statue in detail (*Nat. Hist.* 34.31): although Cato had opposed honoring women with statues in the provinces, one was erected in Rome to commemorate Cornelia, the "mother of the Gracchi and daughter of Africanus." This statue portrayed the matron sitting, wearing strapless sandals. It was first placed in the public portico of Metellus (built by Metellus Macedonicus around 146 B.C.) and was later moved to the *Porticus Octaviae* (the lavish complex of structures still standing today). Plutarch associates it with a specific event: Gaius's withdrawal at his mother's request of the law that would have prevented Marcus Octavius from holding public office. Her intervention—recounted in *Life of Gaius Gracchus* 4.4—was met with great approval by the people "who honored Cornelia for her sons no less than for her father. Afterward (*hýsteron*) they raised a bronze statue to her honor and inscribed it 'Cornelia, mother of the Gracchi'." There are different theories concerning the dating of the statue. Some scholars who believe that political motives underlay this official recognition of Cornelia date this event to around 100 B.C., or even later, at a time when the *populares* once again dominated the political scene (Coarelli). Plutarch's use of the word *"hýsteron,"* however, does not exclude its having happened much earlier, even, according to some, while Cornelia was still living. Plutarch tells us of statues erected to commemorate the Gracchus brothers (*Gaius Gracchus* 18.3) and also mentions a statue of Tiberius Sempronius Gracchus, their father: the night before Gaius's death, the young man was said to have wept in silence while contemplating this statue (14.4). Cornelia's statue, first set in the *Porticus Metelli* and later more prominently displayed in the *Porticus Octaviae,* was probably intended to immortalize her image as a supreme symbol of fertility, chastity, *univirate,* and maternal love for the edification of posterity. And, in fact, records of the erection of statues in honor of women indicate that the females concerned (for example, Clelia, Tanaquilla, Gaia Taracia, Quinta Claudia) either had proved themselves particularly capable in the services they performed for the state or had embodied to perfection the canonical wifely virtues celebrated by tradition. This would have been perfectly in keeping with the moral climate of the Augustan period, when attempts were made to restore the wholesome values of long ago: family, marriage, procreation, and stern attitudes toward children and their education. Pliny must have seen Cornelia in this light, for he emphasizes her strapless sandals (*sine ammento*) and plain attire, inspired by the simplicity of the past. Could this statue also have been a warning to women, expressing rigorous opposition to luxury and lavish excess? Or is it another specific reference to her exceptional fecundity (Bettini 1988)? It is well known, in fact, that the ancients firmly believed that a woman giving birth should avoid contact with knots of any kind whatsoever. It was held that a knot represented an obstacle to the loosening and opening up of the pregnant body at the moment of giving birth. This explains the scrupulous care with which all forms of binding were avoided: fingers, arms and legs were not to be crossed, while belts and boot fastenings and even hair had to be worn loose. Can it be inferred from this that sandals without laces (*ammenta*) were a symbol of ability to procreate?

We cannot say for certain how long the statue lasted. It may have been damaged in the fire of 80 B.C., or (as some scholars have tried to show) the statue itself, or a copy of it, may have still existed in the third century A.D. By the fourth century, the solemn image of a woman sitting (such as Aphrodite seated, by the sculptor Phidias) had become a model commonly used by sculptors to portray Roman women, including Helena, the mother of Constantine (Coarelli).

In 1878 in the area of the *Porticus Octaviae,* the base of a statue was found. It was wide enough to have been the pedestal for a bronze statue representing a seated figure. On the front two inscriptions appeared: *opus Tisicratis* (dating from the third century A.D.), and (dating from the Augustan era) *Cornelia Africani f. / Gracchorum.* This was probably the base of the statue described by Pliny.

This finding poses many problems. We will not discuss the ones related to the inscription *opus Tisicratis* (does this suggest that the artist's signature had been recovered in the Severian period, or is it a false attribution, or an indication that the base had been used for another statue?). The letter forms of the other inscription (*CIL* 6.31610) date from the Augustan period, but there are obvious signs that a previous inscription had been removed. The later inscription may be a faithful copy of the original one, or may have modified it (Coarelli, basing his theory on Plutarch's account, suggests that it originally read *Cornelia Gracchorum*). Could this previously have been the pedestal of another statue (Kajava's unlikely suggestion)? We cannot answer these questions. What interests us here is the curious formula: *Cornelia Africani f. / Gracchorum.* In inscriptions relating to women it was customary to put the husband's name immediately after the father's name. Here *Gracchorum* alone (referring not to her husband but to her sons) without the word *mater* is unusual (we have no other record of similar inscriptions) and has led some to believe that the statue of Cornelia was only one of a group of statues dedicated to illustrious mothers (Lewis).

This statue was a monument intended for the public, and it is extremely unlikely that its inscription would have been worded incorrectly or ambiguously. Cornelia was so famous that no one could have failed to recognize her, and the plural *Gracchorum* eliminates any ambiguity, as it can only refer to her sons (Kajava). This inscription faithfully reflects the formula traditionally used to refer to Cornelia in the sources.

Plutarch explains this by claiming that Cornelia owed her public prestige to being the daughter of Africanus and mother of the Gracchi. Pliny (who also claims that the statue represented "Cornelia daughter of Africanus and mother of the Gracchi"), mentions Cornelia as an example of exceptional fertility, along with Agrippina Major (*Nat. Hist.* 7.57) and refers to Cornelia only as *"Gracchorum mater,"* while referring to Agrippina as *"Agrippina Germanici,"* that is, wife of Germanicus (Agrippina Minor, mentioned in another context is cited as "the mother of Nero"). It was standard practice to use the husband's name to identify a married woman, for women could be identified only through their connections with men. This was the passport required for a woman's entry into history. Men, who were more visible, had to provide the point of reference for women. After her husband died and her sons were still boys, Cornelia was known as "Aemilianus's mother-in-law," as he was the most important male in the family at the time. In Cornelia's case, her sons' fame soon surpassed their father's (this is one reason why Sempronius Gracchus, a leading figure in his day, is less frequently mentioned by the sources). Once she had become a widow, she could be remembered only in connection with her prestigious paternal descent (in the inscription Scipio is in fact cited as "Africanus"), and in connection with her sons, major figures on the stage of history.

In connection with the omission of the word "mater," the expression *mater Corneliae Gracchorum,* in Valerius Maximus 6.7.1, refers to Tertia Aemilia. Inserting another *mater* or *parentis* before the word *Gracchorum* would have been stylistically unacceptable (Lewis). It would be appropriate, in any case, at this point to explode the longstanding and popular theory that the expression *Gracchorum mater* never once appears in the whole of Latin literature. Also, Jerome's statement (*Commentarii in Sophoniam prophetam, Prologus* 655 Adriaen = *PL* 25.1337c) leaves no doubts: *"Corneliam Gracchorum id est, vestram, tota Romanae urbis turba miratur."*

At the beginning of 1779 a bust believed to represent Aspasia was unearthed during excavations of Civitavecchia, and near Tivoli a bust of Pericles also came to light (both were placed in the Vatican). An archaeologist, Ennio Quirino Visconti, suggested to the poet Monti that these events might serve as inspiration for a poem. Monti accepted the challenge and composed his famous ode *Prosopopea di Pericle,* celebrating Aspasia and her consort. This woman, praised for her intelligence and beauty, had at last been given a face (whether it really was a bust of Aspasia is of little importance).

When another noble matron named Cornelia died—wife of Aemilius Paulus Lepidus—she was not forgotten: in one of his most moving elegies (4.11), Propertius immortalized her image.

The last glimpse we have of the Gracchi's mother is of a woman still vital, burdened but not broken by old age and destiny, telling the story of the men in her life to a group of listeners. We do not know when she died. No poet was present that day to honor her memory or to describe her life with Gracchus, a life made of days and moments of which no record remains.

Nor was her statue celebrated by poets. Time and fate have dispersed the last testimony to her form and her face, never described in the sources. Only the pedestal of her statue has survived. Its inscription has passed down to us—as only stones can do—the essence of her entire existence:

Cornelia, Africani f. / Gracchorum

THREE

FULVIA THE WOMAN OF PASSION

Catherine Virlouvet

Very few women who lived at the end of the Roman republic have found their way from the history of women to the shores of history, *tout court.* Fulvia is one, yet the textbooks we continue to recommend to our students merely mention her in connection with Mark Antony, her third husband, describing her as an "ambitious woman of perverse influence." Contemporary historians have realized that to grasp Antony's real personality, they must see through Cicero's invective and the antagonistic testimony of later authors who were influenced by Augustan propaganda. Concerning Fulvia's role in the Perusian War they wrote, "As for Fulvia, she had not lost her taste for power and by exploiting the prestige of her absent husband, she exercised a detrimental influence over her brother-in-law." From the times of Augustus to our own, historians have tacitly shared the same opinion about Antony: they reassuringly stress that this great Roman general would never have come to such a bad end if it hadn't been for the women in his life! Fulvia and Cleopatra (even more so) were his evil geniuses. In these few pages I hope to do for Fulvia what others have done for her husband: to capture the essence of this woman's life concealed by the conflicting evidence.

What little we know about Fulvia's youth is briefly reported in records concerning the latter part of her life, when she was married to Mark Antony. Fulvia was the only daughter of Marcus Fulvius Bambalion, the Stutterer, "homo nullo numero" whom Cicero despised and ridiculed. Her father was from Tusculum and it is very likely (although this has never been proved) that he descended from the famous Fulvii who were consuls in Rome between 322 and 125 B.C. before their family name disappeared forever from the *fasti,* the list of high-ranking officials in Rome. Perhaps Bambalion was the last male in the family to bear the name, and indeed he may never have held public office. Fulvia's mother was Sempronia Tuditana, the youngest daughter of a distinguished plebeian line, the Sempronii Tuditani. Her maternal grandfather had held

66 no public office (according to Cicero he died insane), but his father had

been consul in 129 B.C. and was an uncle by marriage of the orator Hortensius. Fulvia came from a noble lineage in decline, which, as a woman, she could not hope to restore to its former glory. In an era when children were expected to model themselves on the illustrious examples in their families, she inherited a political tradition that inclined, at least partly, toward the *populares*. These were the reformers who sought to resolve the crisis of the republic through measures inspired by the earlier attempts of Tiberius and Gaius Gracchus at the end of the second century B.C. Lastly, and more prosaically, as the sole representative of two families in gradual extinction, she inherited a sizable fortune. Some modern scholars believe she had a half-brother, Lucius Pinarius Natta, the pontifex who "became the guarantor," of the dedication to *Libertas* on Cicero's house on the Palatine, on the request of Publius Clodius, tribune in 58 B.C. The existence of a half-brother would have diminished Fulvia's inheritance from her mother but would also have made her the stepdaughter of the consul in 62 B.C., thus giving her an active role within the circle of the political elite.

Wife of Publius Clodius

Fulvia's background fully justified her first marriage, to Publius Clodius. Cicero briefly tells us that they were already married in 58 B.C., the year Clodius was made tribune. They were probably married in 62, if Fulvia was indeed stepdaughter of Pinarius. The wealthy Fulvia must have been a good catch for Clodius, for although he was also from an illustrious family, his father had not left a large enough fortune to satisfy the needs of three sons, all eager to begin their political careers, and of two daughters not yet married. What we wish to stress here is that her family's political views were close to those of the *populares*. This must have enhanced her charm even more in the eyes of Publius Clodius, the future tribune of the plebs, Caesar's friend and Cicero's adversary. Moreover, from what we can judge across the span of two thousand years, Fulvia must have been a fascinating and unusual woman.

Some attempts have been made to identify her in the figure of Victory stamped on a number of coins dating from the time of Antony. We must abandon this idea however intriguing it may be, for the portrait on this coin is too vague to tell us much: large eyes, aquiline nose, thin lips, and thick locks arranged in the fashion of the time. No writer of the period describes Fulvia as attractive, and her looks most certainly did not correspond to the classical canons of beauty. We learn from Suetonius that her face was asymmetrical, with one cheek fuller than the other, yet despite this flaw, she inspired devotion in all three of her husbands. Cicero informs us that Clodius never left her side and also condemns Antony for his unseemly passion for his wife, as intensity of feeling between spouses was thought inappropriate. We will discuss this point later. There is no doubt that much of her appeal depended on her strong personality. Plutarch tells us that she was by no means a woman "of humble thoughts, content to spin wool and tidy the house." He continues, "She was not satisfied with dominating her husband in private but wanted to dominate him as a magistrate and have command over him while he commanded legions and huge armies."

This comment refers to Fulvia fifteen years later, when she was married to Antony. In the interim she had no doubt become more determined and self-assured. In her youth, Fulvia must have been a strong but charming woman. Her marriage to Clodius was happy and fertile: they had two children, a son and a daughter. We do not know with any certainty that Fulvia was faithful to her husband, but in any case we cannot trust the rumors alluding to an affair she allegedly had with Antony while Clodius was still alive. The only source to mention this is Cicero, in the *Philippicae,* which are full of slanderous gossip about his enemies. When Clodius was murdered on the Appian Way by Milo's men and his bloody body taken to Fulvia in their home on the Palatine, she gave full vent to her sorrow and rage. Asconius reports that she began to scream wildly and pointed out the wounds to the crowd that had rushed to see what had happened. At Milo's trial, where she was called to testify (this was her first public appearance on record), her pain and anger touched all those present and won out over Cicero's harangue in defense of the accused.

Thus in 52 B.C. Fulvia appears as an irreproachable young woman, ever at her husband's side while he was alive and ready to avenge his death afterwards. These are all praiseworthy qualities, but not exceptional for a woman of her rank. Given her future role as decision-maker, first at Antony's side and later during the Perusian war, is it legitimate to think that she also had great political influence over Clodius, her first husband? There are no ancient records that might help us determine just how much influence she may have had. Valerius Maximus criticizes Clodius for allowing her to dominate him, but his remark is meant in a general sense. We have no proof that she played any part in the political decisions made by her first husband when he was tribune in 58 B.C.

Wife of Curio

Scholars who believe Fulvia's influence pervaded the careers of her first two husbands base this claim on the similarity of these two men and of the legislative issues they supported. Fulvia's second husband was Gaius Scribonius Curio, tribune of the plebs in 50 B.C. Unlike Clodius, he was not descended from an illustrious family, but his financial situation was better than that of her previous husband, even though Curio was also a lavish spender always in need of money. Cicero's *Philippicae* contain the only record of this marriage. It must have been of brief duration, as Curio left Rome at the beginning of 52 B.C. to join Caesar and was sent to combat Pompey's partisans in Africa, where he died. We do not know exactly when Curio and Fulvia were married, but the marriage lasted long enough for Fulvia to have a child. Perhaps the marriage took place a few months after Milo's trial, at the end of 52 or at the beginning of 51 B.C. We must not be surprised that Fulvia's period of mourning ended so quickly or try to justify this by imagining that she had previously been involved with Curio. At the end of the Roman republic, marriages between members of the ruling oligarchy were, above all, political alliances. Fulvia was probably no less appealing in 52 B.C. than she had been ten years earlier, and she was also quite wealthy. Moreover, she was the widow of Clodius, Curio's friend, and marrying her meant taking sides with the *populares*. Curio's family tradition did not lean toward the ideas of the reformers and his father was Cicero's friend. Some have supposed that Caesar won the support of Curio for his party by means of a generous gift. By marrying Fulvia, however, Curio showed that he had definitely taken a stand.

The political views and activities of Clodius and Curio were similar in some ways. They both looked after Caesar's interests in Rome while he was away in Gaul. They both adopted similar political measures, such as rationing laws (*leges annonariae*). These measures may well have been dictated by the needs of the time, but traditionally they were part of the political agenda of the *populares*. This is not enough to show that Fulvia had a hand in her husbands' political decisions.

In 49 B.C., Fulvia became a widow for the second time, after a brief marriage of which we know almost nothing, except that she had another child. Cicero's poisoned stylus took this opportunity to accuse Fulvia of having a fatal influence over her husbands and to predict in menacing tones a similar fate for Antony. The wicked picture of Fulvia recorded in the ancient sources and even mentioned by modern historians may be traced back to Cicero's negative depiction of her. It is not easy to draw a detailed portrait of Antony's future wife at the end of 50 B.C. She had been widowed twice and now lived with her mother, as was appropriate for a woman of good family. She had the self-assurance necessary to appear in public when her deceased husband's honor demanded it and was most certainly involved in the political life of her times, if only through Clodius during his term as tribune of the plebs. Her personal inclinations and family traditions leaned most decidedly towards the *populares*, which in those days meant siding with Caesar. This last fact played an important role in her third marriage, to Antony. Given the absence of detailed records, our sketch of this period of her life ends here. Most importantly, it is impossible to evaluate accurately just how heavily she influenced the political decisions of her first two husbands, but we are strongly tempted to believe that this influence did indeed exist.

Wife of Mark Antony

Fulvia enters history as the wife of Mark Antony. This third marriage also occurred within the circle of Fulvia's political connections. Antony and Clodius had known each other since early youth and Curio was also Antony's friend. Antony succeeded Curio as tribune of the plebs in December, 50 B.C., and both joined Caesar in Cisalpine Gaul when civil war broke out in 49. Fulvia was well acquainted with Antony, an old friend of her previous two husbands, but there is no reason to believe Cicero's malicious insinuations that she and Antony had previously been involved in an illicit love affair. At the time of their marriage, Antony was Caesar's *magister equitum*, "Master of the Horse," which meant that he was the second most important person in Rome. He governed in Caesar's place while the dictator was away routing what was left of Pompey's army to the four corners of the empire, his main occupation at that time. Antony's prestigious position must have made him very attractive to Fulvia, Caesar's staunch supporter.

Antony had his own reasons to find her appealing. Like Clodius and Curio he was probably attracted, in part, by her wealth. Like them, he also needed large sums of money, not only because of the important office he held, but also because of his extravagant tastes. Once in their youth, Curio had had to vouch for Antony's debts. In October, 47 B.C., shortly before Antony married Fulvia, Caesar had forced him to pay to the public treasury the complete amount at which Pompey's property had been assessed, which he had never paid in full. He may have married Fulvia also in the hope of having children, for he still had no legitimate son. She gave him two. Lastly, it is very likely that Caesar pressured Antony into marrying Fulvia. At the end of 47 B.C., Caesar had just returned to Rome to solve a few public and private financial problems that were in danger of exploding. He took this opportunity to reproach Antony for his dissolute way of life, and Antony, wishing to please Caesar, broke off his relationship with the actress Cytheris, repudiated his wife (and cousin) Antonia, who was probably guilty of adultery, and married Fulvia.

Caesar obviously hoped that a woman like Fulvia could keep Antony in line. Plutarch describes her as "a grave and stern matron." She was probably about thirty at the time, while Antony was thirty-seven. Their union, formed primarily for political reasons, later developed into a sincere and reciprocal passion. Paradoxically, it is Cicero who records the most touching episode in their tempestuous marriage. In March, 45 B.C., after Caesar's victory over Pompey's last few supporters, Antony set out to meet the triumphant general, but immediately turned back after having heard a false rumor that Caesar was dead. The important position Antony occupied in the Roman state was such that he could not return to Rome except in full daylight, accompanied by an escort. At the end of the day, he stopped nine miles from Rome on the Flaminian Way at a place called Saxa Rubra, but he was so anxious to see Fulvia again that he paid a secret visit to her at night in her home on the Palatine. Cicero recounts: "With his face hidden by a hood, he went up to the house. The doorkeeper asked, 'Who are you?' and he replied, 'Mark Antony has sent me.' He was immediately taken to Fulvia, to whom he delivered a letter. She wept as she read it, for its message was sweet. The letter informed her that he had broken off his affair with the actress and was now ready to concentrate all his love on his wife alone. As Fulvia continued to weep even harder, the tender-hearted Antony could resist no further. He uncovered his face and rushed into her arms." Cicero mentions this anecdote to discredit Antony and to show that he let his private feelings outweigh his sense of public duty. Twenty centuries have passed since Antony's unexpected return, which (according to Cicero) plunged Rome into terror, but all that remains is this moving story concerning Antony's tumultuous marriage (bringing an end once and for all to his affair with the actress had apparently not been easy).

The Greediest and Cruelest of Women

After the Ides of March, Fulvia became a leading figure on the political scene, alongside Antony. After the assassination of Caesar, who had been Antony's colleague, he found himself alone, occupying the highest governmental position for that year. Although in his will the dictator had adopted his nephew, Octavian, and made him heir to his enormous fortune, Antony was Caesar's spiritual heir. He had Caesar's archives transferred to his own home and put into effect a series of measures that he claimed Caesar had been planning before he died. Cicero affirms, however, that these measures were entirely Antony's idea, with Fulvia's full support. "In his home," writes Cicero, "there was a bustling marketplace in which an entire State was being built, and a woman luckier for herself than for her husbands, held provinces and kingdoms in thrall." Elsewhere Cicero describes Antony's home as a "gynaeceum" (part of the house reserved for women) "where anything could be bought and sold."

Cicero gives a specific example of Antony's political dealing. Deiotarus, king of Galatia, had become vassal to Rome and had fallen under Pompey's influence during his conquest of the East. In 47 B.C., during his military campaigns in the East, Caesar had taken some property from Deiotarus and given it to other allied kings as a reward for their support against the minor kings. Deiotarus now hoped to take advantage of the civil war that had broken out in Rome in order to regain his independence. He mobilized all his friends in Rome, including Cicero, seeking help to get his kingdom back, and in April, 44 B.C., his property was returned to him. The deal had been concluded by Antony in Fulvia's presence, and the delegates representing the king of Galatia had promised to pay the sum of ten thousand sesterces in exchange for their kingdom. Hence Cicero's indignation, for he never missed an opportunity to point out Fulvia's greed. Although the deal was probably not a very honest one, and certainly was very advantageous for Antony and Fulvia, it was no exception in a society in which the current political practices encouraged the giving of lavish gifts. Cicero does not condemn the deal itself, but the way it was conducted. In a letter to Atticus written at the time of this event, he says of Deiotarus, "It is true that he is fully worthy of such a kingdom. But to obtain it from Fulvia!" In *Philippicae,* he remarks that "the obligation of ten thousand sesterces was agreed upon by the delegates, all good people but timid and inexpert, without our own opinion being asked, nor those of the king's hosts." What most irked

Cicero was that Deiotarus owed the return of his kingdom to Antony and Fulvia rather than to himself, although he was the one who should have been defending the king's interests in Rome.

Cicero reports that in this period Fulvia not only showed herself to be greedy but also cruel. In the autumn of 44 B.C. the breach was growing wider between Antony, on one side, and Octavian and the senate on the other. Antony had passed a law that gave him control of the province of Cisalpine Gaul for the following year, while Caesar had assigned it to Decimus Brutus. Antony rallied an army to escort him to the province, and brought to Brundisium four of the six legions that the dictator had sent to Macedonia shortly before his death, while preparing an incursion against the Parthians. Some of these men disobeyed Antony and answered Octavian's call to arms instead. To put down the mutiny, Antony began the traditional process of decimation, executing one out of every ten men. Cicero says he "lacks words" to describe the cruelty of that scene, where the most terrible thing was Fulvia's presence at the place of execution: "in the house of his host in Brundisium, [Antony] gave the order to slit the throats of very valiant men, excellent citizens, who died at his feet, after spattering the face of his wife with their blood. The affair is well known." He then proceeds to blame Fulvia for what had happened and goes on to show that Antony's wife was "not only the greediest, but also the cruelest of wives."

Cicero's vengefulness was openly manifest. Antony was acting as consul, commander in chief, punishing men who had answered the call to arms of an ordinary citizen, Octavian, and thus he was acting in accordance with the law. The same scene is also described by other writers of antiquity, in particular Appian and Dio Cassius. Appian's account, based on the testimony of Antony's friend Asinius Pollio, is illuminating. Firstly, he informs us (and this is confirmed by Dio Cassius) that Octavian had hired the mutineers. Secondly, he tells us that Antony had applied the military principle of decimating deserters' units very moderately. Lastly, he does not mention Fulvia's presence. This does not mean that Cicero invented this detail, which is also mentioned by Dio Cassius. It only suggests that Fulvia's role in the scene was relatively minor. The only authentic information to be gleaned from this story is that Fulvia was not a woman who fainted at the sight of blood, as she demonstrated during the Perusian War, which we will discuss shortly.

During the winter of 44–43 B.C. Antony surrounded Decimus Brutus in Modena in order to take Cisalpine Gaul from him. In the spring the situation seemed unfavorable for him and he retreated toward the Alps.

Meanwhile in Rome the senate had declared Antony an enemy of the people. During these long months, Fulvia had remained in the *Urbs,* actively seeking to reconcile Antony and Octavian, with the help of her husband's friends, such as the consul Lucius Calpurnius Piso, Caesar's father-in-law. She never left little Antillus, Antony's two-year-old son, and did her best to sway the senators' views. The day the senate was to discuss Cicero's proposal to declare Antony a public enemy, she presented herself in the forum, along with her son, her mother-in-law, and other relatives, and threw herself weeping at the senators' feet as they made their way to the curia. Her action had no impact on the senate's decision, but at the end of the summer, Lepidus, governor of Narbonensis Gaul and of Nearer Spain, organized a meeting with Antony, Octavian, and himself, which took place near Bologna. The three men drew up a new pact against the senate and the republicans: Octavian changed sides and a second triumvirate was born. Our sources do not say whether Fulvia was present at this meeting, but she managed to use her influence. To seal the pact of their reconciliation, under pressure from their armies, Antony and Octavian also tightened the bonds between them by creating new ties of marriage. Octavian married Clodia, Fulvia's daughter by her first marriage to Publius Clodius. Very likely, Fulvia played an important role in this decision.

The Proscription of 43 B.C.

The triumvirs' first, sinister act was to make a long list of their enemies and put a price on their heads. Forty years after Sulla a second period of proscription had begun. Their victims were illustrious men, and the first on the list was Cicero. Years later, when Octavian became Augustus, he had the history of this period rewritten concerning the proscriptions of intellectuals belonging to his court, not wishing to leave posterity a bloodthirsty portrait of himself. The official version shows Antony and Fulvia as the ones really responsible for these proscriptions, while Lepidus is portrayed as more moderate and Octavian is shown trying to save as many lives as possible. Dio Cassius's history faithfully follows this version of the facts. In his account, Fulvia is personally responsible for the deaths of many of the proscribed victims, whom she caused to be executed out of sheer hatred and greed. If she spared anyone at all, it was only because she hoped to get more money out of them alive than dead. Dio Cassius describes a gory incident in which Fulvia defiled Cicero's remains. Antony had ordered that the orator's head and right hand (which had written so many invectives against him) be displayed in the forum, on the Rostra, from which politicians addressed the citizens. Later when the head was being removed from public display, Fulvia spat on it, ripped out the tongue, and stuck a hairpin through it, while cursing Cicero venomously.

These ghoulish details do not appear in Appian's record, which views Antony and his circle more favorably. Nonetheless Appian does accuse her of being directly responsible for the death of Rufus. This man was denounced because he had refused to sell Fulvia his house, located on the Palatine near her own, and that is where she allegedly displayed the victim's head when Antony brought it to her, telling her to dispose of it as she saw fit. This is the sort of rumor which gave rise to the stories that Fulvia had many people proscribed simply because they were rich. Appian also emphasizes Fulvia's hard-heartedness toward the women of the proscribed victims. The triumvirs had taxed the patrimonies of wealthy women to finance their campaign against Brutus and Cassius. These women first appealed to the triumvirs' women to ask that this tax be abolished. Octavian's sister and Antony's mother received them politely, but Fulvia treated them haughtily, so that they had no other recourse but to appeal directly to the triumvirs themselves.

Fulvia took an active part in the proscriptions, although the large number of condemnations for which she has been blamed is greatly exaggerated. The macabre desecration of Cicero's head, if it really did take place, and her refusal to hear the pleas of the proscribed men's wives show that she may indeed have been a bit cruel. Rather than condemn her behavior we can try to understand it, and must remember that just a few months earlier the senate had turned a deaf ear to her own pleas during its persecution of Antony. We must also consider what Cicero represented to her: a political enemy who had been forced into exile by her first husband, and who, upon returning, had defended her husband's murderer. For over a year Cicero had been heaping insults and abuse upon Antony and herself in *Philippicae,* and had asked the senate to declare her husband a public enemy. At the end of 43 B.C., Fulvia found an opportunity to retaliate for all the humiliation she had borne in recent months. For the next two years she would dominate the political scene in Italy.

The Perusian War

In 42 B.C. Octavian and Antony set out for the East to deal with Brutus and Cassius. Antony would not return to Rome until after Fulvia's death. After the defeat of the republicans in October at Philippi, a new pact

drawn up by the triumvirs required them to make war against the Parthians, as Caesar had been planning to do before he died. Octavian took
Italy, where he had a very delicate problem to solve: finding land to
distribute to the veterans of Antony's army and of his own.

Considering Fulvia's loyalty toward her husband in previous years,
her experience of Roman politics, and her position as Octavian's mother-
in-law, it is very likely that Antony counted especially on her to look
after his interests in the West and see to it that Octavian fulfilled his part
of the bargain.

While Rome awaited Octavian's return, Fulvia was one of the most
influential people in the city. In 41 B.C., the consuls were Lucius Antony,
her brother-in-law, and Publius Servilius Isauricus, but according to Dio
Cassius, whom we may suspect of exaggeration in these matters, it was
Fulvia who was really running things, with no respect for Lepidus, the
only triumvir in Rome. In this period the senate refused to honor Lucius
Antony for his (undeserved) triumph in the Alps until Fulvia withdrew
her veto, an indication of just how much power she had.

Once he had returned to Italy, Octavian began assigning lands to his
veterans, confiscating some of this territory in eighteen Italian cities,
which would be required to welcome his former soldiers. This is where
the conflict between Caesar's adopted son, on one side, and Antony's
brother and wife, on the other, arose, leading to the so-called Perusian
War of 41 B.C. The exact causes are not very clear. In part, it seems that
Fulvia and Lucius were afraid that Octavian's soldiers would receive
preferential treatment in the distribution of land. Moreover, they feared
that Octavian would take all the credit for a gesture that was sure to
make him very popular with the military. This is why they tried unsuccessfully to have Antony's friends distribute the land intended for his
veterans. Fulvia and her two sons went to speak to the veterans to remind them of the gratitude they owed her husband. She then sent Lucius
Antony and her sons to accompany Octavian on his mission and keep
an eye on him. Friction was increasing between Fulvia and Octavian,
who could no longer put up with his mother-in-law. He now repudiated
Clodia on the grounds that their marriage had not been consummated.

Lucius Antony was probably more than just the loyal supporter of
Fulvia portrayed by the sources. Appian describes him as a supporter of
the republic, which he wished to help restore as soon as Brutus and Cassius had been eliminated. In his view, that action would make the triumvirate's existence no longer necessary. From the beginning his ideas differed from those of Fulvia, who wanted above all to defend Antony's

position in Italy, while Lucius Antony wanted to strengthen ties with the Italians from whom Octavian had confiscated the land distributed to the veterans. Lucius Antony's position conflicted with the actions taken by Fulvia on behalf of Antony's veterans, and this at first created tension between Fulvia and her brother-in-law. Later, however, she embraced Lucius Antony's cause out of her jealousy of Cleopatra, as the sources unanimously agree, in order to start a war that would force Antony to break off his love affair with the Egyptian queen and return home. Fulvia and Lucius Antony came to the assistance of the angry Italians but tried to do this without creating more ill-feeling within the army: rather, seeking other ways to distribute land to the veterans.

Thus as the year 41 B.C. passed, Octavian found himself in an increasingly difficult predicament. Once again Italy had risen up against Rome. In the Capitol itself, some of the senators, who supported Antony, nostalgic for the republic, inclined favorably toward Fulvia and Lucius Antony. The populace of the *Urbs*, greatly increased with the hordes of angry farmers who had flocked to Rome to protest the confiscation of their land, did not look kindly upon Caesar's adopted son. Supplying the capital with food every day was becoming more difficult, and the menacing specter of famine loomed ahead. Sextus Pompeius, one of the sons of Pompey the Great, had carved himself out a kingdom in Sicily, and from there his fleet kept the ships loaded with grain from reaching Rome. Much of the province was in control of Antony's friends. In Africa, on Fulvia's orders, the old governor, Titus Sextius, had launched a successful campaign against the current governor Fuficius Fango, an ally of Octavian, in order to regain control of the province.

Growing isolation prompted Octavian to begin negotiations with Fulvia and Lucius Antony through the intermediation of the veterans, who had remained his most loyal followers and who wished to bring about a reconciliation between their leaders. Fulvia and her brother-in-law, together with their friends and supporters, including some senators, had set up their general headquarters in the town of Praeneste, claiming that Rome was not safe enough for them. As a triumvir, Octavian had his own personal guard corps, but they had no such protection. If we believe Dio Cassius's report, Antony's wife personally conducted the negotiations with Octavian's soldiers, "strapping on a sword, giving orders, and arguing with the men." Negotiations failed and war broke out. After marching on Rome, where he was warmly welcomed, Lucius Antony led his army northward, hoping to unite with Antony's generals who governed the Gallic provinces. From the military point of view, Octavian had the advantage of larger numbers in Italian territory, but if Antony's supporters had managed to unite their forces, Octavian would have found himself in deep trouble. This, however, never occurred, perhaps due to the differing opinions that divided Antony's friends. In the autumn Lucius Antony sought refuge in the fortified town of Perusia (the modern Perugia), hoping that the siege would be brief thanks to reinforcements expected to arrive from Gaul. Instead he found himself having to hold out there for months. Some of the missiles that the warring sides threw back and forth at each other have been found: the ones thrown by Lucius Antony's besieged followers were inscribed with the name of Mark Antony and the title *imperator,* commander in chief. The ones thrown by Octavian's soldiers are inscribed with insults addressed to Lucius Antony and Fulvia. Octavian even composed some obscene verses in honor of his former mother-in-law. Perugia fell in February, 40 B.C., Lucius Antony and his army were pardoned, but the city was harshly punished.

During the siege, Fulvia had done her best to turn the tables in favor of her brother-in-law. She sent messages to Asinius Pollio and Ventidius Bassus begging them to come from Transpadane Gaul with reinforcements. She ordered Plancus, another of Antony's men, who was busy settling veterans near Benevento, to gather troops together and come northwards to assist Lucius Antony. But all was in vain. Antony's generals chose not to come to Perugia's aid and did not engage in a single battle. This was perhaps because relations among them were not good, and their own soldiers wanted peace. Their attitude, however, may have been influenced by Antony's silence. Fulvia, Lucius Antony, and even Octavian had sent him dozens of messages, but from the East no clear signal came in reply. Was Antony so besotted with Cleopatra that he did not care? Probably not, as we will see. It is likely that as he had taken no part in these events, he was uncertain about their outcome, and was preparing for the future.

Antony had been the brains behind the victory at Philippi. He spent the following winter basking in glory and reinforcing Rome's government in Asia. When he sent for Cleopatra to meet him in Tarsus in 41 B.C., it was to demand an explanation of her overfriendly behavior toward Brutus and Cassius. She convinced him of her loyalty to Caesar's supporters, using means that mostly likely went beyond diplomatic arguments. When Antony later joined her in Alexandria for the winter of 41–40 B.C. after quickly taking care of a few matters in Syria and Palestine, there is no reason to suppose that their relationship was more than a pleasant romance, similar to the one he had had during the previous winter with Glaphyra, a woman in Cappadocia. Antony left Alexandria at the beginning of spring in 40 B.C. Four years passed before he saw Cleopatra again. The moment had come for him to launch his attack against the Parthians, but when news reached him that Perugia had fallen, he was forced to react before Octavian had time to make full use of his advantage. Thus he set out for Italy, by way of Greece.

Fulvia's Death

Antony met Fulvia in Athens, where she had come from Brundisium after the fall of Perugia, accompanied by her children and a large group of Antony's supporters. He rebuked his wife harshly for the initiative she had taken in his absence and blamed her for the difficulties in which he now found himself. Nonetheless, he set sail to confront Octavian with a numerous army and a fleet of 120 ships and to lay siege to Brundisium.

It was there that the news of Fulvia's death reached him. He had left her behind in Sicyon, where she had fallen ill. He was very distressed about this, it appears, and bitterly reproached himself for having parted from her with such cruel words. Did she die of sorrow after her last encounter with her husband? That would make for a good story, but Fulvia was such a tough and vigorous woman, and her illness and death were so quick and violent, that we may assume she died of some nasty viral disease. Fulvia continued to serve Antony's interests even after her death. Antony had not really wanted a confrontation with Octavian. Moreover, as we have noted, the soldiers themselves were against any new fratricidal struggles, and Octavian was willing to negotiate. For two reasons, Fulvia's death made this easier. Firstly, in the negotiations between the two opposing parties that followed, it was easy to lay all the blame on her. Secondly, now that Antony was a widower, the triumvirs could reinforce their alliance through marriage. In the "peace of Brundisium" concluded in October, 40 B.C., Antony married Octavian's sister, Octavia.

A Jealous Virago?

In October, 40 B.C., Antony and Octavian, to their mutual satisfaction, agreed that the Perusian war had been merely a jealous woman's ploy to get her husband back. This explanation was repeated by all the ancient authors, even by those who view Antony more kindly. We should consider this explanation for what it really is, a good excuse, and explore the legitimate political motives behind Fulvia's actions.

Antony's peccadillos probably made Fulvia unhappy. We saw her weeping at the beginning of her marriage while reading a declaration from her husband in which he promised to break off his affair with his recent lover and dedicate himself entirely to her. She could not have been happy about his infatuation with the queen of Egypt, but Cleopatra was only one of Antony's many adventures. She certainly could not have been pleased by Antony's affair with Glaphyra the previous winter.

It should also be noted that when Antony and Cleopatra met for the first time in Tarsus, tensions between Fulvia and Octavian in Italy were at their peak. While her husband was away, Fulvia looked after his interests in Rome and in Italy. She no doubt took her role very seriously, as she was a scrupulous and stern person. Her experience of political life over the previous twenty years allowed her to realize that the triumvirate could not last long, and that the moment had come for power to be concentrated in the hands of one man, that is to say, in the hands of Caesar's successor. She wanted her husband to be Caesar's successor and she believed that it was time to act. Her calculations were right: Antony was undoubtedly the most powerful man of the moment, but she had underestimated how tired the veterans of Philippi were. Another reason her plans failed was the absence of Antony's explicit support. His friends would have obeyed orders coming directly from him, but they turned a deaf ear to Fulvia's appeals.

By becoming a war commander, Fulvia entered legend as the fierce, archetypal amazon "whose only feminine aspect is her body," and, at the same time, overstepped the bounds of her role as Antony's wife. At the end of the republican era the game of politics, with its subtle web of alliances, obligations, favors, friendships, quarrels, and reconciliations, allowed this aristocratic Roman woman to wield considerable influence in politics. Fulvia knew how to play her part alongside Clodius, Curio, and Antony, but by daring, out of loyalty to Antony, to make her own decisions, exercise her own power in his place, she trespassed beyond the limits, established by men, that kept women from participating in politics. The ancients never really forgave Fulvia for this and they have passed down to posterity a negative picture of her, in which their admiration for her intelligence and courage is outweighed by their moral con-

demnation of her audacity, her jealousy, and her cruelty. Modern scholars have frequently passed this image on unquestioned, very likely
because many of those same scholars shared the Romans' prejudices
concerning how much space women should be allowed to occupy in serious matters of public life.

FOUR

LYCORIS THE MIME

Giusto Traina

Memory from the Sands

In 1978, during the excavation of the Nubian town of Primis (modern-day Qaṣr Ibrīm, south of Aswan), the remains of a papyrus in Latin came to light. This papyrus, which may have belonged to a Roman soldier, contained a few fragments of poetry. Their language and style showed that they were erotic elegies, a literary genre that first came into fashion in Rome in the first century B.C., was developed by the *poetae novi,* and reached its peak in the age of Augustus. The hallmark of this literary form was elegance of style and language; it was called "erotic" because its main theme was love (*eros*) for a woman.

The woman celebrated in the Qaṣr Ibrīm papyrus was named Lycoris. This detail has allowed scholars to identify the author of these fragments as Cornelius Gallus, a leading figure of the Roman revolution and also a famous poet whose compositions marked the transition between the neoteric and elegiac styles. Until the papyrus of Primis was discovered, only one of Gallus's poems was known to be preserved. The name of Lycoris (to whom Gallus had dedicated four volumes of *Amores* around 40 B.C.) is also mentioned in other sources. In his tenth Bucolic, Virgil described the love-struck Gallus pining away for her, while Ovid declares, "Gallus will be famous in the East and West/ and his Lycoris will share his fame" (*Amores* 1.15.39; *Art of Love* 3.357).

Ovid's prophecy came true, for Gallus's fame reached as far as this remote African outpost, located beyond the Roman *oikoumene.* In his public career, Gallus was the first prefect of Egypt. The diffusion of his poetry throughout the area under his control was surely no random matter, and although it may have satisfied his desire for self-glorification it was also, nonetheless, a way of spreading Roman culture.

If the lines mentioning Lycoris's name had not survived, the author
of the Qaṣr Ibrīm poems would have remained anonymous. The glory of

Lycoris has outlived the fame of Gallus, for it is thanks to her own fame that we owe the discovery of the authorship of these poems.

Lycoris/Cytheris

Lycoris was a pseudonym. In love poetry, it was customary for the poet to refer to his beloved by a nickname, generally inspired by Hellenic models. In his poetry, Catullus concealed the noble Clodia behind the fiction of Lesbia. The social rank of these inspiring muses has often been discussed, but it is very difficult to come to any definite conclusions because poets' mistresses, real or imaginary, cannot be classified as a homogeneous category. Lycoris did not belong to the upper classes. Her real name was Volumnia Cytheris, which tells us that she was a freed slave. Her former master was a Roman knight, Publius Volumnius Eutrapelus. Cytheris (for which Lycoris is a prosodic equivalent) was a *cognomen* reflecting Hellenized tastes, one of those names often given to slaves (who were not necessarily of Greek or eastern origin). The names Cytheris and Lycoris are *cognomina* with mythological resonance: *Cytheris* alludes to Aphrodite, the goddess of love who was also the goddess of the Greek island Cythera; *Lycoris* alludes to Apollo who was also known as "Lycoreus," deriving from the name of a place near Delphi. Gallus had given Volumnia a poetic name far more illustrious than her real one.

We know little of her physical appearance or of her personality, but we can imagine her as a very beautiful, refined, and gifted actress, dancer, and singer. Generally, the life stories of people like Lycoris were never recorded, although they may have been celebrities in their own times. Her own case, well documented by various literary sources, is an exception, thanks to the fame of her lovers. As a matter of fact, Lycoris's fame endured until the times of late antiquity. Her name was linked to Marcus Brutus (one of Caesar's murderers) in the compendium *De viris illustribus* which tells us: "He loved the mime Cytheris, as Antony and Gallus did" (82.3).

Cytheris/Lycoris was a *mima*, an actress specialized in the art of mime, a semiliterary genre of the theater, which in that era reached the height of its popularity and was appreciated by the ruling classes. The brief mention of Lycoris in *De viris illustribus* clearly defines her role in Roman society: an actress-courtesan. All of her lovers were key figures in the Roman revolution: Gallus, Brutus, Mark Antony. This will allow us to follow her traces, not always very distinct, in spite of her status as a relatively marginal figure, something generally very difficult to do when dealing with ancient history.

An Apprentice of the Art of Mime

Lycoris was born a slave, possibly around 70 B.C. Her artistic career must have begun early. A mime could make her debut on stage as early as the age of twelve and often ended her career by playing the roles of old women, sometimes even as an *archimima,* or head comedienne. An inscription (*ILS* 5213) commemorates the actress Eucharis, who died at the age of fourteen and who had already danced in a *ludus nobilium,* a performance for members of the nobility. The *cognomen* Cytheris, with its allusion to Aphrodite, may be a stage name. H. Solin, who has collected evidence of the use of Greek names in Rome, has classified both the names Cytheris and Lycoris as typical *cognomina* (such as Lesbia, Thaissa, etc.). In the absence of more complete documentation dating from the Republican period, we cannot confirm this. The *cognomina* Cytheris and Lycoris recur in various Roman inscriptions dating from the imperial period and seem to refer to women who were slaves or freedwomen, but not necessarily actresses or women of loose morals.

Lycoris may possibly have been of Hellenic origin. Performances of Greek mime shows had been held in Rome before her time. The spread of Hellenistic culture made this art form more and more popular, and the growing wealth of the city attracted famous actresses. An epigram dating from the second century B.C., dedicated to the lovely mime Antriodemis, concludes, "To Italy she traveled, hoping with soft charms to make Rome desist from battle and the sword" (Antipater of Sidon, *Palatine Anthology* 9.567). Here the poet, expressing his hope that the charming actress would succeed in taming Rome's warlike nature, may be referring to the suppression of the Greek revolt, which ended with the destruction of Corinth in 146 B.C.

The Roman public loved Hellenistic culture in all its varied forms. A Roman mime of high standing had to know how to sing and recite in Greek. Moreover, Greek actors, as foreigners, were not treated with the same disapproval as Roman ones. In his *Lives of Famous Men* (completed in 39 B.C.) Cornelius Nepos wrote, "[in Greece] going on the stage or acting in public performances was not considered dishonorable for anyone, things that for us are partly disgraceful, partly humiliating, and partly contrary to decorum" (Praef. 5). Even though their talents may have been appreciated by a wide public, actresses were still outsiders living on the fringes of society.

Roman Mime

From a sort of farce originally intended as an entr'acte, mime evolved gradually into an autonomous genre, becoming very popular in late republican Rome. Distinct from the genres of serious theater such as tragedy and comedy, mime was a mixed art blending singing, dancing, and acting. Much of the performance was improvised and the actors of mime relied on their "mimetic"—in the true meaning of the word—skills, gestures, and facial expressions, to get their meaning across. Pantomime, a more complex variation of Greek origin, became popular in Rome around 30 B.C.

It is not known whether the actors of serious theater always wore masks when they performed. Mimes did not, and they appeared on stage barefoot to distinguish themselves from comic actors, who wore the *soccus,* and from tragic actors, who wore the *cothurnus* (Diomedes 1.490.3 Keil). Hence the name *planipes,* or "barefoot," given to mimes. The *cognomen* Plautus seems to have had a similar meaning. In other words, mimes had no need for a uniform, as they were not bound by the rules of serious theater.

Unlike comedy and tragedy, which were Greek forms transposed into Latin, mime was a typically Roman form, and thus legitimately subject to change. An author of tragedies or comedies could be accused of *contaminatio* (improper mixing) if, for example, he altered the plot of the Greek original (as Terence did), but not the author of a sketch based on improvisation, in which mythology, politics, obscene jokes, and slices of daily life were mixed. As Beare has remarked, "Free from the obstacles of social status, technical traditions, and written texts, mime had no law other than itself."

Perhaps it was this naturalness, along with the inspiration it drew from daily life, that made mime so popular in Rome. Augustus himself is said to have asked on his death bed, "Have I played my part well in the mime of life?" (Suetonius *Life of Augustus* 94). Following the examples of philosophers (see the fragment of Cleobulos in Fulgentius *Mythologia* 2.14), the *princeps* was declaring his condition as a mortal by comparing his life to a mime performance. Such a comparison was neither random nor banal. For a Roman living in the times of Augustus, acting in a serious play meant interpreting relatively free Latin versions of Greek plays whose meaning had become more and more remote—Caesar looked haughtily upon Terence and called him a half-baked Menander (Suetonius *Life of Terence* 34). By contrast, performing in a mime meant improvising a sketch, entering spontaneously into action, amusing and moving the audience, and surprising the public with unexpected twists.

Scandalous Mimes

Long barred from serious theater, women acted in mime performances from the very beginning, as was the Greek practice. Their presence was fundamental, for they lightened the tone of the performance and made it more sensual, if not openly erotic. It was no mere coincidence that the mime representations performed in Rome (which had originated in Magna Graecia) were linked from the very beginning to the *Floralia,* a feast first celebrated in 238 B.C., which became an annual affair in 173 B.C. The plays connected with the *ludi Florales* were apparently rather scandalous.

Nor was it a coincidence that the origins of this feast were connected with the *meretrices* who took part in the festivities. The goddess Flora, to whom the feast was dedicated, was later transfigured by Christian authors into a prostitute who had become wealthy through the practice of her profession and who had left her fortune to Rome in order to create the *Floralia.* Servius, the grammarian of the fourth century A.D., introduces the story of Gallus and Lycoris in his comment on the *Bucolics* (10.1) by saying, "This Gallus, in fact, was in love with a *meretrix,* a freedwoman of Volumnius." This shows that many people used the word "mime" as a synonym for "prostitute."

The licentious nature of mime has been confirmed by the fragments of a few texts that have been preserved. These were not mere sketches on which to improvise, but were complete scripts composed expressly by poets. This form reached the peak of its development in the times of Lycoris, during the golden age of mime. The following lines of a play entitled *Aries* (the ram), written by Decimus Laberius (ca. 106–43 B.C.), have survived: "The hairy ram, with butting horns, drags his balls behind him," and "I can hardly keep my arse up" (18–20 Bonaria). Another fragment reads: ". . . come on, knock down in one blow the passive youth and the whore in heat" (fr. 70 Bonaria). From the mime *Compitalia,* we have "Come into the bath with me and I'll give you a taste of the Cynics' doctrine" (fr. 42 Bonaria).

Mime performances did not consist only of ribald jokes; they often alluded to daily life or to the political issues of the time. Some were based on mythological themes. The dimension of mime was not so distant from that of tragedy or comedy, and after all, nothing kept the actors, always on the fringes of society, from performing in any of these types of theater. Moreover, the sense of humor expressed in these plays (at least in the "literary" ones) was no cruder than what we find in the comedies of Plautus. Rather, the ancients extolled the wise sayings often uttered by the actors in these plays.

Furthermore, mime differed from other types of farce (in particular, from the *fabula Atellana,* which it came to replace) because of its urban nature, more sophisticated and open to the influence of similar forms deriving from the Greek world. The mixture of improvisation and traditional themes, along with brevity of performance, were the main ingredients of its great success, which in the time of Lycoris was enormous. This was partly because traditional Roman mime was able to make the most of Hellenic elements, thanks to the influx of Greek actors and actresses, without losing its own traditional characteristics. There were no rigid distinctions between mime performers and serious actors, and in the period of the late republic, women also began to perform before more refined audiences. In her epitaph, Eucharis is commemorated as the first female mime to appear "in public on the Greek stage," that is to say, in serious performances, perhaps of comedy.

Cato Blushes

Toward the end of the republic, the licentiousness of these performances was extremely marked. In these shows, the actresses acted, danced, and sang, all pursuits considered "tools of lust," unseemly for honest women (see Sallust *The Catilinian Conspiracy* 25.1). For Romans, the display of the body was in itself scandalous, and anyone who behaved histrionically in this sense was immediately branded as licentious. Not even Hortensius, the greatest orator of the age, escaped such censure. During a trial his opponent, Lucius Torquatus, mocked him by calling him Dionisia, the name of a famous dancer (*saltatricula*). This was a reference to Hortensius's habit of accompanying his speeches with broad, theatrical gestures.

Perhaps as an adolescent, Lycoris participated in the famous festival of Flora of 55 B.C., in which some of the mimes performed what nowadays would be called a striptease. This probably did not entail complete nudity (the Romans were very constrained on this point), but the event caused a big scandal all the same. Records tell us that Cato the Younger was present at this performance. Shocked at seeing the mimes naked, he blushed and ran out of the theater, but the people shouted out to call him back and demanded that the show proceed in the traditional manner (Valerius Maximus 2.19.8).

Later, however, *nudatio mimarum* became obligatory during the *ludi Floralia,* and the audience demanded striptease shows as encores. At the end of the first century A.D., Martial commented on the episode involving Cato, "Why did you come to the theater, austere Cato? / Did you leave only to return again?" In Martial's eyes, Cato's behavior must have seemed dictated by old-fashioned Roman morality, personified by this aristocrat who we know had difficult relationships with women and was a deserving descendant of his great-grandfather Cato the Censor, considered by the Romans the "most eminent man of his times in virtue and reputation" (Plutarch *Life of Cato the Elder* 27.7).

In reality things were quite different. Cato at that particular time was engaged in a struggle with the emerging political class, represented by the so-called first triumvirate. In Rome, theater and politics were closely connected. Powerful men found it to their interest to sponsor performances and promote the careers of actors and actresses. In 55 B.C. Pompey had inaugurated the first stone theater built in Rome, thereby stirring up a great scandal among the more traditionally minded. In that period, Cato's career had been obstructed by the triumvirs, and on February 11 of that year they had successfully boycotted his election as praetor.

When Cato rushed out of the theater during the mime performance (probably held in the theater Pompey had recently built), this was clearly a political message. It was a genuine coup de théâtre, performed in the most appropriate place to protest the setback he had received and to show his enemies that people of the better sort were on his side and not on the side of the men who sponsored such immoral performances (Plutarch *Life of Cato the Younger* 41). Cato continued to promote morality in the theater. Three years later he sought the help of his friend Favonius, aedilis in 52 B.C. (and thus responsible for organizing the *ludi*), in organizing scenic games, marked by moderation and temperance, without resorting to the spectacular effects so much in fashion. The actors and actresses were given gratuities of wine and food (ibid. 46.3).

A Freedwoman's Services

At some point in her career, Lycoris was freed by Volumnius Eutrapelus. As a slave she had had various obligations, including, perhaps, prostitution. As a freedwoman she was still under obligation to furnish services (*praestare operam*) to her former master, now her patron. This mainly entailed giving free performances for Eutrapelus and his friends—but there were other ways she could show her loyalty, for example, by becoming the mistress of the powerful men with whom he associated. No doubt Lycoris owed her liberty to this. Thanks to her grace and beauty she became one of the most popular courtesans in Rome, but it would have been unseemly for any man to keep company with an actress who was not a free woman. Thus in giving Lycoris her freedom Volumnius was not acting in a wholly disinterested manner. Freeing her was a necessary move in order to introduce her into society. The wealthy Eutrapelus expected to gain something from his interest in the theater, if only in political terms. And he was not the only one to exploit the great popularity of theater in Rome. Many other leading politicians, including Sulla, had promoted the careers of actors. Knights such as Eutrapelus could mix and mingle with the world of the theater, but senators were subject to greater restrictions in order to protect their honor. For example, a senator could not marry an actress (*Digesta* 23.2.11.6), but knights like Laberius could even be the authors of these plays. Actors who may have felt misunderstood by the vast public found refined and appreciative critics among the members of the equestrian rank. This was the case with the mime Arbuscula, named thus ("little tree") for her height. Booed in the theater by an audience of the *vulgus,* she proudly declared that she could content herself with the applause of the knights (Horace *Satires* 1.10.77).

Despite the close link between theater and politics, the social separation between the two worlds was very clearly marked. According to the law, a Roman citizen who acted in the theater was branded with "infamy," or a bad reputation. A person who had been branded *infamis* lost of some of his rights and became in fact a second-class citizen. This happened to Laberius in 46 B.C. Laberius had ridiculed Caesar in some of his plays. During the *ludi* organized by Caesar, he forced Laberius to perform publicly in one of his own plays, thereby causing him to lose his rank as knight automatically. The dictator immediately restored him to his lost rank as a reward for his performance, but Laberius was deeply humiliated (Suetonius *Life of Caesar* 39; Gellius 8.15; Macrobius 2.3.10).

Despite her important lovers, Lycoris also remained on the fringe. Her newly gained freedom granted her new rights, but being a freedwoman could not erase the infamy of being a mime. Very few freed slaves could move in any high social circle. Most Roman mimes of the era could at best associate with wealthy freedmen, as did the singer Tigellius, scorned by Horace for his wanton extravagance. When he died, Tigellius was mourned by "a company of flutists, grocers, beggars, mimes, jugglers, a whole brood of that sort" (Horace *Satires* 1.2.1). Lycoris's romantic affairs, although exceptional, cannot be considered attempts at social climbing, for she could not aspire to climb very far.

Most of her colleagues had little hope of bettering their circumstances except by joining together in professional associations. A college of mimes, which included actors, musicians, and servants, comprised a fairly large number of members. The inscription of Lucius Acilius Eutiche (*CIL* 2408) lists sixty members. Various imperial-age inscriptions testify to the existence of colleges of actresses that may have been originally organized in the time of Lycoris. By banding together in a *collegium* under the protection of a patron, mimes attempted to look after their interests—and perhaps, their personal safety as well. Women like them, of no reputation, were often exposed to violence and abuse. In a speech delivered in 54 B.C., Cicero refers to the rape of a mime in Atina by local youths, an act of violence that he considers of little importance of itself and not unusual in Italian provincial towns (*Pro Plancio* 12.30). Aside from the threat of rape, the life these girls led was not very healthy and they often died young, as many tomb inscriptions show.

Lycoris, however, enjoyed two great advantages: personal charm and Eutrapelus's powerful friends. These allowed her to keep company with influential men and, according to S. Pomeroy, she was even "independent enough to choose her own lovers." This last point is debatable, and reveals limited knowledge of the strict conventions governing Roman society. A mime, no matter how charming, had too many obligations to her patron to live her love life as she pleased. As a mime, which more or less explicitly meant *meretrix*, Lycoris's social ascent was limited. She was considered *infamis* by law and by respectable people. In her case she was lucky enough to be on the right side, for Eutrapelus was connected to Caesar's circle, the winning party.

Our mistaken idea of Lycoris as a liberated woman derives in part from the tradition concerning Cornelius Gallus. Virgil had described his unhappy love for the mime, and Gallus himself complains in the Qaṣr Ibrīm lyrics of the woman's *nequitia*, her wickedness, obviously in an amorous sense. If we interpret the tradition literally, we might be misled by this poetic allusion. In reality Lycoris's *nequitia* was more imaginary than real and depended more on the conventions of the elegiac genre than on the mime's real character or behavior.

In other words, we must not try to modernize Lycoris and to see in her the forerunner of some of the familiar heroines of modern literature, such as Baudelaire's Fanfarlo or Proust's Odette de Crécy. She did not enjoy the same freedom as these the nineteenth-century demimondaines, who could choose their lovers-protectors and even play the tyrant to them. Our mime was only a high-class courtesan, better respected than most of her colleagues but always ready to render services when needed.

By making love to influential men, she did reap some benefits. All of Lycoris's lovers belonged to Caesar's entourage. Eutrapelus chose her lovers for her and she remained bound to him. Her allegedly freely chosen love affairs were in reality only special but not unusual services a freedwoman could be asked to perform.

A Scandalous Cortege

We have sketched out thus far a possible biography for Lycoris based on supposition and information from varied sources. Our first dated piece of evidence is an epistle written by Cicero on May 3, 49 B.C., when Lycoris, by then an adult, had already begun to play leading roles and receive public acclaim. As was normal for a woman of her social position and profession, Eutrapelus's mime was already very active outside the theater, leading a busy love life. The day after Caesar's victory over Pompey she became the lover of an undeniably influential man, the tribune Mark Antony.

After Caesar's entry into Rome, Antony had become his lieutenant for Italy at the age of thirty-three. In a letter to Atticus (10.10.5), Cicero complains about Antony's excessive behavior. It seems that Antony traveled around Italy on public business with Lycoris at the head of a procession of litters. Cicero's language is a bit ambiguous, but his scorn for the young tribune and for the dubious company he kept is clear enough. In another letter (*To Atticus* 10.16.5), Cicero adds in a scandalized tone that Lycoris had been carried on a litter accompanied by an escort of lictors, sharing with Antony, as his official lover, the *insignia* used by magistrates in service.

That Antony relished the company of mimes is well known. He is said to have spent his days carousing and took pleasure in attending the wedding feasts of mimes and buffoons. Plutarch reports: "They say that once, after having eaten and drunk all night at the mime Hippias's wedding feast, the next morning when the people summoned him to the forum, Antony showed up with his belly full of food and vomited while a friend held a mantle before him" (*Life of Antony* 9.6).

These testimonies reflect a negatively biased tradition and must be interpreted carefully. If we want to know more about the relationship between Antony and Lycoris, we must understand why Antony enjoyed having mimes around him. Freedmen or women were always at the disposal of their patrons for whom they had to provide services. If they possessed useful qualities, they could become indispensable, or at least become part of an entourage of parasites, hustlers, and errand boys that existed in the Hellenistic courts (some managed to do this even while remaining slaves, like the mime Ecloga, who belonged to king Juba of Mauretania: *ILS* 5216). Antony's pseudotriumphal cortege, symbol of Hellenistic luxury, is one example of this type of entourage. It is clear that the excessive display of arrogance was real, and not simply a distortion created by the opposing party for propagandistic reasons.

Eutrapelus's freed actors were part of Antony's entourage, a public-relations apparatus. The social position of mimes required them to furnish services not necessarily connected with their profession. For example, one of Eutrapelus's freed mimes fought at Philippi against Caesar's murderers (Plutarch *Life of Brutus* 45.4). Moreover, it would seem that Eutrapelus himself in 43 B.C. was Antony's own *praefectus fabrum* (chief of armory) at the battle of Modena, and probably followed him to the East.

Another mime, Sergius, also had great influence over Antony. According to Plutarch, he came from the same *palaistra* as Lycoris (*Life of Antony* 9.7). Sergius was also a freedman and former slave of Eutrapelus, like Lycoris. Plutarch, in speaking of a "gymnasium" was referring to a school for training mimes, such as those that Eutrapelus passed on to Antony. Mimes were not limited simply to livening up Antony's debauches. Both Sergius and Lycoris, although *infames*, were intimate enough with the tribune to influence his relations with the public.

A few years later Cicero was openly engaged in war against Antony. In *Philippicae* (2.23 and 57) Cicero describes the episode of the cortege and specifies its composition. Lycoris was at the fore, escorted by lictors, followed by Antony's chariot, and then by another vehicle (transporting "pimps and panders, really nasty fellows"). The tribune's mother, left to herself, trailed behind. During this journey gold vessels were ostentatiously displayed, and at every stop tents were set up and banquets laid as in the manner of Hellenistic kings. The local authorities were required to lodge the tribune's women friends in their respectable households (Plutarch ibid. 9.8). We can imagine the shame of these Italian *munici-*

pales (dwellers in small provincial towns), whose tradition was to treat actresses as mere objects of pleasure! Scandal may have turned to fury when Antony assigned plots of fertile farmland in Campania to these actors and actresses (Cicero *Philippicae* 2.39).

Cicero records a detail which he found particularly detestable. The local authorities who encountered Antony's cortege addressed Lycoris by the name Volumnia. A mime like Lycoris, a common but successful actress, could thus be treated as politely as though she were an honest matron and greeted with deference by honest men who called her by her extremely respectable *nomen*, rather than by her Hellenized *cognomen*, as was the custom.

"Marriage and Divorce" from Antony

Lycoris remained Antony's "wife" for quite a long time, and his enemies liked to point out the pseudomatrimonial nature of their relationship. What scandalized Antony's enemies was not that he had had an affair with an actress, but that he had treated her with the same dignity normally reserved for honest women. In Rome, libertine mistresses had to be kept out of public view. The wealthy Marseus went so far as to give the mime Origo his father's farm and house, declaring, "May I never have anything to do with other men's wives" (Horace *Satires* 1.2.47). Horace criticized this, taking the side of the moralists, but it is obvious that Marseus was indeed adapting to the morals of his time. Giving up part of his inheritance to an actress was less compromising than committing adultery with a matron would have been, for adultery entailed far more serious losses than the loss of one's reputation—and also exposed the lover to the risk of the deceived husband's revenge.

Antony had transgressed even further. Having an actress for a lover could be tolerated. Having a matron for a lover was reprehensible but one could cover up the scandal. But having an actress for a lover, treating her as an honest matron, and maybe giving her land in Campania as if she were a veteran—that was too much to bear. Antony enjoyed taking Lycoris with him everywhere, almost carrying her in triumph. According to Cicero, this may have left the inhabitants of the towns indifferent, but it offended the soldiers. In the period when Antony was fighting in Italy and Illyricum, the veterans saw him appear in the military port of Brundisium together with the mime (*Philippicae* 2.25.61). Cicero goes on to make a pun that I will try to preserve here: "You came to the gulf of Brundisium, engulfed in the arms of your petty actress."

Yet not even Cicero could avoid dealing with this woman whom he so abhorred and scorned. In a letter to his wife, Terentia, dated January 4, 47 B.C., he complains about her relationship with a certain Volumnia, to whom Terentia had appealed for help but with little success. "Volumnia should have been more polite to you than she was, and she could have acted with greater caution and discretion" (*To His Friends* 14.16).

It has been supposed that the Volumnia to whom Cicero refers was indeed our Lycoris. The circumstances are not very clear. It was a difficult moment for Cicero, and it was in his interest not to irritate Antony. Very likely he wanted to test Antony's mood by flattering his mistress in the most effective way possible, by treating Lycoris as if she were really Antony's wife and inviting her to play the role of intermediary, as a proper Roman matron might have done. Lycoris probably received Terentia rather haughtily. Although she agreed to intervene on Terentia's behalf, she probably did so without much tact, an art not taught in the training schools for mimes. Thus we can see why, three years later, Cicero was so indignant at the thought of others respectfully calling her Volumnia, knowing that he had been forced to do so himself.

At a certain point events forced Antony to cut off his relationship with his mistress. His political position, now consolidated, would not allow him to go on leading an immoral life. Caesar, who had other reasons for doubts about Antony, certainly believed that Antony's weak spot lay in his affair with the *mima uxor* (Pliny *Nat. Hist.* 8.55). Antony wanted to avoid a break with Caesar. After Caesar's return to Italy in September, 47 B.C., he abandoned his old way of life and acquired a soberer and more moderate public image. This entailed a break with Lycoris, and Cicero defined the end of the relationship as a "divorce" (*Philippicae* 2.28.69). Antony remained for a while in disgrace and then once again, in 45 B.C., managed to regain the dictator's favor shortly before Caesar's assassination. Yet even afterwards, the nickname Cytherius, "Cytheris's boyfriend," clung to him (Cicero *To Atticus* 15.22).

His affair with Lycoris ended in 47 B.C., and there is no evidence that the relationship continued after that. Even if the mime had some influence over him, we cannot imagine her as an Aspasia. No matter how much Antony was smitten by her, no Lycoris, no former slave, could overcome the insuperable barriers that existed within Roman society. Star-crossed or illegitimate lovers could be united in a happy ending only on the stage.

In the *palliatae* (a form of comedy in which Greek actors appeared in Greek costumes), we often find the convention of a respectable young man foolishly falling in love with a slave. In the end, her deserved recognition always comes: the woman is revealed to have noble origins and the obstacles to their union fall away. This could not happen in real life: in Rome a relationship between a man and woman could not be legitimate without marriage. If the senator Antony had married Lycoris, he would have lost his rank, as she was *infamis.* He too would have become *infamis* and would have lost his political rights. For a public personage of Antony's stature, no recognition of Lycoris could have salvaged this illegitimate and unjustifiable relationship.

Freedwoman or Artist?

Freedmen or women, though rich and powerful, never achieved the status of parvenus and had to content themselves with living in the shadow of their free protectors. Those who were born in, or who had lived in slavery were always kept at a distance from the nobles, and even at a greater distance from *homines novi* like Cicero. Yet these categories could meet or come into conflict on certain occasions. For example, we will find both Lycoris and Cicero among the guests at a famous banquet given by Eutrapelus in November, 46 B.C., described in a letter from Cicero to his friend Lucius Papirius Paetus:

> I am at table at the ninth hour, writing this note on my tablet. You will ask: where? At Volumnius Eutrapelus's house. Atticus and Verrius, your friends, are on either side of me. But listen to this. Cytheris reclines stretched out below Eutrapelus. At such a banquet, you say, Cicero is among the guests? The man "Whom I admired and upon whose eyes / The Greeks gazed."
>
> By Hercules, I never suspected she would be here. However, not even the famous Aristippus, Socrates' pupil, blushed when reproached for his affair with Lais and said, "I possess Lais, she does not possess me." In Greek it sounds better, translate it if you want. But in reality this kind of pleasure did not excite me when I was young, so just imagine now that I am old (*To His Friends* 9.26).

Eutrapelus remained a loyal supporter of Antony until the end. Yet at the same time he had excellent relationships with members of the opposing party. Horace, many years later, drew a malicious portrait of the man (*Epistles* 1.18.31): a corrupter, a keen judge of character, and the ruin of those youths who did not know how to resist the temptation of luxury. Such a man was quite suited to the times. Eutrapelus knew how to survive and make the most of the delicate political balance of Caesar's era. Cicero snubbed him but also associated with him. Titus Pomponius Atticus protected him on several occasions and at the time of the proscriptions, Eutrapelus returned the favor by hiding him in his home (Cornelius Nepos *Life of Atticus* 9.4).

Cicero could not refuse to include Eutrapelus among his familiar associates. Perhaps, when Cicero's wife asked Lycoris to act as intermediary between Antony and her husband, Eutrapelus had promised Cicero his own support. After Caesar's assassination, when Cicero believed he had recovered his political influence, he vented his poison on Antony and his circle and did not spare minor characters such as Sergius and Lycoris. Even Eutrapelus stood accused of being one of Antony's chief "associates and accomplices" (*Philippicae* 13.2.3).

What happened at that banquet? Despite Cicero's usual ambiguity, there is little doubt that during the banquet Eutrapelus's loyal freedwoman, momentarily disengaged from other important lovers, was performing a special service for her patron. Cicero, who had already been forced to treat Lycoris as a respectable matron, perhaps pretended not to notice anything amiss, but the tone of his letter belies the embarrassment of a man who knew he had been invited to a banquet for men only and thus could not even pretend to be scandalized. In a moment of need he had not hesitated to seek the help of Lycoris, respectfully addressing her as Volumnia. Now he could do no better than to call her Cytheris, pretending to a stoic indifference and entrenching himself behind the respectability of his age. By inviting Cicero to a genuine surprise party, Eutrapelus (which in Greek means "joking,") proved he was indeed worthy of his name.

Cicero continued to despise Lycoris, who thanks to her skill and charm, remained a prestigious component of Eutrapelus's "team." Her connection with Marcus Brutus seems to date from this period, but nothing is known of this relationship and it may have been only a brief affair. Sometime between the Saturnalia of 45 and November of 44 B.C., Lycoris gave a performance, singing Virgil's sixth *Eclogue,* and Cicero, who was among the select audience, was much moved by those verses (Servius *Commentary on the Bucolics* 6.11). Some say that this performance took place in the theater of Pozzuoli, but others claim that it might have been held in the villa of Vedius Pollio in Posillipo, where Cicero was a guest in that period, in which case, this would have been a private performance.

Lycoris's Relationship with Gallus

P. Veyne has written, "Gallus sang Lycoris's praises: he loved Cytheris, but if we are to read Lycoris for Cytheris and find a key to the interpretation of the story, we must imagine Lycoris as a realistic and well-defined figure depicting a real and specific woman—but in elegiac poetry, women are vague and idealized figures." As we have seen, Lycoris's cruel treatment of Gallus was poetic fiction. In real life Lycoris was by no means free to love whom she pleased.

Gallus's love for Lycoris cannot be taken literally, nor must we draw a parallel between elegiac love and courtly love. The code of Roman erotic elegy was based on fiction. Our only real historical data is the fact that Cornelius Gallus had a love affair with Volumnia Cytheris. The grammarians who recorded this fact did not bother to add details, which were considered irrelevant for a poet's biography. Everyone was familiar with the code whereby Lycoris was to be understood as Cytheris and vice versa. Moreover, the ancients knew that Lycoris, and thus Cytheris, had inspired Gallus's poetic genius: *Ingenium Galli pulchra Lycoris erat,* "The genius of Gallus was the beautiful Lycoris" (Martial 8.73.6).

We cannot assign a specific date to her affair with Gallus, but it probably occurred between 43 and 41 B.C. The soldier poet possessed all the prerequisites for a love affair with Lycoris. First of all, he belonged to Caesar's party, although he was destined not to follow Antony but Octavian, Caesar's adopted son and the future Augustus. Like many of Caesar's supporters, he was fond of the theater, and of the very kind of theater abhorred by traditionalists like Cato.

One of the fragments of the Qaṣr Ibrīm papyrus may allude to this controversy over theater. Gallus claims that he had been inspired by the muses to compose poetry worthy of Lycoris, and further boasts that he did not fear Cato's judgment. Several attempts have been made to identify this Cato. Gallus may be referring to the neoteric poet Valerius Cato (in which case, he means he does not fear his rival's literary judgment of his work). There is another possibility: he may be referring to Cato the Elder, the famous censor of the previous century, a stern judge of moral behavior (two fragments of Cato's speeches seem to refer to mimes rather scornfully). Gallus may be saying that he does not fear Cato's condemnation of his mistress, the mime Lycoris.

The distichs of the papyrus are too fragmentary to allow us any categorical conclusions, but perhaps it would be useful to think that Gallus was referring to the now deceased Cato Uticensis. Cato had committed suicide in 46 B.C. to protest the new political groups who used *luxuria*, represented by the mime's shameless display in the theater, as a means of propaganda. Gallus laughed at his respectable morality, for although Cato may have been an authoritative opponent, he was quite powerless in a world in which a simple mime could (at least in the fiction of erotic elegy) be transformed into a *domina*, a lady in command of her lover. Even after his death, Cato continued to be a source of trouble to some. Many of Caesar's adversaries, including Cicero, composed biographies full of high praise for Cato, to which the Caesarians promptly replied, and Caesar himself wrote an operetta, *The Anti-Cato*.

Gallus, in celebrating his love for a scandalous and famous mime, most certainly irritated the traditionalists, the people like Cato. The new poetic language he created offered a more open dimension, in which a woman could move and act much more freely. This applied only to high-class courtesans like Lycoris, however, not to honest women. Later, in the stern climate of Augustus, Ovid would pay the price for this double morality and from his exile mournfully write, "'Twas not the praise of Lycoris, Gallus's ignominy / but his tongue, unleashed through too much wine" (*Tristia* 2.45).

The Last Traces of Lycoris

Virgil's tenth eclogue, written at the beginning of the third decade B.C., tells of Gallus's sorrow after being abandoned by Lycoris. Virgil imagined him lamenting: "Here are cool streams and soft meadows, O Lycoris, / and the woods; here I will pine away for you as I while away the time. / Oh, foolish love keeps me in the arms / of cruel Mars amid his arrows, facing the enemy; / you so far away from your homeland (if only it were not true), / alone, without me, you see the snows of the Alps / the ice of the Rhine. May the ice not offend you / and cutting as it is, may it not wound your tender feet" (*Bucolics* 10.43).

Lycoris, indeed, had a new lover, a soldier who received her services, not in villas and private homes, but in uncomfortable camps. Who was this man and what facts or events may be connected to Virgil's context? Gallus, in Virgil's poem, is shown fighting in his homeland, in Italy. This may be a reference to the Perusian war, which occurred during the winter of 41/40 B.C. Lycoris's new lover must have been one of the officers who were in Gaul at the time. Mazzarino suggests that it was Quintus

Fufius Calenus, or more likely, his son. Eutrapelus's freedwoman had been chosen, once again, by one of Antony's men.

Bucolic fiction aside, Gallus must indeed have suffered the pangs of unrequited love for Lycoris, as Propertius informs us (2.34.91). Even Antony, it would seem, was greatly infatuated with her but political reasons forced him to abandon her. It was the poet, however, who had the last say by glorifying her memory through an idealized image. Other mimes and freedwomen continued to use the *cognomina* Cytheris and Lycoris up to the third century A.D., and there is no doubt that they did so in honor of the mime and of her exceptional career.

The sources stop speaking of her when she was in her thirties. What happened to her afterward is hard to say. She may have died in a foreign land like a Manon Lescaut of ancient times, amid the ice of Germany or on the sands of the desert, while following yet another soldier. Or she may have survived the civil war and grown old to become a wealthy and much appreciated *archimima,* continuing to receive applause from the new Augustan ruling class. Whatever befell her, we can be sure that to the last she made the most of the slim possibilities open to a woman of her status within the rigid social structure of Roman society.

⟨᎑ FIVE ᎑⟩

LIVIA THE POLITICIAN

Augusto Fraschetti

Escaping from the Civil War

In the year 40 B.C., a young Roman matron named Livia was forced to flee secretly from Rome to escape from Octavian, the cruel triumvir, Caesar's adopted son. Livia's husband, the noble Tiberius Claudius Nero, had been proscribed. This meant that his name had been put on a list of persons who could be murdered by anyone, as whim dictated. The murderer would even receive a reward.

Tiberius Claudius Nero deserved such punishment because he had fought against Octavian in the Perusian War. This war had been caused by the conflict between Octavian, on one side, and Fulvia and Lucius Antony (wife and brother of Mark Antony, the triumvir) on the other, concerning the distribution of land in Italy to the veterans of earlier wars. For the Roman army commanders, finding a solution to this problem was extremely crucial. But for Fulvia and Lucius Antony, the Perusian War was a disaster.

While Livia was trying to escape from Rome and join her fugitive husband, she doubtless looked back on her father's tragic death, just two years earlier. Livia's father was the nobleman Marcus Livius Drusus Claudianus. On the battlefield of Philippi (*civilia busta*, "sepulchre of citizens," Propertius called it [II.1.27]), where Caesar's assassins, Brutus and Cassius, had fought against the triumvirs Antony and Octavian, in 42 B.C., Livia's father had fought on Brutus and Cassius's side. After their defeat, he had committed suicide in his tent so as not to fall into the hands of his vanquishers. Many years later, however, in the time of the emperor Claudius, the memory of Marcus Livius Drusus Claudianus was rehabilitated, and an inscription in his honor placed on the Greek island of Samos. This inscription hailed him as the "origin of many great and good works for the world" (*megiston agathon aition . . . en toi kosmoi*), in reference to the fact that as Livia's father, he was also Claudius's ancestor. Her father had met a tragic and glorious destiny; her husband was equally courageous. After the Ides of March, Tiberius Claudius Nero had boldly suggested to the senate that the city should reward Caesar's assassins. Cicero, a close friend of Brutus and Cassius, asked, with far greater caution, for an amnesty to be granted so that all the evils of the past, experienced on both sides, could be forgotten.

Troubled Times at Her Husband's Side

These were men's affairs that necessarily involved their women. Livia had tragically lost her father just two years earlier, and now, faced with the anguish of her husband's proscription, she had fled from Rome to join him. Such gestures of loyalty (in rushing to her husband's side, Livia accepted the dangers of exile) were not rare during the bloody civil wars following Caesar's death, yet they were considered exemplary. Another celebrated example of this was the anonymous matron who saved her husband from proscriptions. She was rewarded with her husband's gratitude and loyalty for as long as she lived, even though she was childless, sufficient grounds in Rome for a man to repudiate his wife (as often occurred). Many other wives actually denounced their legitimate husbands to get rid of them and most likely, come into control of their fortunes.

The marriage of Livia and Tiberius Claudius Nero was clearly a strong one. He was her cousin, a member of the noble *gens Claudia*. The marriage most likely had been arranged by their fathers in accord with the marriage strategies typical of the noble Roman elite. Through this union, Marcus Livius Drusus Claudianus had carved out yet another place for his daughter in the *gens* of her origins. Furthermore, in these years of civil war, the marriage helped reestablish a more solid alliance between these two families in opposition to their enemies, the triumvirs.

In 40 B.C. Livia escaped from Rome with a baby in her arms, the future emperor Tiberius, and with only one other person accompanying her. While in Naples, with their enemies in hot pursuit (Suetonius *Tib.* 6.1), the child's crying nearly gave them away twice as they were trying to board a ship and sail to safety. In the end, she managed to join her husband and travel with him to Sicily. At that time, the island was under the control of Sextus Pompeius, son of Pompey the Great, who was also Octavian's enemy. Despite the enmity he and his host shared for the triumvirs, the haughty Tiberius Claudius Nero did not feel welcome in Sicily and complained that Sextus Pompeius had not treated him with proper respect. He decided to go with his wife to Greece, which was then in Mark Antony's sphere of influence. At this time Antony was not on good terms with Octavian, either. While in Greece, Livia and her son were guests of the city of Sparta. This city had once been under the protection of the Claudii, and Livia was doubly connected with that family, both by birth and by marriage. Much later, during a journey to Greece in 21 B.C., Octavian, then called Augustus, gave the island of Cythera to Sparta and granted the Spartans the honor of participating in banquets held by the Romans. This was intended as a gesture of gratitude toward the Spartans for having given refuge to Livia, her husband, and children when she had fled from Rome. He seemed to have forgotten that he was personally responsible for Livia's exile—but in the meantime she had become his wife. During her Greek exile, Livia encountered other misadventures. One night, while she was passing through a wood after leaving Sparta, a fire broke out, and the noble matron just managed to escape alive with her clothes and hair singed (Suetonius *Tib.* 6.2).

Livia and her son were finally allowed to return to Rome with her husband only in 39 B.C., when a general peace had been established between Octavian and Antony, on one side, and Sextus Pompeius on the other. Before this time we know nothing of Livia's political views, and it is impossible to guess what they might have been (generally, of course, with a few rare exceptions, Roman matrons were not expected to have political opinions). Her father had committed suicide at Philippi, and her husband had been forced into exile. No doubt she blamed Octavian, the powerful triumvir, for her own misfortunes and those of her family.

Marriage to Octavian

After returning to Rome, Livia must have resumed her daily life, a life befitting a woman of her rank as the wife of Tiberius Claudius Nero: looking after her household, supervising the work of her many slaves, caring for her son, Tiberius. After such troubled times, this must have seemed a calmer routine, and she was expecting a second child. Then something extraordinary happened, an event described two centuries later by one historian as the greatest of all paradoxes. The cold-blooded Octavian, whose previous marriages had been arranged for purely political reasons, fell madly in love with Livia. He was so irresistibly attracted to her that he repudiated his wife the very same day she gave birth to a daughter, Julia.

In 38 B.C., Octavian asked Livia's husband to surrender her to him so that he could marry her. Tiberius Claudius did not need to be asked twice. He gave his full consent to the divorce and to Livia's remarriage and at the wedding banquet was treated with the honors traditionally paid to the bride's father or other close family member. Attitudes and practices such as these within the Roman aristocracy should not surprise us. A few decades earlier, probably in 56 B.C., the stern-minded Cato Uticensis, viewed by later generations as the paragon of all Roman virtues, had given his own wife, Marcia, mother of his three children, to his friend, the great orator Hortensius Hortalus. Hortensius also had two children by Marcia. When Hortensius died, Cato promptly remarried her. The chief purpose of marriage in upper-class Roman society was the procreation of children to guarantee continuation of the family line. Thus a wife who had already borne enough children to one husband could be conceded to a close loyal friend. One advantage of this was that sons born of the same mother, as half-brothers, would find it easier to act as allies in the fierce political struggles of ancient Rome.

Tiberius Claudius Nero seemed quite willing to surrender Livia to Octavian. Tacitus (*Ann.* 5.1.2) suggests that Livia herself was not adverse to her new, extremely prestigious marriage. But there was a problem, a mere detail, and yet difficult to solve: Livia was pregnant again, and according to both law and custom a pregnant woman could not enter into a second marriage until the child in her womb had been born into her legitimate husband's home. Thus Livia and Octavian had to wait a while (it seems to have been three months) so that they could be married after the child was born. Octavian was not only a deeply infatuated man, but also a feared and powerful triumvir, who held the entire city in his power.

Three months must have seemed far too long for him to wait. As he was pontifex, he consulted the pontifical college and asked if the marriage could take place immediately. The college replied that if there were no doubt about the period of conception or the father's identity, they could celebrate the marriage without waiting for the child to be born. To justify such a surprising answer, they claimed that this was an ancient practice (and, we might add, a practice of which all trace had been lost). Tacitus indignantly called this a great mockery (*Ann.* 1.10.5), while Dio Cassius (48.44.2) merely states that to avoid angering Octavian, the pontifical college had been forced to give the triumvir a favorable answer.

Once Octavian had obtained permission from the pontifical college, despite the scandal caused in the more conservative circles, the wedding was celebrated in Rome on September 17, 38 B.C. Many years later, by senate decree, this date was entered in the calendar as a holiday. This was after Augustus's death and subsequent deification (and after Livia had been adopted, by her husband's express wish, into the *gens Julia*). Their haste in marrying was criticized even by Octavian's brother-in-law, the triumvir Mark Antony (who was by no means a model of conjugal fidelity). Afterward, Livia, still pregnant, moved from Tiberius Claudius Nero's home to the home of her new husband, where she gave birth to her second son, Drusus. The newborn infant was taken to Octavian and as lord of the household where it had been born, he lifted it from the ground, as was the Roman custom. By means of this ritual gesture, he implicitly gave the order that the child was to be fed and, consequently, kept alive (rather than face the hideous, but legal, fate of death by exposure, frequent in the poor classes). Since the pontifical college had established that Livia's first husband was the child's father, and that only on those grounds could the marriage have been celebrated, the triumvir hurriedly sent Drusus to his father's house, to join his brother Tiberius.

As often happened in marriage strategies among the Roman elite, by remarrying and passing from Tiberius Claudius Nero to the adopted son of Gaius Julius Caesar—a man partly responsible for her father's death—Livia helped reconcile tensions between two families, in this case, the Julian and the Claudian clans, which were subdivided into several branches and which had often fought on opposite sides during the civil wars. Tiberius Claudius Nero's willing surrender of his pregnant wife to the triumvir need not surprise us and does not suggest that he was afraid of Octavian or that he had a weak character. It may be explained as a political move, albeit a crude one. Like all his Claudian forerunners, Tiberius Claudius Nero seems to have been a difficult person with an extremely high opinion of himself, almost obsessed with pride of rank. When he was praetor, the prestige of his office was so important to him that he wished to keep the *insignia* of his rank even after the permitted time had elapsed. As we have seen, even when a fugitive, he felt slighted by Sextus Pompeius and decided to go to Greece, to be near Mark Antony.

Through her second marriage, Livia became the mediator of reconciliation between the omnipotent triumvir and a powerful Roman clan, which was in turn related to other important noble clans whose members were senators. As Sir Ronald Syme has noted, "the nephew of a small-town banker" (referring to Octavian who was from Velitrae, modern-day Velletri) had married into the powerful clan of the Claudians. His party began to attract ambitious aristocrats, first among whom was a Claudian from another branch, Appius Claudius Pulcher, one of the consuls for that year (38 B.C., the year Octavian and Livia were married).

In order for this reconciliation to be genuine, a policy of oblivion had to be adopted, especially over the next few decades, when civil wars were to flare up and burn out. We have already mentioned that Augustus, during a journey to Greece, rewarded the citizens of Sparta for having welcomed Livia during her exile, almost forgetting that he had been responsible for her exile in the first place. Through her marriage to Octavian, Livia became the main exponent of this policy of pacification and reconciliation.

Honors and Power

Although their marriage has been described as a close and happy one, rare in Roman society, it was also childless. At one point Livia lost a child by miscarriage, and she never became pregnant again. This was unusual (but not inexplicable, in that we know nothing at all about the details or effects of this miscarriage) for a woman who had given her former husband two sons and who could thus be considered fertile. The lack of children, specifically, of sons, to guarantee the continuity of the father's name, did not lead in this case to a divorce, as usually happened in Rome (giving an indication of Octavian's deep attachment to his wife). It did, however, have very important consequences on how historians later viewed Livia's attitude towards Octavian's nephews, Marcellus, Gaius, and Lucius Caesar (Gaius and Lucius were later adopted by Octavian) and how they viewed her role in defending her aspirations for her own sons by her previous marriage, Tiberius and Drusus.

In the year 35 B.C. Livia, together with her sister-in-law, Octavia (Augustus Caesar's sister and Mark Antony's wife), were honored in a way that was exceptional for Roman women. They were granted the authority to act in legal matters without the assistance of a guardian, as only vestal virgins could do, and were allowed the right to be honored by statues. They were decreed *sacrosanctae,* a privilege enjoyed by the tribunes of the plebs, which meant that no one could harm them physically, or even touch or insult them. This was exactly the same privilege the tribunes of the plebs had been granted to help them in their role of defending the rights of the common people. So as to evaluate correctly the importance of this honor, we may reflect that the only other persons to have received a similar honor were Caesar, in 44 B.C., the last year of his life, and Octavian in 36 B.C., the previous year, after the defeat of Sextus Pompeius and the elimination of Lepidus.

These honors placed Livia and Octavia well above all other Roman matrons (although Octavia must have made little use of such status after Antony repudiated her). Later Livia's role in her husband's political dealings became decisive, though always under cover, since she was, after all, a woman. She is said to have been an obliging wife, always collaborating in her husband's intrigues, quite capable of plotting her own conspiracies. Her grandchild, Caligula, must have known something of her intrigues, as he was raised in her home and once defined her as "Ulysses in skirts." Augustus had his own personal council of advisors, including Agrippa and Maecenas, but for the most important decisions, he usually consulted Livia in writing. By formalizing his requests for advice from his wife in writing, Augustus gave this correspondence between them a more official air. According to Dio Cassius, in 37 B.C., just one year after their marriage, a portent occurred—offering a good indication of Livia's real power over her husband. A white bird bearing a laurel twig was enfolded by an eagle in its bosom as if to protect it. The eagle took the bird into its care and planted the laurel twig, which grew into a tree, the leaves of which were used thenceforth by the triumphant. According to Dio Cassius's sources the portent signified that Livia (the eagle) had enfolded Caesar's power (the white bird with the laurel twig) and that she would dominate him in everything. Significantly, the omen gave pleasure to Livia, while inspiring fear in others.

Despite the power hinted at by this omen, Livia participated in Roman politics the only way Roman women could, operating from behind the scenes through her replies to Augustus's notes, influencing men's decisions, and not only her husband's. It would be a mistake to think that her role was negligible. After Antony and Cleopatra's death, when in 27 B.C. the title of Augustus was conferred upon Octavian, the empire was firmly in his possession. The senate and popular assemblies still existed but it seems unlikely that they would have dared oppose the will of the *princeps*. Without ever going to the senate or, much less, to the people's assembly, but by receiving Augustus's written requests for advice and furnishing him with answers appropriate to her own aims, Livia soon became more powerful than any woman in Rome had ever been before.

Her status and power were defined in other ways. Livia, who shared her husband's stern moral views, loved to display herself as an old-fashioned Roman matron. Contrary to the prevailing fashions, she had the cloth for her husband's clothes spun and woven at home. She ruled from within the *domus Augusta,* the ruler's household, in all daily matters. This household included both Augustus's immediate relatives (for example, his daughter Julia, and his adopted sons Gaius and Lucius Caesar) and more remote ones, at least all those who lived on the Palatine. She also had a say regarding the roles and functions that some members of the *domus Augusta* were to have in public life. Some very amusing letters have survived in which Augustus asks his wife for advice about what public office Claudius, future emperor, could be given, considering that everyone agreed he was "the family idiot."

In appearances, Livia's household resembled the other noble households of the Roman aristocracy, but in actual fact it was quite different. As early as 28 B.C. Augustus's home already contained a genuine temple of its own (the temple of Apollo Palatine), and after 30 B.C., the *domus Augusta* had its own annual celebrations connected with milestones in the ruler's life. These festivities were entered in the calendar as public feasts observed by the entire Roman people, and thus, the lives of all citizens followed the rhythm of these holidays. In these celebrations, whenever possible, Livia played an important role, which distinguished her from the other matrons. The ruler's house, where she lived, was full of symbols reminding her of her husband's power, from the oak crown and the laurel trees that adorned the main entrance after 27 B.C., to the statue of Vesta dedicated in Augustus's house when he was named Pontifex Maximus in 12 B.C.

Livia was also surrounded by this rich symbolism whenever she accompanied her husband on journeys to the provinces, and in their visits to the Eastern Empire this was particularly evident. Augustus was welcomed in the East as a god and received honors normally reserved for the gods while he was still alive. Livia was also honored and hailed as a goddess, or at least compared to one, as, in an emblematic manner, to Hera or Demeter.

This woman, venerated in the East as a goddess, in Rome was forced to deal with very practical problems, such as arranging for her sons marriages that would help them advance their careers (with some intervention by Augustus) and at the same time keep them out of danger, given their ambiguous position as Livia's children but not her husband's. Livia was a good arranger of political marriages. With excellent timing, she married her older son, Tiberius, to Vipsania, daughter of Mark Vipsanius Agrippa. Agrippa had not only been Augustus's closest and most faithful friend since their school days, but had shared all his most dangerous moments ever since his return to Italy after Caesar's assassination.

Moreover, next to the *princeps* himself, Agrippa was the most powerful man in the empire. When Augustus fell seriously ill in 23 B.C. and was not expected to recover, he gave his seal to Agrippa as his designated successor, whom he preferred even to his own nephew Marcellus.

By marrying Vipsania, Tiberius could count not only on Augustus's protection, but also on Agrippa's help, no matter what happened. The exquisitely political nature of this marriage was made even more evident by the great difference in rank between the bride and the groom. The noble Tiberius married a woman whose father was not of noble birth and whose mother was the daughter of Pomponius Atticus, the famous friend and correspondent of Cicero who decided to remain a simple *eques* [knight] for life, although he was an outstanding member of the equestrian order. Later, in arranging the marriage of her second son, Drusus, she astutely chose Antonia Minor, Augustus's niece, whose father was Mark Antony and whose mother was Augustus's sister Octavia. Through these marriages Livia protected her sons from potential danger: Tiberius became the son-in-law of the powerful Agrippa, while Drusus became part of Augustus's own family. Any children of Drusus and Antonia Minor would also have been grandnieces and grandchildren of Augustus himself.

Plans for the Dynasty

This leads us to an important issue. After the death of Marcellus in 23 B.C., part of the ancient tradition insists that Livia was determined to make sure one of her sons would become Augustus's successor. As her son Tiberius did indeed succeed Augustus in A.D. 14, the course of events prior to that date has been interpreted in light of this fact. At this point, we must examine the numerous and closely recurrent deaths in the *domus Augusta,* which continually posed the problem (and for some, the hope) of succession. Two things must be borne in mind here. The first is that the term "succession" must be used very cautiously in this context: Augustus, while not hesitating to create institutional mechanisms that would guarantee him an heir, aspired to be known as the "first citizen." Secondly, we must say that in this series of very tragic deaths, Livia was inevitably portrayed by most of the ancient sources as the secret poisoner who cleverly eliminated Augustus's closest relatives one by one in order to pave the way to power for her own son, Tiberius.

Let us briefly review these deaths. Augustus had given his only daughter, Julia, in marriage to his nephew Marcellus, son of his sister Octavia.

In 23 B.C. Augustus, believing he had successfully repacified the republic, suddenly found himself the victim of a very sinister conspiracy. The noble Varro Murena, a consul that year, plotted against Augustus, but his plans were discovered and he was executed. This grave episode also indirectly involved Maecenas, who was brought to his ruin. Maecenas had imprudently told his wife, Terentia, Varro Murena's sister, that the plot had been discovered. Augustus did indeed become very ill and was not expected to recover. By the end of the year Marcellus had died, and many suspected that Livia was to blame for his premature death, as she was convinced that Marcellus would have had precedence over her own sons. The historian Dio Cassius, writing more than two hundred years later, mentions these suspicions, but adds that the year 23 B.C. was a particularly unhealthy one, and its inauspiciousness had been revealed through omens.

After the death of Marcellus, Julia was given in marriage to Agrippa. She bore him several children, including three sons, creating more obstacles for Livia's plans. Augustus did not delay in adopting the eldest two nephews and named them Gaius and Lucius Caesar, to dispel any doubts about his intentions. Then when Agrippa, Tiberius's father-in-law, died unexpectedly and providentially in 12 B.C., a ray of light suddenly pierced through clouds that had darkened Livia's aspirations for her sons. With Agrippa's death, she had lost a faithful ally but had also gained an opportunity for her son, Tiberius. Tiberius was forced to divorce from Vipsania and marry Julia. This arrangement may have satisfied Augustus and Livia, but it did not seem to please the groom himself, as he was sincerely attached to Vipsania, by whom he had a son named Drusus after his own brother. He did receive some compensation: thanks to his new position as the ruler's son-in law, Tiberius, like Agrippa before him, received the power of the tribunate, which rendered him a colleague of Augustus, although with lesser powers. Tiberius was not Augustus's true heir, but in the future he was very likely to become the guardian of Augustus's grandchildren and adopted sons, Gaius and Lucius Caesar, as they were Julia's sons, and therefore Tiberius's own stepsons.

In 9 B.C. Livia suffered an enormous and irremediable loss: the death of Drusus, her younger son, who had been born in Augustus's own home just a few months after their marriage. Drusus was a young, valiant, and legendary commander who at Augustus's behest (and theoretically under orders of his brother Tiberius) had led the Roman army as far as the Elbe and had fallen ill in a land very far from Rome, in distant Germany. Tiberius rushed to Drusus's bedside as he lay dying in Germany and was just in time to hear his brother's last words. Although it was winter, Augustus and Livia came to meet the body of Drusus in Ticinum (Pavia) and from there they accompanied his remains to Rome.

Fifty years later, Seneca depicted the rivalry existing in the family of the *princeps* by describing Livia's and Octavia's very different reactions to their sons' deaths. Octavia "buried and hid herself" and wore her mourning robes for the rest of her life. She hated "her brother's grandeur, which surrounded her with too much splendor" and also detested all other mothers, particularly Livia, for Octavia believed that the happiness promised to Marcellus now awaited Livia's own son. This happiness was obviously the dream of succeeding Augustus, and it was Tiberius who actually attained this after many vicissitudes. Although Seneca's account of this event was written after the succession had occurred, it is nonetheless important. In the bitterest moment of her sorrow after Drusus's death, Livia had turned to Areus, her husband's philosopher, for consolation, but after the ashes of her beloved son had been deposited in the mausoleum of Augustus, her period of mourning ended. Seneca's explanation for this is very simple: Livia considered it neither just nor dignified to prolong her mourning beyond that point, given that both her husband and her other son were still alive.

Some statues were dedicated to Livia to console her for her loss and she was granted the special prerogatives given women who had borne three children, the *ius trium liberorum*. The death of Drusus had not diminished her status as fertile and prolific Roman matron in the public imagination. On the contrary the stoicism with which she had borne her loss reinforced that status. As part of a clever strategy, she now welcomed Drusus's widow, Antonia Minor, and her children to Augustus's home on the Palatine. Antonia Minor was also Augustus's niece, and her children, Germanicus, Claudius, and Livilla, could be useful as pawns in future marriage strategies.

She and Tiberius dedicated the "porticus Liviae," in the year 7 B.C., and on that occasion Tiberius organized a banquet for the senators on the Capitoline, and Livia, another one for the matrons elsewhere. Now that Marcellus was out of the way and Tiberius was married to Julia, Livia's dream of seeing her son rise to power may have seemed more within reach, but her son's difficult character momentarily put a check on her aspirations, for Tiberius was a true descendant of the haughty, aristocratic Claudii. Augustus's adopted sons, Gaius and Lucius Caesar, were by now nearly grown up and this put Tiberius in second place.

Following the example of Agrippa, who had once accepted a mission to the East in order not to overshadow young Marcellus in Rome, Tiberius asked his mother and stepfather if he could go to Rhodes to study rhetoric. Although Augustus and Livia begged him to stay with them in Rome, in 6 B.C. Tiberius made an irrevocable decision. Although invested with the powers of a tribune, he set out for Rhodes in a sort of voluntary exile. This period of self-imposed exile on an island in the Aegean anticipated his later retirement to the island of Capri.

The relationship between Tiberius and his wife Julia's children as they began to grow up was by no means ideal. A zealous friend who had followed Gaius Caesar on a mission to the East, offered to go to Rhodes and bring back the head of "the exiled" to Gaius. In 2 B.C. there was an enormous scandal involving Julia, Augustus's daughter, who was accused of immoral behavior and banished to a remote island off the coast of Apulia. It has been suspected that Livia was the author of this scandal, but this hypothesis does not seem very likely, considering that Augustus next forced Tiberius to divorce Julia, thereby depriving Livia's son of his status as the ruler's son-in-law. Tiberius managed to return to Rome (on condition that he could live as a private citizen) in A.D. 2, thanks only to his mother's intervention.

At this point, all of Livia's schemes to see her son become Augustus's successor, or at least to guarantee him a brilliant career as the guardian of the two young princes, seemed to have come to nothing. Then suddenly death struck twice in the *domus Augusta*. First Lucius Caesar died in A.D. 2, and next, his brother Gaius in A.D. 4. Both young men had been sent to get some experience of command in places far from Rome. Their unexpected deaths rekindled Tiberius's hopes, but also contributed to the suspicion that Livia had had them poisoned (similar doubts had been cast on Marcellus's death), but these suspicions were unfounded. After the deaths of Lucius and Gaius, Augustus's adopted sons, Tiberius was also adopted by Augustus, and invested not only with powers of tribune but also with proconsular powers, a status that made him Augustus's colleague, just as Agrippa had been in the past. However, a clause was added to mitigate this recognition (which could not have displeased either Livia or Augustus)—that Tiberius was to adopt Germanicus, son of his dead brother, Drusus, and Antonia, while Augustus adopted on his part (indicating that not all the schemes had been in favor of his wife's children) Agrippa Postumus, son of Agrippa and Julia, born after his father's death.

For Tiberius and for the Country

While Tiberius, newly invested with proconsular powers, set out for Germany and Illyricum, Livia kept the situation in Rome under control. Agrippa Postumus, who represented a potential rival to her son, as he was now Augustus's adopted son, was eliminated in A.D. 14. Like his mother, Julia, before him, Agrippa Postumus was banished to an island. Among the many accusations against him was that he had accused his stepmother of cruelty. Now that Augustus was growing older amid so many family misfortunes, Livia could begin to consider her son Tiberius the designated heir. Already very powerful thanks to her influence over Augustus, she believed she would be even more powerful under Tiberius's reign. Then in A.D. 14 a sudden *coup de théâtre* occurred. The old prince, accompanied by his most loyal friend, Fabius Maximus, paid a secret visit to his nephew and adopted son, Agrippa Postumus, on the island of Planasia, where a moving reconciliation took place. As soon as Fabius Maximus's wife, Marcia, learned of this reconciliation from her husband, she informed Livia. Livia is said then to have resorted to her usual means and not only had Fabius Maximus poisoned—thereby eliminating the only witness to that reconciliation—but also Augustus himself, so that he could not reconsider the designation of his successor.

In scheming for her son's success, Livia was accused several times of poisoning: first Marcellus, then Gaius and Lucius Caesar, and lastly Augustus himself. All these accusations are in reality unfounded, but in Livia's case, the sources view the recourse to poison as a wicked and occult political tool, a typically feminine expedient frequently used by women wielding power in the labyrinth of court policies. Moreover, in A.D. 14 Livia was accused of having concealed Augustus's death for several days until Tiberius's succession had been guaranteed beyond all doubt. In this, Livia was following an illustrious precedent. It is reported that Tanaquil, the Etruscan wife of Tarquin Priscus, did not reveal her husband's death until it was sure that the succession would pass safely into the hands of Servius Tullius, the only person she believed worthy of succeeding her husband. Immediately after Augustus's death, Agrippa Postumus was killed on the island where he had been banished, on the orders, it is said, of Tiberius and Livia.

When Augustus's will was read before the senate, it was discovered that not only was Livia listed among his heirs, as was natural, but also that she had been adopted by her husband into the *gens* of the Julii and authorized to used the *cognomen* of Augusta. This change of name (from

Livia to Julia Augusta) entailed a substantial change in status. At first Tiberius was extremely respectful of his mother, knowing that he owed everything to her. He instructed the senators to draw up a written proposal for the funeral ceremonies honoring Augustus so that the decisions would not have to be made on the senate floor, and so that he and his mother could examine the proposal in their palace.

At the end of the long and extremely elaborate funeral ceremonies for the dead *princeps,* Livia, now Julia Augusta, personally performed the heart-wrenching task of gathering her husband's bones from the pyre, assisted by the most illustrious of the knights. Here Augustus's policies were being stressed, for he had always especially honored and esteemed the equestrian order, second only to the senate. After the consecration of her husband and his ascent to heaven as the *divus* Augustus, she was chosen as his priestess, with the right to her own lictor during the celebration of sacred ceremonies. She also gave private *ludi* for three days on the Palatine, and these *ludi* inaugurated in honor of the deceased Augustus would continue to be held on each year on the Palatine, under all the emperors of later times.

Livia, Tiberius, and Sejanus

Immediately after Augustus's death, Tiberius tried to limit the honors that the senate wished to bestow upon his mother Julia Augusta. He did not want her to be called "Mother of the Country"—an ambiguous title, since it could be used in the masculine gender as *parens patriae,* or in Greek translation, *gonèus tes patrìdos.* Nor did he want the title "son of Livia" to be included in the title "son of the *divus* Augustus," which had now been added to his own name. In an address to the senate, Tiberius claimed that honors granted women should be restricted and that he wished to set an example by rejecting these excessive honors that the senate had proposed for his mother.

Livia, now Julia Augusta, probably did not agree with her son's ideas. Well aware that Tiberius owed everything to her, she desired to rule at his side, or even take precedence over him. In fact, early in the period following her husband's death, she sometimes received members of the senate or representatives of the plebs at home. These audiences were recorded in what could be called Rome's official daily records, the *acta diurna.* Moreover, in this same period, as Dio Cassius tells us, letters written by Tiberius were also signed by Livia, and those addressed to him were also addressed to her. Julia Augusta, as perhaps she had already been doing when her husband was alive, now began to make and break careers with greater arrogance. Among the men she helped were the future emperor Galba and Afranius Burrus, destined later to become commander of the praetorian guard under Nero. One day when her son refused to give into his mother's wishes, Livia threatened to blackmail him. Suetonius gives a detailed account of this episode (*Tib.* 50–51).

> Unable to bear his mother, Livia, whom he accused of wanting to share his power with him, he avoided visiting her too often or spending much time with her, so that people would not think that he ruled according to her advice, although he did often ask her for advice and follow it. Then Livia begged him to include in a list of judges the name of a man whom she had recently helped to obtain citizenship. Tiberius replied that he would do this only on condition that she agreed to have it written in the register that he had been listed "as a favor to his mother." Livia, indignant, took from her archives some of Augustus's letters, in which he referred to Tiberius's intolerant and wicked character, and read them to him. Tiberius was furious that these letters had been kept for so long and then waved before his nose in this fashion. Some believe that this was the main reason he decided to retire to Capri.

Tiberius was against honoring women on principle, and he soon became completely intolerant of his mother. Most of the sources claim that this intolerance is what compelled him to retire definitively to the island of Capri in the year A.D. 26, where he hoped to escape the stern control of Julia Augusta, who observed his every move. Just a few years before Tiberius withdrew from Rome, however, we have record of an episode illustrating great complicity between mother and son in the circumstances regarding Germanicus's death.

Germanicus was the son of Drusus and the adopted son of Tiberius. In this period their relationship had begun to deteriorate, or at least it appeared rather cold to outside observers. Germanicus had married Agrippina, a woman well aware of her heritage as daughter of Agrippa and of Julia (who had been banished by her own father, Augustus, to an island and repudiated by her husband Tiberius) and this could not have helped ease the tensions between Tiberius and his adopted son. Tiberius sent Germanicus on a mission to the East where he came into conflict with the governor of Syria, Calpurnius Piso. The governor was a friend of Tiberius; his wife, Plancina, was an intimate friend of Julia Augusta. It was rumored that Tiberius and Livia had instructed Calpurnius Piso and Plancina to make things as difficult as possible for Germanicus and his wife. It was even said that Tiberius and Livia had ordered the governor and his wife to poison Germanicus. As Tiberius had a son of his own (Drusus Caesar), he and Livia feared that Germanicus might be a potential rival for Drusus Caesar in the right to succession.

Germanicus fell ill in Daphne, near Antioch, and died shortly afterwards. Plancina and her husband were blamed for his sudden death. When they returned to Rome, they were brought to trial for poisoning Germanicus. During the trial, Tiberius and Livia, who were also suspected, could not help but being accusers themselves. Calpurnius Piso committed suicide, but Plancina was spared, thanks to her close friendship with Julia Augusta. The "scandal" of Germanicus's death and of the trial of Calpurnius Piso and his wife Plancina (with the tacit but implicit accusation of Tiberius and Livia as the minds behind the crime) made a great impression in the city and even caused riots. Moreover, the sources tell us that this was one of the last occasions on which Tiberius and his mother collaborated, and in this case it was to prepare the way to succession for Drusus Caesar, Tiberius's own son.

It is not easy to discover, even partially, the truth behind court conspiracies and animosities of this kind. In the specific case of the *domus Augusta,* all the members were related to each other. Just a few years later in A.D. 23, Drusus Caesar also died, thus putting an end to Tiberius's hopes that a son of his would succeed him. This time blame for Drusus Caesar's death (once again, death by poison, as in all self-respecting royal courts) was laid on Sejanus, the powerful commander of Tiberius's praetorian guard, and on Drusus's own wife, Livilla, the sister of Germanicus and Claudius, and supposedly Sejanus's lover. Even before Tiberius withdrew to Capri in A.D. 26, Julia Augusta's power and influence had dwindled greatly and the cause of her decline may surely be attributed to Sejanus's ascent to power. For a while, however, the prince's mother was the only one able to keep Sejanus in check, at least to some extent. Sejanus controlled the praetorian guard in Rome and had completely won Tiberius's trust. A provincial from the Etruscan town of Volsinii, Sejanus was a member of the equestrian order and hoped to become a member of the prince's family, thereby reinforcing his rank and power.

One sign of Julia Augusta's decline in power was that she was no longer able to protect her closest friends. Years earlier, a member of the powerful Piso clan had brought suit against one of her most intimate friends, Urgulania, whom, as Tacitus tells us, "Augusta's favor had raised above the law." Urgulania was given refuge in the palace itself while

Tiberius, at the request of his mother (who considered this lawsuit to be a very grave insult to herself) went in person to the lawcourt to defend the accused. One of Urgulania's nieces, Urgulanilla, had married Claudius, the future emperor and Livia's own great-grandchild, as he was Drusus's son. Furthermore one of Urgulania's sons, Plautius Silvanus, had already been consul in 2 B.C. in the time of Augustus.

Later however, in A.D. 25, when the father of another intimate friend, Marcia, was brought to trial, Julia Augusta failed to obtain Tiberius's help. Marcia's father was the senator and historian Cremutius Cordus, the author of a history of Rome that glorified Caesar's murderers Brutus and Cassius. Accused of treason by two of Sejanus's followers, Satrius Secundus and Pinarius Natta, Cremutius Cordus committed suicide to avoid the shame of a trial. On this occasion, Livia must have remembered the death of her own father, Marcus Livius Drusus Claudianus, who had fought alongside Brutus and Cassius (styled by Cremutius Cordus as the "last of the Romans") in the battle of Philippi and had also committed suicide. By the year A.D. 25 not even Julia Augusta had power to influence her own son, if that entailed opposing the political intrigues of the now powerful Sejanus.

A Sad Old Age

Julia Augusta's health declined as she grew older. Born in the remote year of 58 B.C., she lived to be a very old lady, in terms of the average life expectancy of the time. Once when she became seriously ill, in the year A.D. 22, Tiberius rushed home from Campania to her bedside. Tacitus tells us that he did this "either because there was still great harmony between mother and son, or to cover up the conflicts." The senate decreed that prayers should be offered to the immortals for her and special *ludi* organized to honor the gods and help restore the elderly matron's health. The games were organized by the four most important colleges of priests in the city: the pontifical college, the college of the augurs, the college of the Sibylline books, and the college of sacred banquets. Another college was to join in the ceremonies, the confraternity of Augustus, which was in charge of the cult of the god Augustus, considered to be the family's own special priesthood.

After he withdrew definitively to Capri in A.D. 26, Tiberius detached himself completely from Julia Augusta, abandoning her to a sad, isolated old age in her home on the Palatine where she lived by herself. During this period, Rome was in Sejanus's uncontested control.

For the remaining three years of his mother's life, he saw her only once, for a few hours on one particular day. Afterward, he had nothing to do with her and was not present when she fell ill or when she died [in A.D. 29]. In the hope that he would come, her funeral was delayed for several days and was celebrated when her body was already corrupt and decomposing. He did not allow her to be deified and claimed that this had been the deceased's wish (Suetonius *Tib.* 51.5).

Tiberius, apparently, chose not to leave his island even on the occasion of his mother's funeral. Caligula, his grandnephew, presided at the funeral ceremonies, which were said to have been modest, and praised Livia in the forum. Her son did not respect her last wishes as expressed in her will, nor the wishes of the senate, which had decreed that an arch be raised to commemorate her (an unusual honor for a woman), in recognition of the help she had offered to many senators, as well as to their children. As Santo Mazzarino has observed, the daughter of Marcus Livius Drusus Claudianus and the wife (by her first marriage) of Tiberius Claudius Nero, had been an important agent of reconciliation between Augustus and the senate at the end of the civil war.

Only somewhat later, Tiberius's successor, Caligula, began to pay her designated heirs the legacies specified in her will. In A.D. 42 the emperor Claudius had her name listed among the goddesses. We know that previously, while alive, she had been revered as a goddess in the provinces. Claudius ordered that a statue of Livia be raised in the temple of the *divus* Augustus, her husband, and that sacrifices in honor of the new goddess be performed by the vestal virgins. This is a paradox, that Livia owed her new status as a goddess to her grandnephew Claudius, whom she had never thought well of, but on the contrary, had always scorned.

Six

PERPETUA THE MARTYR

Emanuela Prinzivalli

for Valentina De Angelis

On March 7, A.D. 203, the noblewoman Vibia Perpetua died for her faith at the age of twenty-two in the amphitheater of Carthage, leaving behind an infant son and a life of comfort. Her martyrdom is no surprise for historians of antiquity, as reliable sources record the deaths of Christian martyrs, both men and women, as early as the previous century. Under Nero and Domitian, women martyrs were dressed up for the occasion as Danaids or in other costumes offensive to Christians, and put to death in the circus of Rome, as we learn from Clement's first letter (dated A.D. 98) from the Christian community of Rome to the community of Corinth. In A.D. 112, Pliny the Younger, dutiful governor of Pontus and Bithynia, wrote to Trajan (Letter 96) to enquire what procedure should be followed in bringing Christians to trial. He admits that two women in his custody, both slaves and *ministrae* of the cult, showing remarkable strength of character under torture, had refused to confess they had done anything wrong. Good old Pliny, in full conscience, however, could not describe their stubbornness and willingness to die as courage since they were unable to account for their attitude in philosophical terms. Instead, he defined their attitude as superstition, obstinacy, and madness. The anonymous and ignorant crowd, generally quite bloodthirsty, could at times prove more generous than he had: When another slave, Blandina, was publicly tortured and killed in Lyons in A.D. 177, the onlookers all agreed that "never in their town had a woman been capable of bearing such suffering" (*Acts of the Martyrs of Lyons* 1.56). Christian women of low social rank were not the only ones persecuted. Blandina's mistress was right beside her down in the arena. In Rome, under Domitian, Flavia Domitilla, a member of the imperial family, was banished to the island of Ventotene, and a matron was denounced by her own husband, although we do not know with what consequences, in the latter half of the second century A.D., as Justin, the Christian philosopher and himself a future martyr, informs us. There is nothing remarkable about Perpetua's martyrdom, although we may wonder why this Roman citizen (as she was, most likely) was summarily condemned to death *ad beluas,* "by wild beasts."

A Woman Writer

What is remarkable about Perpetua and what makes her one of the most outstanding women, not only among the Christian communities of the era, but of the entire ancient world, is the fact that she recorded her story while in prison. Despite the extremely precarious conditions of her imprisonment, she continued to keep a diary until the day before she died. Her diary concludes with an explicit invitation addressed generally to her community to finish her story for her. This task was taken up by a very skilled editor-compiler, whose identity is unknown. The editor composed a prologue full of doctrine, followed this with Perpetua's diary, added another brief memoir written by her fellow martyr, Saturus, and concluded with a detailed narrative of the martyrdom of Perpetua and her companions. Thus was born the *Passion of Perpetua and Felicity* (*Passio Perpetuae et Felicitatis*), a rare jewel of early Christian literature and a literary prototype for a specific genre of *Passiones* in Africa. The amazement aroused in scholarly circles by this woman's achievement has sometimes bordered on incredulity, and some have wondered if her diary were not a clever piece of literary forgery. Meticulous analysis of the various sections of the *Passion of Perpetua* has shown that there are such great stylistic differences between the language used by the compiler-editor and the language used by the author of the diary, that it is extremely unlikely that they were written by the same person, unless he (or she) were the cleverest forger in the whole of antiquity.

Perpetua wrote only a few pages, and yet how valuable they are, given the impenetrable silence surrounding women in ancient times. It is remarkable enough that a woman left any written record at all, but the content of her testimony is even more significant. Perpetua was not a poet. She was not attempting to immortalize her experiences or to endow them with universal value. She simply kept a diary, a chronicle of daily events, something very close to historiography (for all the distinctions of classical treatises), a genre that precluded authorship by women in ancient times. She wrote about herself, focusing on her feelings, as is natural for someone undergoing the dismaying experience of being in prison and grappling with her fears. It is moving to see this woman of the ancient past daring to appropriate a form of narrative expression generally denied her sex—and by this act, placing herself at the center of a public turmoil (and at what a price!), outside that cycle of child-bearing and care-giving reserved for women since time immemorial, a way of life that gave them no opportunity to influence current events or politics.

There can be no doubt that it was Perpetua's Christian faith that encouraged her to express herself in writing, making her realize that her experiences deserved to be recorded. As a member of the upper classes—*honeste nata, liberaliter instituta* ("respectably born, gently educated"), as the compiler of the *Passion of Perpetua* presents her to us—she had received the training necessary for that self-expression. The entire text of the *Passion* is pervaded by a remarkable self-confidence in dealing with the outside world, a characteristic she probably owed to her upbringing. Her social status cannot explain, however, her deep self-awareness: otherwise we would have seen many more writings produced by women. On the contrary, as a matron, and a member of an extended family in which the paterfamilias had special authority and in which modesty and discretion were deeply rooted values, her family status could easily have been an obstacle keeping her from self-determination and self-expression. Family pressure to keep silent is, in fact, one of the main themes of her diary. "Do not dishonor me," her father admonishes her on his second visit to prison and then concludes, "If anything happens to you, none of us will ever be able to hold up our heads again."

When her father exhorts her to return to the bosom of her family, Perpetua must make a choice on the basis of *what* she is, *who* she is: that is, a Christian. She must make this choice in the solitude of her conscience with only God to guide her, putting aside the family relationships that define her existence in society as daughter, mother, and wife. Her deep conflict leads her to a greater understanding of herself in relation to the world, and in particular to the world of men. It is striking that Perpetua—at last a woman capable of writing about herself, of giving a personal interpretation of the facts—records in her diary the words and actions only of men. She gives us merely a fleeting glimpse of her mother, whom she begs to look after her baby (and receives no reply). Her father briefly mentions an aunt. All her interlocutors are male, yet they exist in her diary primarily in relationship, positive or negative, to herself—or they are excluded, like her husband, whom she never mentions, not even to explain his strange absence. In her diary Perpetua does not define herself in relationship to men, rather she defines men in relationship to her. This ceaseless confrontation will find its conclusion in her final vision, when she sees herself transformed into a man during her battle with the devil: at last on equal terms with men, without ever losing the feminine identity maintained in the diary through her narrative "I."

A Subtle Intellect

Perpetua's brief diary opens with a clash with her father, one of the recurring themes:

> When we were still in the hands of the guards, my father wanted to convince me to deny my faith and insistently tried to persuade me by reminding me how much he loved me. So I asked him, "Father, do you see that pot, or vase, or whatever it is, on the ground over there?" "Yes," he replied. I said, "Can it be called by any name other than what it is?" "No." "Well, neither can I be called by any name other than what I am, and that is a Christian."
>
> Upon hearing that word, my father became furious and threw himself upon me as if to tear out my eyes, but he only managed to hurt me, and then he left, defeated, taking with him the devil's arguments. For the next few days he did not come to see me, and I thanked the Lord and breathed more easily, glad that he had not come.

Perpetua's line of thought has reminded some modern readers of syllogistic reasoning or of Platonic theory concerning the essential relationship between name and thing. Here she is practicing Socratic dialogue with her father, overturning the roles of the traditional family code, and thereby creating an alienating effect, especially considering the gravity of her situation. Her father is intrigued first, and then rudely awakened by her unexpected conclusion. "That word," *Christian!* The word shocks him, for he is unfamiliar with the language of his daughter's faith. Her shocking conclusion is in fact foreshadowed by her reference to the vase at the beginning of her argument, probably an intentional allusion to the writings of St. Paul, where the image of a vessel refers to the Christian soul filled with the Holy Spirit. In this opening exchange Perpetua depicts herself as a woman whose dialectical skills anticipate her victory over the forces of evil, which she hopes to attain through martyrdom. Later, in mentioning her relief at her father's absence, she shows just what price she has paid both mentally and physically for the self-control necessary to win this struggle with her father.

The Genesis of a Visionary Experience

Her failure to mention the circumstances of her arrest, even in passing, is almost inexplicable. It may become understandable, however, if we consider that in the diary the "controlling function," to use a term a literary critic might employ here, is quite clear. Perpetua narrates only those facts that have special inner resonance for her. It is her feelings that give form to the factual exposition: her physical relief when her father does not come to see her after their quarrel, then later, after her baptism (at the time of her arrest Perpetua and her friends were still only catechumens), her even more determined resistance. She describes her fear of the thick darkness in her cell, her sensation of suffocating in the dank, close air—all new experiences for her—the guards' attempts to extort money from her, and above all, her constant anxiety about her baby (3.4–8).

After the darkest moment of despondency has passed, Perpetua's spirits revive. The deacons Tertius and Pomponius, whose work includes assisting Christians in prison, manage (by paying) to obtain a better place for all the Christian prisoners and bring Perpetua her little son "who had nearly starved to death." A few days later Perpetua writes, "I have been given permission to keep my baby with me in prison. I immediately felt better and am relieved to be taking care of the baby myself. For the moment, this prison has become for me a king's palace. No place could be more beautiful." This conclusion, arresting in the simplicity of its style, gives us a fleeting glimpse of her imagination.

Next, her brother, also a catechumen, enters the scene, and like the deacons and other members of the community, visits his sister in prison. Trajan's policy (which we may gather from the context was evidently still in effect) permitted charges to be laid by name only, and did not countenance any automatic seeking out of Christians. A curious situation consequently arose for the future martyrs in prison upon whom were focused the aspirations of their entire community. Their fellow Christians could freely flock to the prison to see them, having managed to escape prison thanks to their greater caution or discretion, perhaps to their cowardice, or else simply by chance. These solicitous visitors suffered for them and yet rejoiced in the anticipation of their heavenly rewards, to which only martyrs (as was believed then) acceded directly upon their death.

Perpetua's brother exhorts her, now that she has become worthy through the confession of her faith, to ask God for a vision so that she may know her future: "Venerated sister, by now you are worthy to ask for a vision, and to know whether or not you will be granted martyrdom or freedom" (4.1). There is nothing strange about her brother's request. People in ancient times believed that their dreams foretold the future and that through visions they could communicate with the divine. Special practices were sometimes used to induce this phenomenon. The eschatological tensions pervading early Christianity encouraged prophetic rapture, in which visions played an integral part. This was particularly true of the African community. Peter's first speech in the Acts of the Apostles opens with a reference to the prophecy of Joel (2:28–32): "I will pour out my spirit upon all flesh and your sons and your daughters shall prophesy, your old men shall dream dreams and your young men shall see visions." The compiler of the *Passion of Perpetua* was obviously very familiar with this verse, for he closes his prologue with it. Moreover, martyrdom, which had its own particular charisma, was inextricably linked to visions, as Stephen, the first martyr in the Christian tradition, illustrates: "But he, being full of the Holy Ghost, looked up steadfastly into heaven, and saw the glory of God and Jesus standing on the right hand of God" (Acts 7:55). Furthermore, there existed an apocalyptic literature that was partially transmitted through catechism, offering stimulus to fertile imaginations. Perpetua was young, like her brother, a condition conducive to having visions according to Joel. Older people were not excluded, however, for the elderly Bishop Polycarp of Smyrna, while absorbed in prayer, had a vision of his imminent martyrdom by fire (*The Martyrdom of Polycarp* 5.1). Perpetua's firm conviction that she would receive a revelation from God if she asked for one is disarming, and fully understandable, given the historical context. "I knew I was able to converse with the Lord," she says simply. After her brother's visit, she records four visions in her diary, alternating with major episodes of her life in prison. Modern readers are unsure whether they should consider her visions as genuine visions or as dreams: both were regarded in ancient times as forms of communication with the divine, although the latter was less direct. Christians were very circumspect about the vagueness of some dreams. Some scholars have noted that Perpetua's first two visions occur in the night and that the expression she uses to indicate the end of the experience is ambiguous, for *Experta sum* may mean either "I woke up" or "I roused myself." This does not necessarily prove that they were dreams. The darkness may simply have provided a background from which the images emerged. In any case, her brother had asked her for a vision, and Perpetua considered her experience to be a vision. In her first vision, she sees a narrow, bronze stairway reaching up to heaven, with sharp iron points all along the sides and a snake at the bottom blocking her ascent. She steps on the head of the snake and climbs up to a garden where a white-haired shepherd, standing in the midst of a crowd of thousands all robed in white, welcomes her with fatherly affection and offers her a morsel of cheese. Perpetua thereupon rouses, with a pleasant taste in her mouth. When she tells all this to her brother, they both realize that martyrdom awaits her: "intelleximus passionem esse futuram" (4.3–10).

Family Affection

After her visionary experience, she is plunged back into the bleak reality of prison. She receives the news that she is to be brought to trial soon, and her father reappears (5.1–6). In her first encounter with her father, she recorded only his aggressive behavior toward her. Now his anxiety has become aggression against himself and this can be seen in his appearance. *Consumptus taedio,* "spent by fatigue," she describes him. The moment has come for supplication, and this is the only point in the diary where Perpetua fully records his words in direct speech. Her father reminds her that she has always been his favorite child, his only daughter. He mentions their various relatives and finally alludes to her unweaned baby. With this veiled threat, he is reminding her of her paramount duty as a mother ("How will he survive without you?"). Then he tells her that he himself and the whole family will be dishonored ("Do not expose me to dishonor"), held suspect by others, pulled down from their position of self-respect in society, because of her ("None of us will ever be able to hold up our heads again"). This is pure egoism, not love, some modern scholars have pointed out, but Perpetua evaluates his motives more generously. "He spoke this way out of affection" (*pro sua pietate*). We are familiar with the accusations and suspicions, sometimes quite vulgar, that surrounded the Christians of that era, as well as the scorn displayed toward them by the cultivated upper classes. Almost a hundred years earlier, the refined Pliny had spoken of Christianity as superstitious madness, and even the sagacious Marcus Aurelius showed little respect for Christian martyrs, disapproving of their "theatricality" in the face of death. This was precisely the point: the unreasonable faith of Christians and the atmosphere of fervent rejoicing that accompanied their martyrdom were far too removed from the Roman *gravitas* and from the *logos* so dear to the Greek spirit. Perpetua's father, the head of the household, probably shared those judgments and prejudices. Perpetua confirms that he is the only one in the family who is truly hostile to her faith. We may recognize in his behavior the same attitude typical of the eldest male in Roman aristocratic families much later—in the fourth century. They saw their role as preserving the rites and convictions of the pagan tradition while the women converted to the new faith. Later, an almost peaceful subdivision of religious faith occurred within the family—but at these first moments of crisis, the clash was violent and the family structure split deeply within.

How does Perpetua reply to her father's beseeching, his prostrating himself before her, his kissing her hands, and his calling her "my lady"? Her answer, superficially comforting in its intentional ambiguity and yet inexorable, was later praised as an example of moderation and filial respect by Saint Augustine (*Sermons* 281.2), who laid no stress on Perpetua's more human aspects in his sermons. She says, "On that scaffold will happen only what God wants to happen. It does not depend on our will, but on the will of God" (5.6). Once again, Perpetua shows how skillful she is at ambiguous word play. This was evident in her first clash with her father, and will later be underlined in the compiler's description of her when she is no longer the narrator, but the subject of the narration. Her father now understands that his requests have been denied and returns home, crestfallen.

The next day was the day of the trial. "Everyone confessed their faith," she records. In her diary Perpetua is completely focused on her individual struggle: she never mentions her prison companions by name except for Saturus, the catechist, who gave himself up to the authorities to be near his pupils. He appeared in her first vision, preceding her up the bronze stairway. During the proceedings, just as she is about to confess "I am a Christian," her father, who has brought his little grandson along to the trial, tries to pull her down from the stand and is punished with a beating on orders from the procurator Hilarian. Perpetua claims to feel real physical pain, as if she were receiving the strokes herself (6.1–5). Her father's prediction that he would lose the privileges and social standing of his class because of her was obviously on the mark.

Once the public trial has concluded with the death sentence, Perpetua returns to her private role as mother. In prison again, she demands that her child be brought to her so that she can nurse it. "My father did not want to give him to me." This brief sentence indicates the tensest moment of their conflict. Did he deny her the child as a last act of revenge, because he felt abandoned by his daughter and by society? Was this gesture a desperate attempt to make her retract? Did he wish to protect his grandchild from a poisoned breast soon to be withered by death? But in the *Passion of Perpetua,* a worldly happy ending is still possible, if only for the innocent child: "As God willed, the child no longer sought my breasts, which were no longer inflamed. I ceased to torment myself with worry about the child and was spared the pain in my breasts" (6.7–8). The God of Perpetua and of the compiler (who later takes care to note that Felicity's premature daughter, born in prison, survived: 15.7) does not oppose the human value of motherhood, and above all, he spares women the accusation of intentional cruelty toward their children. Although in the eyes of her Christian brethren, the indirect sacrifice of a child might possibly have found religious justification, such an attitude was incomprehensible to the pagan society surrounding her. Their opinion was clearly expressed by Hilarian: "Have compassion for your father's white hair, for your child's tender age!" (6.3). In their eyes, Perpetua's willingness to abandon her child made her only slightly less heinous than Medea and absolutely deviant from the ideal of the self-effacing woman, nourisher and keeper of the house. This ideal had never been repudiated ideologically, despite important sociological changes during the imperial era.

After Perpetua has mentioned her child for the last time, her maternal instinct projects itself beyond the terrestrial sphere to the memory of her brother Dinocrates, who died in childhood:

> A few days later while we were all praying together, in the middle of prayer it suddenly came to me to say aloud the name of my brother Dinocrates. This amazed me, because he had never come to mind before, and I felt sad remembering his fate. I immediately understood that I was worthy to intercede on his behalf and that I must do so.

She thus experiences her first vision of Dinocrates: she sees him in a shadowy place; he is dirty, suffering, and thirsty. He tries to drink from a tub of water too high for him to reach, but she cannot help him because they are separated by a great distance. Perpetua awakens from this vision with the awareness of his suffering and yet full of hope. With fervent prayer, she brings on another vision, in which Dinocrates appears healed and clean. The tub has been lowered within his reach, and a brimming cup with an inexhaustible supply of water is placed on the edge. The child drinks from the cup and plays with the water in the tub. "I knew his suffering had ended" (7–8).

After the death sentence has been pronounced, her diary dedicates less space to outer events and focuses more on her communication with God. Between her two visions of Dinocrates, she briefly mentions that the group of Christians has been transferred to the military prison and put in shackles (8.1). After concluding the account of her second vision of her younger brother, she describes the sympathy shown by Pudens, the guard, toward the prisoners, and then recounts her father's last visit. *"Consumptus taedio"* she repeats, recording his gestures of desperation and his incoherent, heartbroken protests. There can be no happy ending between father and daughter, as there had been with her innocent child. Perpetua's last words have a cold, sepulchral ring: *ego dolebam pro infelici senecta eius* (9.3), "I grieved for his unhappy old age."

"Facta sum masculus"

In her fourth and last vision (10.1–3), the day before her death, Perpetua has a foretaste of the joys of victory. She sees herself in an amphitheater where she must fight not wild beasts, but a hideous Egyptian fighter. In her vision young assistants undressed her and massaged her with oil, and she "became a man" (*facta sum masculus*). The arbiter is a very tall personage dressed in purple, holding the rod of the *lanista* (an instructor of gladiators). He promises her a branch of golden apples as a reward. After a fierce battle, the Egyptian falls to the ground, Perpetua tramples on his head and is rewarded with the branch and receives the kiss of peace from the *lanista,* who says to her, "Peace be with you, daughter."

> I awoke and realized that I would have to fight not with beasts but with the devil, but I knew that the victory would be mine. This is what I have done up until the day before the games. Someone else may write the story of what happens during them, if he wishes (10.15).

Thus ends Perpetua's diary. Her visions are the most controversial part. Modern critics have done their utmost to interpret them, viewing them within the limited context of the diary and within the overall context of the *Passion of Perpetua.* The core of the problem is whether they should be evaluated as expressions of the subconscious or as rational constructions. The attempts by some modern scholars to interpret them as rational constructions are weakened by those scholars' compulsive need to justify and explain every detail. The interpretations of her visions as manifestations of the subconscious are based on a more realistic evaluation of Perpetua's mental condition. Given the dramatic and dangerous circumstances, her visions/dreams are symbolic and reassuring; they compensate for her fears and project her outwardly. Moreover, in the visions she has recorded, despite the inevitable editing they have undergone in the process of being transcribed in her diary, visual, spatial elements, proper to the subconscious sphere, prevail over narrative, causal elements.

Yet an interpretation based on the subconscious should not, due to its very nature, be an overinterpretation. To my mind, this point has not been sufficiently understood. We may read the contents of her text according to many different psychoanalytical approaches, but all results would be fallacious because Perpetua thought in terms quite different from those of the modern reader. Moreover, in the logic of the subconscious many meanings may coexist on different levels, and situations may be reversed as they cannot be in real life. Confronted with the actual text, all psychoanalytical interpretations are equally valid and invalid, for the text both allows such interpretations and at the same time disavows them. They are valid insofar as concerns our knowledge of how the subconscious imagination works (in oneiric or hallucinatory modes) and yet false because these meanings could not exist in the imagination of an author producing these texts in such a remote past (unless we postulate the existence of an archetypal, atemporal dimension). Nevertheless, we can identify some elements which a psychoanalytical interpretation might take into consideration, for example, conflict with the paternal figure, which produces a double register in her text: antagonists (dragon, Egyptian) who end up stretched out at Perpetua's feet (as her own father did) and comforting figures (the white-haired shepherd, the *lanista*). Another interesting element is her transformation into a man. It does not cancel out her female nature, recognized by the *lanista* ("Peace be with you, *daughter*"), but it brings out the double identity—both male and female—of every human being. The obvious presence of a few religious symbols in this context is perfectly explicable in that she experiences her faith deeply both on a conscious and on a subconscious level, in which basic symbols may be fused or overlaid (food—the morsel of cheese—may symbolize the bread of the Eucharist). Equally explicable are such pagan vestiges as the symbolic branch of golden apples.

Perpetua in a Man's Dream

The *Passion of Perpetua* continues with a vision written by Saturus (11–13), who describes the garden of paradise the martyrs yearned to reach.

Perpetua accompanies Saturus in his discovery of heavenly joys. She is the only one he singles out by name among his companions in prison. When the elders in heaven say to them, "Go and play" (indicative of Saturus's desire to regress to childhood), he exclaims to Perpetua, "You've got what you wanted." She replies, "May God be praised, for just as I was happy (*hilaris*) in life, so now will I be even more so" (12.7). Perpetua's *hilaritas* is above all the joy of her faith and of the divine gift of martyrdom, but Saturus is also referring to one of the personality traits of this extroverted young woman. Saturus then sees, bursting into the midst of this company of blessed ones, the bishop Optatus and the priest Aspasius, who ask the martyrs to mediate a quarrel: "Reconcile us. You have abandoned us here like this." For many reasons, conflict within the Christian community was frequent and did not diminish even in times of persecution. Saturus's intention to punish Bishop Optatus is very clear, for the bishop is sternly reproached by angels (13.6). The martyrs comfort and embrace the two men, but Perpetua then takes them aside and speaks to them in Greek (13.4). As we can see from these details, Perpetua played a major role in Saturus's imagination.

Perpetua's Story Continued

Saturus's narrative is followed by the compiler's account (14–21) of the earthly phases of the victory which has been foreshadowed by Perpetua's and Saturus's visions of paradise. This account now focuses on the martyrs as a group, providing a happy ending for everyone, as at the beginning of the *Passion* it had also focused on them as a group when recounting the arrest of the young catechumens, Revocatus, Felicity, Saturninus, Secundulus, and Vibia Perpetua (2.1). As the story had then narrowed in to concentrate on Perpetua and her family, here too, in the closing section, she stands out while the others recede into the background.

Two main themes are entwined throughout the entire text of the *Passion of Perpetua*. The first is intentional and is stated in the prologue: the exaltation of the martyrs' witness through the celebration of their eschatological rewards—foreshadowed in their charismatic powers of prophecy and intercession (Perpetua successfully intercedes for Dinocrates beyond the grave)—and through the celebration of their shedding of blood. The second theme, unifying the text at a poetic level but perhaps less intentional, is the portrayal of Perpetua as a very strong personality. This is evident in the compiler's description of her martyrdom. We are informed that Secundulus died in prison (14.2) and that Felicity received special grace and gave birth prematurely so that she might be with her companions on their day of triumph. In the compiler's narrative, Felicity (the only other woman in the story, who has been in the shadows till now) cries out in the midst of her labor pains, "Now I am suffering what I am suffering. But later someone else will be in me and suffer for me because I will be suffering for him." Her words effectively express her faith in the notion of the Christian as part of the body of Christ. The compiler then relates the final events, beginning with the last day in prison. The tribune accuses the Christians of practicing magic (a frequent accusation made by the pagans against Christians) and tries to deny them the traditional liberties granted on the day before execution. In the compiler's account, Perpetua speaks out boldly: "And thus you will not allow us to refresh ourselves with food? We, nobles of Caesar, condemned and destined to fight on his feast day? Is it not to your own glory if we arrive there in flourishing health?" Irony and ambivalence are mingled in her words: the health she is thinking of is no doubt also spiritual. Perpetua silences the tribune with her irony, while Saturus, with sarcasm and veiled threats, alarms the curious pagans who have come to watch them enjoy the banquet she has obtained for them. In the compiler's narrative, male figures tend to evoke the threatening aspect of God: this happens again when Revocatus, Saturninus, and Saturus threaten the crowd in the arena, while Perpetua calmly advances toward her destiny, her mind fixed on her future glory (18.7). In the compiler's stylized narrative, all the martyrs appear happy and beautiful on that great day, but as always Perpetua is his central focus.

> The day of victory shone. They went from prison to the arena as if to heaven, happy, their faces calm, trembling not with fear but with joy. Perpetua followed them calmly, her face glowing, like Christ's matron, God's favorite, and the strength burning in her eyes made everyone else lower their own.

In the author's mind, Perpetua, "matron of Christ," combines the dignity of the great Roman ladies with Christian virtue. Once again, she humiliates a tribune who wanted to dress the condemned group as priests and priestesses of Saturn and Ceres, and once again her subtle and compelling argument reduces a man to silence:

> We have come to this of our own free will, so as not to be bound by anyone else's will. We have committed our lives to not doing anything of this kind. We agreed on this with you.

The authorities attempt to humiliate the women by the rather unusual means of exposing them to a wild cow, but Perpetua and Felicity, her companion in the arena, are victorious.

Perpetua was the first to be thrown down, and she fell on her back. She sat up and adjusted her tunic, now ripped on one side, to cover her legs, not out of pain but modesty. Then she picked up her hair ribbon and tied her hair back, for it was all undone. It would not have been dignified for a martyr to undergo her trial with hair loose, as if she were in mourning, rather than going to meet her glory. At last she stood up, and seeing Felicity on the ground, went over to her, reached out to her and helped her to her feet (20.4–5).

This scene is described as if in slow motion. The author underlines Perpetua's state of ecstasy, for when the first encounter is over and she has escaped unhurt, she asks, "When are they going to expose us to the cow?" She immediately returns to herself, counsels her brother and another catechumen, Rusticus: "Be firm in your faith and love one another. Do not lose heart because of our suffering." Saturus, on the other side of the arena, says a few encouraging words to Pudens, the converted prison guard (20.10–21.6). Saturus prophesies that he will be wounded by a leopard, and he is the first to die (21.8), thus fulfilling Perpetua's vision in which she had seen him preceding her up to the top of the stairway (4.5). Perpetua does not even receive the *coup de grace* at the hand of a man. The gladiator, in an overwrought, emotional state, is unable to strike hard enough to dispatch her. Perpetua herself, crying out with pain but lucid, guides his right hand to the mark. The author concludes, "Perhaps a woman like her, who was feared by evil spirits, could not have been killed unless she willed it."

We do not know how much the compiler embellished reality, but in his account he is careful to name the witnesses who actually heard what the martyrs said. If Perpetua were a fabrication, she would be an admirably consistent one. Her hieratic pose and her gesturing, which to some scholars have seemed unconvincing (adjusting the folds of her gown, fastening back her hair) were in fact the conditioned reflexes of a matron's education, which stressed modesty and dignity above all, as ancient pagan sources tell us. At the supreme moment, when she stood facing the impassioned verdict of the crowd, this lifelong training came to the fore and dictated her actions. An Arria or a Porcia would have done the same, even though for Perpetua, these gestures were given deeper meaning through her new faith.

A Woman's Experience in Early Christianity

This is Perpetua of the *Passion*. We cannot stress enough how rare and important a figure she is. We know more about this woman as a person, more about her real character and her social background than we know about all the other female martyrs of ancient times. We will not compare her to other female figures who are fanciful fabrications of later times: illustrious names like Agnes and Cecilia were used in stories telling of spurned and vindictive lovers, or faithful ones who shared their beloved's choice of virginity, to celebrate a system of values and behavior belonging to a later era. We cannot even consider Crispina, another African matron like Perpetua, as a real person, for as early as the *Acts of the Martyrs*, she is already crystallized into a stereotype. Perpetua most closely resembles the women martyrs of the most trustworthy *Acts*, although of those women we have record only of a word or a gesture.

Remaining in Perpetua's own era and setting, we may compare her to Donata, Vestia, and Secunda, three women among the Scillitan Martyrs executed in Carthage about twenty years before. We read with admiration Donata's outspoken reply to the proconsul Saturninus, "Honor to Caesar as Caesar, but fear before God." This is a synthesis of Christian political thought, and one wonders how she acquired such expert lucidity. Vestia and Secunda are equally admirable, and in their words "I am a Christian" (Vestia) and "What I am is what I wish to be" (Secunda), two statements that reinforce each other, these women seem to be claiming their full capacity to make their own choices. Perhaps Perpetua, who must have been familiar with the testimony of the Scillitans, intentionally echoed Secunda's words (with a variation on the theme) in her first clash with her father.

We know nothing about Vestia or Secunda. The only personal data we are given in the *Acts of the Scillitan Martyrs* are the names and sex of the martyrs: three women and three men. This only tells us that being a Christian was equally dangerous for women and for men. We do not know to what extent these women, in converting to Christianity and appealing to a supernatural authority against all human bonds, were consciously expressing a need for greater personal freedom, which they believed could be found in the Christian community. Nor are we able to evaluate how far the Christian community was able to satisfy such aspirations. We may ask ourselves if the numerous testimonies of women martyrs and their veneration by the church indicate that women in the Christian community enjoyed a more satisfying condition of life than in pagan society. What prompts us to ask this difficult question is that in the early centuries there were far more women converts to Christianity than men. Attempts have been made to explain this by claiming that women have a greater affinity toward mystery religions.

To attempt an answer to this question, we must examine the facts. First, Perpetua is indeed the dominant figure in the *Passion of Perpetua*. This may be demonstrated not only by analyzing the text. Tertullian, who lived in this era, provoked the dismay of latter-day critics (who believed he was the compiler of the *Passion of Perpetua*) by attributing Saturus's vision to Perpetua (*On the Soul* 55.4). This oversight may be easily explained (without going into the problem of authorship): the figure of Perpetua was simply the only one that endured in his memory, hence the mistake.

It would be inappropriate to explain Perpetua by means of sociological reductionism. It is true that her upperclass status was an important element in her character, but it would be an oversimplification to affirm that the moral authority she enjoyed in the community, both during her lifetime and after her death, depended solely on her family status. Contemporary stories of other saints prove this point: Blandina, a slave, is the main figure in the *Acts of the Martyrs of Lyons*, the image of Christ himself crucified (1.41), while the name of her noble mistress, also a martyr, is not even mentioned. Felicity, another woman of humble origins, plays an important role in the *Passion of Perpetua*. Although an elevated social position may have been of help to some Christians, this phenomenon was not limited to women. Cyprian no doubt owed his rapid rise through the ecclesiastic ranks to the important position he occupied in Carthaginian society, but it would be absurdly reductive to say that he owed his influence and his role to his social background. It is more difficult to reply to the assertions of functional reductionists who claim that Perpetua's authority (or that of any other female martyr) depended entirely upon the fact that she was a martyr. It is true that martyrs were admired for purely human reasons, as well as considered edifying religious models. This admiration is underlined in the *First Epistle of Clement*, written in Rome at the end of the first century: "They [women martyrs] have reached the goal in the race of faith and have received the highest prize, they who were weak in body" (6.1). Elsewhere he writes, "Many women, made strong through the grace of God, have performed manly acts" (55.3). For the men and women of antiquity, the values of a lifetime received maximum confirmation at the moment of death. The literary tradition of the *exitus illustrium virorum,* "the passing of famous men," clearly bears this out. In the times of persecution, Christian women demanded of themselves, as routine practice, a heroic attitude which in the Roman tradition had been achieved by very few. Tertullian, in two passages (3–4) of his *To the Martyrs,* a work written in more or less the same period as the *Passion of Perpetua,* exhorts women to become martyrs. Drawing on the mythic and historic traditions of Rome and Africa, he cites examples of women who died for human causes (honor, homeland, conjugal love) and then extols the greater glory destined for martyrs. A Montanist "oracle" (no. 7) also specifically addressed women, inviting them "not to die in their beds of miscarriage or fever, but as martyrs," emphasizing the difference between a natural destiny passively accepted and a choice freely made.

Returning now to the question of whether Christian women enjoyed a more satisfying situation in life than pagan women, we must make distinctions between various epochs. In the earliest phases of evangelization, women were conspicuous in the Christian community. Their importance gradually dwindled as the ecclesiastical hierarchy solidified and as episcopal authority came to outweigh the charismatic component in the church. It would be instructive here to compare St. Paul's epistles (those of certain authorship) with the pastoral epistles on this point. As long as charisma and the gift of prophecy were prized by the Christian community (and we have seen that martyrdom signifies great charisma and has always been connected with prophecy), women were allowed to play a more important role. The gift of prophecy could be manifested equally by women and by men, and through the act of prophecy women could become religious teachers, like Philip's four daughters at the end of the first century, or Ammia of Philadelphia in the second century, all women prophets accepted as orthodox. When, in later epochs, charisma became less important or was repressed, the honor with which martyrs were invested no longer signified any special importance for women.

In Perpetua's community the charismatic element was very strong. The writer of the Prologue to the *Passion* stresses the close connection between martyrdom and prophetic charisma in Perpetua's circle. Perpetua, her catechumen brother, Saturus, and others, all show their complete faith in the action of the Holy Spirit within their community. It is the Holy Spirit that tells Perpetua to ask, in her baptism, only for courage to endure pain, and her visions show that she not only has prophetic power, but also the capacity to intercede for the dead. Perpetua's charismatic powers lend her an ecclesiastical authority, not just a general moral one. This is evident in the compiler's text, in which he shows Perpetua performing the role of religious teacher in the arena, alongside Saturus. It is also evident in Saturus's tale of his own vision, in which he underlines Perpetua's influence over Bishop Optatus and the priest Aspasius. There is another very significant element in the *Passion of Perpetua:* the compiler never speaks negatively of women. He never suggests that womanhood is a condition that must be overcome. Rather, it is Perpetua herself who touches upon this theme with her evocative, ambivalent, and cryptic statement, "I became a man." In the *Passion of Perpetua,* it is only their adversaries who wish to humiliate the female sex. The organizer of the games exposes the women, "contrary to the normal custom" (20.1) to a cow, and Felicity's heartless jailer mocks her when she cries out in labor: "What will you do when you are thrown in with the wild beasts?" (15.5). The compiler's attitude will appear more striking when we compare it with the attitude expressed by St. Augustine in the three *Sermons* (nos. 280–82) in which the main theme of Perpetua's story is indeed the overcoming of female weakness.

The charismatic elements of the church were openly antagonistic toward the ecclesiastical hierarchy. Cyprian, in the middle of the third century, spent ten years of his episcopate fighting against the lax attitudes of confessors who in prison readmitted apostates to communion, on the basis of a right they had acquired by tradition. In 177 the martyrs of Lyons wrote a letter of introduction for Irenaeus, the future bishop, addressed to Eleutherius, Bishop of Rome. In the letter they express themselves in clear antihierarchic terms: "Be good enough to welcome this man as a zealot of Christ's testament. If we thought that rank and position rendered a person righteous, we would have presented him as a priest of the Church, which indeed he is" (Eusebius, *Ecclesiastical History,* 5.4.1–2). Another early Christian text of the first two centuries is the *Shepherd of Hermas.* This text is based completely on visions, and it passionately praises martyrs (3.9.9–10.1), two aspects which link it closely to the *Passion of Perpetua.* The *Shepherd* also harshly criticizes the presbyters of the Church of Rome, comparing them to practitioners of witchcraft because of their wicked hearts, and takes them sharply to task for quarreling among themselves (3.17.8–9). This same criticism of the clergy's quarrelsomeness and unworthiness is implicit in Saturus's vision (particularly in his portrayal of the Bishop), although his rebellion is not declared openly. This is another way in which the *Passion of Perpetua* reflects its charismatic background.

In his prologue, the compiler further adds to the martyrs' charismatic enthusiasm, and declares that sacred writing is always open to new manifestations of the Spirit. "We welcome and honor prophecies and new visions as promises, and consider all other manifestations of the Spirit as part of the scripture on which the Church is built" (1.5). Whether the compiler's statement should be taken as an expression of Montanist views, and whether these were also held by Perpetua's community, is still subject to debate, and the discussion is heavily influenced by the apologetic intentions of the writers. At the end of the second century the Montanist phenomenon revitalized the role of ecstasy and prophecy in the Church. This development marked a moment of major, openly declared conflict between charismatic tendencies and the ecclesiastical hierarchy. It is very difficult to piece together a complete picture of early Christianity from the documents that have come down to us. These sources allow us to reconstruct vaguely only a few fragmentary moments in the complex and often contradictory evolution of the Church. We cannot hope to identify the wide range of heresies, with all their various nuances, of which early Christians accused each other. The boundaries of deviation were hard to pin down in the actual life of individual communities, at least during the early centuries, given the absence of a juridically constituted central religious power. For example, in the middle of the third century Bishop Cyprian of Carthage and the Bishop of Rome came close to excommunicating each other over a doctrinal dispute concerning baptism, and they were prevented from doing so only by circumstances beyond their control (the beginning of Valerian's persecution). This same vagueness in determining the boundaries of orthodoxy also applies to the Montanist movement, in which women played a major part (Priscilla and Maximilla were the heads of the movement alongside Montanus). This phenomenon, chiefly characterized by its prophetic exuberance and by its rigorous moral attitude, was probably evaluated differently according to place and circumstance. What can be safely assumed about the religious group of Perpetua and her companions is that they were strongly united by their shared sense of purpose. They believed that the Holy Spirit had called upon them to submit to a powerful experience and had bestowed charismatic gifts upon them in the form of endurance to trial and of visionary-prophetic powers. These powers were accorded to both men and women, in rather greater proportion to the women, given that Perpetua had four visions and Saturus only one. We are unable to say if Montanism comes into this, not out of a wish to defend the martyrs' orthodoxy (indeed Montanism did not entail heterodox beliefs) but because we do not know what specific situation existed in the Carthaginian church at the beginning of the third century. Factions did exist (as Saturus attests) and Montanist propaganda was present in this context and had attracted sympathizers (e.g., Tertullian), but there had not as yet been a break in ecclesiastical unity.

In this same period (the end of the second century) the Montanist problem caused turbulence in the Christian community of Rome. Tertullian (*Against Praxeas* 1.5), very attentive to events in Rome, informs us that during this long controversy various bishops took contradictory positions. In Rome, in the latter half of the second century, the monarchic authority of the bishops had gained in ascendency. These bishops naturally viewed Montanism as a grave danger, for it posed an important question regarding the authority of the church. Should that authority be charismatic or institutional? The so-called *Muratorian Canon*, produced in Rome, which listed books recognized as Holy Scripture, was compiled during the same period as the *Passion of Perpetua* and expresses a point of view diametrically opposed to that of the editor of the *Passion*. The *Canon* specifically excludes the *Shepherd of Hermas* (along with a number of other works) from public reading, denying its value as scripture because "the number of prophets is complete." Later, in Rome, in the first half of the third century, the author of another important antiheretical work, *Philosophumena*, expresses scorn for the "little women prophetesses" of Montanism (8.19). By contrast, the great Irenaeus, bishop and theologian (the same man whom the confessors of Lyons had introduced to Rome as a zealot rather than as a clergyman), defended the traditional faith in the charisma bestowed by the Holy Spirit on "men and women" (*Against Heresies* 311.9), basing his argument on one of Paul's epistles to the Corinthians. The anti-Montanists brought a new tendency to marginalize women, and with them, charismatic powers, whereas in the *Passion of Perpetua*, high estimation of women and faith in the charisma of the Spirit are closely linked.

The Normalization of Perpetua

Attempts were later made by the African church to correct the *Passion of Perpetua*. By evaluating these corrections we may grasp the basic problems posed by the *Passion of Perpetua* within the context of Christianity, or rather within the context of later forms of Christianity. Fifty years after Perpetua's martyrdom, Cyprian represented the sum of ecclesiastical authority, prophetic charisma, and martyrdom for the Carthaginian church. Pontius, his biographer, describes the vision experienced by the bishop on the first day of his exile to Curubi, which foretold his martyrdom the following year, and also underlines Cyprian's caution in interpreting it (*Life of Cyprian* 12–13). Cyprian himself describes his visions on other occasions (*Letters* 11). Cyprian served as a model for future martyrs: the *Passion of Marian and Jacopo* and the *Passion of Montanus and Lucius*, patterned on the *Passion of Perpetua* from the literary point of view, found in Cyprian their sole model for martyrdom and in his doctrine a safe justification for the visions of martyrs.

In the prologue of his *Life of Cyprian*, Pontius reveals his polemical intention when he states:

> It would be intolerable to ignore in silence the passion of Cyprian, such an illustrious bishop and martyr, who, aside from the fact that he was a martyr, was able to instruct us, while our elders, who venerated martyrdom in itself, attributed such honor to *laymen and catechumens*, who became martyrs through the grace of God, as to leave an ample and almost complete written record of their tribulations.

The reference to *Passion of Perpetua* here is obvious. Pontius does not merely distinguish varying degrees of dignity between bishops and laymen, but implicitly adds that aside from their experience of martyrdom, these laymen had little instruction to give, compared with Cyprian. Nor should we believe that Pontius in mentioning instruction is referring here only to the books written by the bishop. In a letter (no. 58) to the Christian community of Tibarus, written during a period when renewed persecutions by Emperor Decius's successor, Trebonius Gallus (A.D. 252), were feared, Cyprian includes an impassioned exhortation to martyrdom. He lists the names of glorious martyrs, beginning with Abel and going on to the sacrifice of Abraham, the three youths in the furnace, Daniel, the mother of the Maccabees, and the Holy Innocents. His list ends here and it is hard to understand why when addressing Africans, he does not speak of the martyrs of the Church of Africa and fails to mention not only Perpetua and her companions, but also the Scillitan Martyrs, who had been venerated for an even longer time. Here Cyprian seems to be displaying the very same mentality criticized in the compiler's prologue to the *Passion of Perpetua*, as "imbecillitas aut desperatio fidei," the blindness of those who see the glory of God only in ancient examples, without considering the martyrs of the present time, who are a gift of God, "because God always fulfills what he promises" (1.5).

The events narrated in the *Passion of Perpetua* were reworked in the form of brief *Acta*, in two versions (denominated A and B). The second is more succinct than the first and is rather mannered in tone. It is difficult to say when these briefer versions, which draw on the *Passion of Perpetua* as their only source, were written, but given the conclusion of version B, this probably occurred in the era of Constantine. Perpetua's story was probably reworked for the liturgy, which required a shorter version more suitable for reading aloud to the congregation. In these versions, the figure of Perpetua, who dominates the *Passion,* loses some of her importance to the benefit of Saturus, who takes on the role of a guide during the official interrogation. Perpetua has only two visions concerning her martyrdom, and the visions concerning Dinocrates are not mentioned. Perpetua never appears as the only protagonist in her visions but is always surrounded by her companions. In the vision of the stairway, Saturus invites all the future martyrs to follow him. Perpetua makes no reply, quite unlike the original. Of the episodes following their condemnation, only Felicity's premature delivery is mentioned. No particular details of their martyrdom are given, and it is reported that they were all eaten by wild animals. The ideological slant of these changes cannot be denied, even though they were probably dictated by the need for brevity.

Let us now turn to the sermons dedicated by the great Augustine to Perpetua and Felicity on the anniversary of their martyrdom, delivered following a public reading of the *Passion of Perpetua.* The era of imperial persecution was a distant memory. New dissent and inner struggles among Christians (Donatists versus Catholics) had created serious religious conflict in Africa. In these sermons, the martyrs have completely lost their human side. Augustine stresses Perpetua's filial piety and chastity (*Sermons* 281.2), a more urgent issue in his time than the courage of martyrdom. He mentions only the vision of the stairway (280.1) and explains that the snake Perpetua treads on is the ancient serpent, "abyss for the sinning woman, stepping stone for the woman ascending to God." Augustine is in general diffident toward visionary manifestations, one of the Donatists' weapons. Perpetua's visions of Dinocrates particularly disturb him (*Nature and the Origin of the Soul* 1.10) and he interprets them in the light of his doctrine of original sin, with which they do not fit. Aside from these women's natural inferiority as females, he points out another weakness in them—motherhood—which would have rendered them even less able to endure suffering (*Sermons* 282.2). Two themes recur throughout these three sermons: the weakness of womanhood overcome through divine grace and a pun on their names, the *perpetual felicity* of the righteous. Sermon 280, the most complex, opens with the pun on their names and then develops the doctrine of the mystical body of Christ. Sermon 281 begins with the theme of womanhood (the weaker the sex the more glorious the crown) and ends by again punning on their names. Sermon 282, very brief, opens with the pun and ends with a fusion of both themes. Why were only the women of that group of martyrs remembered? Augustine asks, and answers himself, "Female weakness prevailed against the ancient enemy with great glory, but these men in their strength had to struggle to obtain their Perpetual Felicity" (*Sermons* 282.3).

Thus concludes a long journey, leading from real, flesh-and-blood women on to the enduring transparency of names.

Helena Augusta: From Innkeeper to Empress

Franca Ela Consolino

De stercore ad regnum: The Reticence of the Sources

The blessed Helena, born in Trier, was so noble according to worldly canons of honor and prestige that nearly the entire city, which was huge, could
be considered part of her property, as even today the extent of her palace
proves. . . . And if so much time had not elapsed since the days of the
Trojan War, it would be not too incredible that she took her ancient origin
from the famous Helen of the Greeks, long desired as a bride and finally
united in marriage to the noble Menelaus, king of the Greeks and younger
brother of Agamemnon. . . . There is no doubt that our Helena shone with
equal nobility on the earthly plane, but although she was equal to the
Greek Helen in name and beauty, it cannot be expressed how superior she
was in wisdom, power, wealth, and knowledge. The former was the wife
of a king's son, who owned only a part of the kingdom, while she married
the pious Augustus Constantius, who ruled the Roman empire, which he
had divided in two with Galerius, also Augustus. The Greek Helena was
in possession of part of her homeland, while this woman, truly gifted with
a manly spirit, with just laws and pious moderation, ruled the empire of
the whole universe. For Helen of the Greeks, endless wars were waged,
while our Helena, living and acting with admirable faith, exemplary devotion, modesty, and holiness of character, deserved to reach Christ, who,
through the blood of his cross, brought peace to heaven and earth. She
followed him with the spirit of a believer and with a devoted soul, laying
at his feet all her wealth and power, her whole kingdom, for in her holy
faith she knew she had received all these blessings from Christ. Made
strong through her firm faith and devotion, she was worthy enough to find
the precious yoke of the True Cross . . . and thus with her words, example,
and deeds armed the holy Church against the arrows of the enemy (*Life
of Helena* 1.9–11).

This flattering portrait of Helena comes from the oldest Latin biography dedicated to her, composed around A.D. 850 by the monk Almann   *141*

of Hautvillers—at the request of Incmar of Reims, the archbishop of his diocese—to celebrate the recent arrival of the empress's relics at the monastery. Filling in the gaps of the existing documentation with his inventiveness nurtured by pious reading, Almann created a much more complete biography than the sources permitted, as they leave a number of essential questions unanswered. We do not know the date and place of Helena's birth. It has been debated whether she was the wife or concubine of Constantius (Chlorus) I. Her death has been dated to a period varying between 326 and 336. The discovery of the True Cross, the action on which her posthumous fame and iconographic success are chiefly based, is probably not due to her. Three different locations are given as the resting place of her saintly remains: the abbey of Hautvillers in the diocese of Reims, Santa Maria in Ara Coeli in Rome, and Venice.

The ancient sources say little about her and the only detailed testimony of her life is furnished by one of her contemporaries, who is not above suspicion: the Church historian Eusebius of Caesarea, who devoted to her a brief section of his *Life of Constantine*. All other available information comes from authors who lived in much later times and who were very much influenced by their own religious views. Pagan writers were hostile to her, while Christians extolled her as if she were a saint, transforming the historical personage of Helena into a paradigm of royal virtues.

We do not know in what city Flavia Julia Helena (this was her complete name) was born. Some claim that she was born in Drepanon (or Drepanum), in Bithynia, known today as Hersek, basing their opinion on rather late evidence. The first to affirm this was Procopius of Caesarea, a sixth-century historian, who does not take upon himself responsibility for the data he reports: "*They say* that Helen was born in this village, which formerly was of no consequence" (*Buildings* 5.2.1). It is certain, however, that Constantine gave Drepanum a new name: Helenopolis. Eusebius of Caesarea simply states that this town "was named after his mother" (*Life of Constantine* 4.61), but does not say that she was born there, nor do the sources prior to Procopius make this claim. The fact that Constantine named the town after his mother does not prove that she was born there, and many illustrious examples prove this point: Jerusalem was rebuilt as Aelia Capitolina by Hadrian and Byzantium itself became Constantinople. The assumption that Drepanum was an already existing town enhanced by Constantine, who renamed it in honor of his mother, but was not necessarily the empress's birthplace, is confirmed by Jerome and by Socrates, the fifth-century Church historian.

Socrates informs us that Constantine transformed many villages into towns and gives the examples of Drepane, renamed after Helena, and of Constantia in Palestine, named after Constantia, the emperor's sister (*Ecclesiastical History* 1.17.1). Jerome's *Chronicles* tell us that Drepanum was promoted to the status of city for religious reasons and mentions Helena only because of its name: "He made Drepanum . . . a city to honor the martyr Lucian, who is buried there, and named it Helenopolis, after his mother" (231, 22 ff. Helm). Philostorgius, the Arian author of an *Ecclesiastical History* dedicated to Theodosius II, also mentions the cult of Lucian, who was martyred in Nicomedia on January 7, 303, to explain the importance of Helenopolis. He further claims that Helena was the founder of the city: "Helena, mother of Constantine, founded a city on the mouth of the Gulf of Nicomedia and called it Helenopolis. That place was dear to her for one reason alone: it was there that rested the [remains of the] martyr Lucian, whose body had been brought there by a dolphin after his martyrdom" (*Ecclesiastical History* 2.12). Helena's devotion to Lucian has led many scholars to suppose that she sympathized with the Arians. Lucian had been a presbyter in Antioch and among his disciples there were Arius himself, and the Arian bishop Eusebius of Nicomedia, who baptized Constantine on his deathbed in 337. But Helena's devotion to the martyr does not prove that the empress professed heterodoxy, given that Lucian, scholarly interpreter of Holy Scripture, was not known as a heretic in his own time: on the contrary, he was highly praised for his erudition by Jerome.

The absence of any consolidated historical tradition regarding Helena's place of birth proved stimulating to later authors. Medieval Latin writers soon replaced the east with the west, claiming that Constantine's mother was born in Trier (Almann bases his account on this local tradition), or also in Colchester, according to the *Historia regum Britanniae* (5.6) of the twelfth-century historian Geoffrey of Monmouth, which gives the oldest account of the Arthurian legend.

Helena's year of birth is also uncertain but may be traced by piecing together clues, beginning with Eusebius of Caesarea's statement that she was nearly eighty when she died shortly after her return from Palestine. Coins in her name were no longer issued after the spring of 329, so we may presume that she died in that year. If she was nearly eighty in the year 328/29, she must have been born before 250 A.D.

The silence concerning Helena's date and place of birth may be readily explained by her extremely humble origins, mentioned by both pagan and Christian authors in discussing Constantine's parentage. Ambrose, Bishop of Milan, gives us the most detailed information: when Helena met Constantius Chlorus, she was a *stabularia,* that is to say, at best, the proprietress of a tavern and at worst, a tavern maid. Ambrose emphasizes her lowborn status to point out how God intervened to elevate her *de stercore,* "from the dung of the stable," to the very summit of the empire (*On the death of Theodosius* 42). His insistence on the word *bona* in connection with Helena, aside from underlining what really counts in God's eyes, could also be a polemical reply to pagan attacks on Helena, traces of which appear in the *Passion of Artemius,* a Greek text dating from the end of the fourth century, in which Julian the Apostate is quoted as saying, "Our family has greater right to the empire than the family of Constantius II. Indeed, my father Constantius was begotten by my grandfather, Constantius, of Theodora, daughter of Maximian, whereas Constantine was begotten by my grandfather of Helena, a lowborn woman no better than a prostitute" (Philostorgius, *Ecclesiastical History* 2.16a, 27, 22 ff. Bidez). Julian was apparently speaking of his family to the future martyr, who distinguished himself while defending the Arians alongside the emperor Constantius II.

Helena's low origins, explicitly mentioned by some sources and confirmed by the discreet silence of others, lead us to conclude that given their difference in social rank, Helena was not Constantius's wife by full right, but his concubine—as Zosimus indeed tells us (2.8.2). Their relationship was broken off in 289 when he married Theodora, stepdaughter of the emperor Maximian. The term *coniunx* (spouse) appears in reference to Helena in an inscription dating from about 325, when her prestige at court was already an accepted fact: *divi Constanti castissimae coniugi,* "to the most chaste spouse of the divine Constantius" (*CIL* 10.517). Eutropius (*Breviary* 10.2.2) speaks of her *matrimonium obscurius* to Constantius, while other sources define her as his *concubina* or *uxor* (in Greek *gyne*). The inconsistency of sources in reference to her status suggests that she was not married by full right, since, although it is perfectly understandable that a concubine could have been promoted to legitimate spouse, it is far less likely that a wife fully entitled to that name would have been degraded to the role of concubine. This term implies a discrepancy of social rank between partners that places any children born of their union in an inferior condition compared to those born of legitimate marriage. This was probably the case of Constantine, as is strongly suggested by the arguments used by an anonymous panegyrist in 310 to demonstrate that Constantine was indeed his father's legitimate successor (*Panegyrics* 7.4). Nearly fifty years later, in a funeral oration for Julian the Apostate, the rhetor Libanius of Antioch stressed the nobler origins of Julian's father, "more entitled to rule than he who became emperor [i.e., Constantine]" (*Orationes* 18.8).

We do not know where Helena lived after she was repudiated. A modern biographer of her, Jules Maurice (*Sainte Hélène*, 36), claims that she was in York when the dying Constantius I designated Constantine as his successor, but this assumption is probably more romantic than true. Constantine's accession in 306 marked a great change in his mother's life, for she suddenly acquired a public role that was to become increasingly important. We do not know the exact date of issue of the bronze coins inscribed with her name and the title *nobilissima femina* (limited to the mint at Thessalonica), an honor she shared with her daughter-in-law, Fausta.

Helena Augusta

The highest recognition of Helena came in A.D. 324, when Constantine, who now ruled alone after Licinius's defeat, conferred the title of Augusta upon his mother and his wife. Coins were issued in their honor (the first ones were minted in Antioch). The coin honoring Helena depicted her with a crown and bore the inscription *securitas Reipublicae,* "well-being of the State" (in contrast to the inscription dedicated to Fausta, *spes Reipublicae,* "hope of the State").

Helena was far away from court when Constantine's son, Crispus, was murdered, but she was present when Fausta died—and perhaps contributed to her death. "Since Helena, Constantine's mother, suffered greatly and could find no peace after the youth's death, Constantine, in order to relieve her suffering, remedied that evil with an even greater one." Here Zosimus (2.29.2) is expressing the belief, also shared by the anonymous writer of *Epitome de Caesaribus* (41.12), that Constantine had his wife killed, because she had persuaded him to eliminate his own son, Crispus, and Helena, deeply stricken by the loss of her grandchild, blamed Fausta for his death.

Pagan historians charged Helena with Fausta's death; modern scholars hold her responsible for the long exile in which the sons of Constantius I and Theodora spent much of their lives. "From the beginning of the new reign, Helena, a tavern servant who had become the queen mother, went to live with her triumphant son and he fell under her influence. Recognized as *nobilissima femina,* Constantius I's concubine, previously abandoned for Theodora, had burning rancor to satisfy. The chil-

dren of the empress who had supplanted her were to feel the effects"
(J. Bidez, *Julien,* 7). Scholars who believe that Helena was to blame for
the exile of Theodora's children usually base themselves on Julian the
Apostate's statement that his own father had spent many years wandering in exile (ed. Bidez-Cumont, 26 n.20), but their assumption cannot
be proved, because the ancient sources do not mention Helena in discussing Constantine's decision to keep his half-brothers far away from
public life.

After Fausta died, Helena remained the only influential woman at
court. In the Roman imperial tradition the title of Augusta did not imply
any recognition of political powers equal to those of the emperor. Consequently, when Paulinus of Nola (*Ep.* 31.4) and Sulpicius Severus (*Chronicles,* 2.33.5) describe Helena ruling at her son's side, we must understand
that she shared in the power on a practical rather than an institutional
level. Eusebius tells us that Helena had full access to the imperial treasury (*Life of Constantine* 3.47.3). Further information concerning her
public role may be gleaned from inscriptions. There are eight inscriptions
referring to Helena that we may consider unquestionably authentic. The
very fact that six of these eight epigraphs give her the title of Augusta
confirms that her power increased after A.D. 324. Moreover, she is usually
commemorated as the mother of Constantine and often as the grandmother of the Caesars. Her role as the founder of the dynasty is stressed
in two epigraphs prior to 324, and this emphasis on Helena's line is intended to contrast with the line of Theodora and her descendants. This
suggests that Helena's elevation to Augusta was part of a strategy intended to reinforce the power and prestige of Constantine's dynasty, a
strategy already in effect before the elimination of Licinius. The inscriptions are all in Latin, and all come from south-central Italy, with the
exception of one found in Africa. This would suggest that Helena had
some special influence in this zone, probably connected with her long
sojourns in Italy and particularly in Rome.

Three of these inscriptions were found in Rome in an area between
Saint John Lateran and Santa Croce in Gerusalemme. The *Liber pontificalis* (1.34.22) refers to this same area, and relates that Constantine
had a basilica built in the Palatium Sessorianum of Rome. This basilica
was the church of Santa Croce in Gerusalemme (the Holy Cross of Jerusalem), which is called the *Basilica Heleniana* already in the *Gesta Xysti,*
an apocryphal text dating from the early years of the sixth century (*Liber
pontificalis* 1. n.75, 196). This same text (1.34, 27) claims that Helena
Augusta owned a *fundus Lauretus,* an estate extending from the Porta

Sessoriana to the Via Prenestina, which Constantine later donated to the church of SS. Pietro e Marcellino. Among the treasures donated to this church, there was a large gold basin, a gift from the empress mother. In the Roman inscription commemorating Helena's role in rebuilding the baths near the Palatium Sessorianum after they were destroyed in a fire (*CIL* 6.1136), Helena's name does not bear the title Augusta. That proves that she resided in Rome even before 324.

While Helena's special connection with Rome is very well documented, her connection with Trier is not, even though a local tradition, first recorded by Almann, claimed that she was born in this town and that her home was located near the cathedral which later incorporated part of her house (*Life of Helena*, 1.9). Excavations carried out in the 1940s proved that Almann was partly right, for beneath the cathedral of Trier were found the remains of an imperial residence dating from the times of Constantine. There is no proof, however, that Constantine's mother ever lived in that palace, and the legend concerning her may have sprung from a confusion with the lesser-known Helena, wife of Crispus, who lived in Trier for a few years. The existing documentation allows us only to affirm that she resided in Rome, and there is no evidence indicating that she lived anywhere else. We do not know where she died, but we know that her son was with her at the time and that her body was sent with solemn honors to Rome and buried near the church of SS. Pietro e Marcellino on the Via Labicana, where it rested until 849, when the monk Theogisus took her relics to the abbey of Hautvillers. The porphyry sarcophagus that had previously held her remains was later used to bury Pope Anastasius IV (who died in 1154). Today it is in the Vatican Museum, next to the sarcophagus of her granddaughter, Constantina.

Voyage to the Holy Land

Helena's journey to the Holy Land, undertaken when she was already advanced in years, is the only period of her life for which we have a detailed report, furnished by Bishop Eusebius of Caesarea. His description of her journey provided the general outline for later versions of the legend concerning her discovery of the True Cross. Eusebius's account is important not only because it shows Helena's role at court in the last years of her life, but also because it bears the only contemporary witness on her. The story of her journey is inserted as an excursus in the third book of the *Life of Constantine*. After describing in detail the splendors of the Church of the Anastasis (i.e., the Resurrection) in Jerusalem and the opulence with which the emperor decorated it, Eusebius adds:

> When he came to know that in the same region there were other places venerated because of the presence of two holy caves, he resolved to adorn both with munificence. Thus he honored the grotto where the Savior first appeared to the world and in which Christ took upon himself the burden of incarnation, while in the other cave he solemnly commemorated Christ's ascent to heaven, which took place on the top of the mountain. He conferred the highest of honors on these two places and adorned them with great splendor, intending thereby to perpetuate eternally the memory of his mother, who had become the promoter of much good for mankind (*Life of Constantine* 3.41.1 f.).

Helena's visit is mentioned to explain Constantine's decision to build two churches in the Holy Land: in Bethlehem and on the Mount of Olives, and Eusebius tells us that the Empress made the journey on her own initiative:

> When she proposed to settle the debt she owed to God, the Sovereign of the universe, with her pious devotion, she thought that she must thank in her prayers the Lord for giving her a son who had proved to be a most noble emperor, and for giving her grandchildren, Constantine's sons, who happened to be Caesars themselves, and very dear to God (3.42.1).

In explaining Helena's decision, Eusebius blends private and public concerns, as her gesture of thanksgiving was offered in the name of the whole ruling family. The public character of her journey is confirmed in the next lines of the passage:

> Moved by youthful fervor, the elderly woman wanted to see what the Holy Land was like, and eagerly visited the eastern provinces and the people who lived in them, showing imperial concern (*basilikè promètheia*). After following in the Savior's footsteps and duly worshiping in those holy places, . . . she wished to leave the fruits of her own piety to posterity too (3.42.1 f.).

Eusebius defines Helena's concern for the peoples of the empire with the term *promètheia*—that is, *providentia,* a term that normally referred to the solicitude of the emperors toward their subjects—leaving no doubt that her mission to the East was not just a religious one. We may wonder why Helena, though well along in years, decided to undertake such an arduous journey on behalf of her son and her grandchildren.

Considering that Helena died in 329, shortly after her return, we conclude that her pilgrimage must have occurred in the years 327–28, just after the tragic elimination of Crispus and Fausta. A Pagan source tells us that Helena's contemporaries saw a connection between Constantine's growing pro-Christian religious policies after 326 and the bloody events that had just occurred at court. This source claims that the guilt-ridden Constantine had been refused absolution by pagan priests, and thus had turned to the Christian clergy, who promised to wash his sins away through baptism (Zosimus 2.29.3). We might argue that Helena's journey, which took place immediately after Fausta's murder, did not resemble a pilgrimage of expiation, but we cannot deny the political value of the gesture, intended to restore luster to the ruling family's recently bedimmed image by playing on the Christian piety of Helena and on her status as an imperial visitor.

In approximately this same period, Constantine's mother-in-law, Eutropia, also made a journey to the Holy Land. She later wrote Constantine to express her indignation for the pagan practices still observed in the area of the holy oak of Mamre, and begged him to destroy the pagan altar and idols defiling that hallowed ground. It is difficult to say exactly when Eutropia's pilgrimage took place. We know that she made this journey only because Constantine refers to her letter in an epistle addressed to the bishops of Palestine, in which he asks them to eliminate the idolatrous cults and build a sanctuary in Mamre. The fact that Eusebius mentions this incident (3.52 f.) a few chapters after describing Helena's pilgrimage does not prove that Eutropia's visit to the Holy Land occurred at the same time or even after Helena's pilgrimage, for Eusebius does not mention Constantine's epistle in a chronological context, but rather in a discussion of the emperor's deeds that display his religious zeal. We cannot know if Eutropia visited the Holy Land after Fausta's death, though it would seem more likely that she made this journey at an earlier date, perhaps after the defeat of Licinius, when Constantine's rule was extended to the Eastern Empire. Her journey would have had more political significance if it took place after 326, but in any case, it fits in with Constantine's religious campaign to obtain greater support from the church.

Whatever reasons may have prompted Eutropia to visit the Holy Land, Helena, who played a much more official role, found an excellent opportunity to make a public spectacle of her royal piety:

> Famous for her good works, she did not neglect the other aspect of piety, devotion to the Lord. She was seen frequently going to the church, and it

was her habit to adorn the sanctuaries with splendid works, never neglecting the places of worship even of the smallest towns. That admirable woman could be seen mingling in the crowd, dressed in simple and dignified garments, and showing her faith through every sort of pious and devout deed (3.45).

The key of Eusebius's interpretation is exclusively religious. Aside from being an example of religious devotion, the empress mother, in collaboration with her son, had two churches built, the churches of the Nativity and of the Mount of Olives, and in return for her piety was rewarded with a happy death upon returning home (3.45). Her visit, however, which took place before pilgrimages became the fashion, was not limited to the sacred places or to the good works that rendered her name illustrious, and the deeds accompanying these acts of devotion were not strictly religious ones:

She journeyed across the entire Eastern Empire with the magnificence of her imperial dignity, bestowing gifts upon whole cities and upon people who sought private audiences with her. She gave many gifts to the armies and generous alms to the poor and naked. To some she gave money; to others, clothing to cover their bodies. She liberated the oppressed suffering in prisons and forced labor. Others she freed from the abuse of the powerful and still others she called home from exile (2.44).

Helena not only visited holy places, she also traveled widely across the Eastern provinces with the magnificence befitting her rank. Generously drawing on the imperial treasury, she clothed the naked and fed the hungry, as the Gospel recommends, but also undertook some initiatives that were notably political in character, such as bestowing gifts upon populations and armies and obtaining the release of prisoners and the return of exiles. Scholars have often pointed out the twofold nature of her mission, which was both religious and political. Her journey was an act of Christian propaganda (exercised specially through the benefit of the poor) and also an act intended to consolidate her son's empire as an institution, erasing the lingering traces of civil war and soothing the resentment aroused by Constantine's growing pro-Christian policies. Her liberation of political prisoners and her gifts to soldiers, among whom the cult of Mithra was widespread, would suggest that Constantine's policies were intended primarily but not exclusively to promote Christianity.

Despite its obvious political implications, Helena's pilgrimage became famous solely because of its religious aspects, which were extolled through the portrayal of the empress as a model of Christian piety. Therefore in the early years of the fifth century Paulinus of Nola affirmed that Constantine deserved to be first among Christian princes no less for his mother's faith, than for his own (*Ep.* 31.4). Rufinus of Aquileia gives equally glowing reports of her:

> The venerable queen left also this proof of her religious soul: it is said that she invited to dine with her the consecrated virgins she found there and attended them with great devotion. Feeling it unfitting that they should be served by slaves, she herself, dressed in a servant's garment, gave them food and drink with her own hands, and poured water over their hands for washing. And, although she was the queen of the world and mother of the empire, she considered herself a mere servant of the servants of Christ (*Ecclesiastical History* 1.8).

Helena's fame, promoted by Eusebius and his continuators, was not limited to ecclesiastical histories, for she later became the inspiring model of every saintly queen. In the Eastern empire, in A.D. 451, the empress Pulcheria was declared the new Helena at the Council of Chalcedon. Helena had even greater success in the Roman-barbarian kingdoms: Gregory the Great proposed her as a model worthy of imitation for Berta, the queen of the Angles, and Radegundis, queen of the Franks, was called a second Helena.

And yet, of this woman who in the course of seventy years became the image of royal piety, we do not know when she converted or what religion she previously practiced. Eusebius claims that Constantine converted his mother and educated her in religious matters (*Life of Constantine* 3.47), and therefore it may be inferred that she was not born a Christian. The possibility cannot be excluded that she was of Jewish origin, as J. Vogt has proposed, with questionable arguments (*Saeculum* 27: 221). Some claim that after conversion she had philo-Arian tendencies, indicated by her devotion to the martyr Lucian and also by Constantine's conflict with Patriarch Eustace of Antioch, staunch defender of Catholic orthodoxy. This too is mere hypothesis, founded on Athanasius's statement (*History of the Arians* 4.2) that Bishop Eustace of Antioch was deposed by Constantine because he had gravely offended the emperor. On the basis of so vague a statement, some scholars have thought that Eustace had reproached Constantine for his low birth, while others have concluded that the bishop had offended Constantine with his anti-Arian views. Later ecclesiastic historians do not mention Helena in this context and attribute Eustace's downfall to a plot by his Arian enemies, who attempted to discredit him by bringing false evidence in order to charge him with adultery.

At any rate, the supposition that Helena sympathized with the Arians finds no confirmation in the ancient sources, and even the suspicion that she may have entertained heterodox beliefs never occurred to the Christian authors of the fourth and fifth centuries, who, on the contrary, insist greatly on her piety. Their image of her primarily depends on her discovery of the True Cross, which the ancient sources unanimously ascribe to her.

The Discovery of the Cross

The Council of Nicaea thus concluded, and all the bishops returned to their homes. The emperor was extraordinarily pleased to see that the Universal Church was in agreement over dogma, and in order to give thanks to God for the agreement reached among bishops, and also for himself, for his children and for the empire, he felt it was his duty to build an oratory in the place called Calvary. It was more or less in this same period that his mother, Helena, went to Jerusalem to pray and visit the holy places. Given her pious attitude toward Christian truth, she ardently desired to find the wood of the holy Cross. But it was not easy to find the Cross or even the Holy Sepulchre, for the pagans, who had formerly persecuted the Church, had used every means to eradicate the religion that was just beginning to rise, and hid that place under a great pile of earth. They had filled in the sunken ground and elevated the surface, as can be seen today. . . . However, the holy place was revealed and the deceit woven around it laid bare, some say, because an Eastern Jew made it known thanks to a written document dating back to his ancestors. Others believe that God revealed it through miraculous signs and dreams, and this is more likely to be true, for I do not think that divine things need human help to be discovered, when it pleases God to reveal them. Once the place had been completely cleaned out on orders from the emperor, the cave of the resurrection was found and nearby three crosses were found together with a piece of wood fashioned like a scroll bearing the words "Jesus of Nazareth King of the Jews" written in Hebrew, Greek and Latin. This inscription, as the holy Book of the Gospels tells us, had been placed above Christ's head on the orders of Pontius Pilate, who was at the time procurator of Judaea. It was difficult to identify the holy Cross, since the inscription was broken in pieces and scattered here and there, and the three crosses had been thrown all in the same place and their order had been confused when the crucified bodies were removed. . . . Since the sacred wood had not yet been identified, a sign of a more than human nature was needed, and that is exactly what came to be. Among the people visiting Jerusalem, there was a woman afflicted by a painful and incurable illness. Macarius, the bishop of the local church, went to visit her while she was lying in bed, and took with him the emperor's mother and his own collaborators. After they had all prayed together, they decided that the woman would be healed if she were touched by a fragment of the holy cross, and that by attempting to do this, they would be able to identify which of the three was the True Cross. So they picked up the three crosses and approached the woman. On contact with the first two, nothing happened, and it seemed a cruel joke to play on this woman as she lay dying. But when they approached her with the third cross, she immediately opened her eyes, and with strength regained, bounded out of bed, completely cured. And they say that at the very same moment a corpse was brought back to life. Most of the holy wood discovered is still preserved in Jerusalem in a silver reliquary. The empress took part of it to her son, Constantine, together with the nails that had pierced Christ's body. It is said that with these nails the emperor had a helmet made for himself and a bit for his horse, thereby fulfilling the prophecy of Zechariah, who had foreseen this, referring it to the present-day "Sacred to the Lord Almighty shall be that which is on the horse's bridle."

This version of the *inventio crucis* was written in the middle of the fifth century by the ecclesiastical historian Sozomen (*Ecclesiastical History* 2.1.1 ff.). In his account, he gathered all the details that over the course of fifty years had come to embellish the older, meager version given by Ambrose of Milan in 395. Ambrose mentions—as does John Chrysostom in a sermon (*In Joh.* 85.1), though without mentioning Helena—the piece of wood with the inscription by means of which the True Cross was identified. Ambrose also describes the discovery of the nails, later inserted into Constantine's crown and in the bit of his horse, emphasizing the relationship between faith and the exercise of imperial power, and stresses the fulfillment of Zechariah's prophecy. Ambrose's account, bare of details, was of the greatest importance because of the role attributed to Helena. She is represented as the author of a long discourse in which she attacks the devil and describes her own deeds as the continuation of Mary's work of redemption (*On the death of Theodosius* 44).

The versions that followed Ambrose's account were much more detailed. In his *Ecclesiastical History* written in A.D. 402, Rufinus of Aquileia, who was to be followed by Socrates, Sozomen, and Theodoret, describes the excavations on Golgotha ordered by Helena. She, *divinis admonita visionibus* ("so advised by divinely inspired visions"), had gone to Jerusalem and obtained information concerning the site where Christ was crucified. The place was in such a state of confusion, however, that despite Pilate's inscription, it was impossible to identify the True Cross. Thanks to Macarius, the Bishop of Jerusalem, it was identified through the miraculous healing of a woman. Rufinus also relates that Helena found the nails, but does not mention them in the context of the prophecy of Zechariah (*Ecclesiastical History* 1.7).

Paulinus of Nola sent a fragment of the cross, together with his Epistle 31, dated around 403, to his friend Sulpicius Severus, who later used Paulinus's account in his *Chronicle* (2.34). In this version, the discovery of the cross was not made easier by finding the inscription and no nails were found. Macarius, who plays such an important role in Rufinus's version, does not appear. To prove the authenticity of the relic, Helena, alone, goes looking for a dead person to revive. Sozomen's account blends the two versions, describing both the healed woman and the revived dead person, and briefly discredits yet another version (which will have greater success in the Latin West) in which the Jew Judah revealed where the cross was hidden and then had himself baptized with the name Cyriacus and became Bishop of Jerusalem.

The oldest accounts we have of the *inventio crucis* are all in Latin, but this does not mean that they were based on western sources. Rufinus, who spent a long period in Palestine, used as his source an *Ecclesiastical History* written by Bishop Gelasius of Caesarea around 390–400, which was a continuation of Eusebius's history. Paulinus of Nola received a relic of the True Cross as a gift from his cousin Melania the Elder (a Roman aristocrat who had gone to live in the Holy Land) and must have learned from her the story as to how it was discovered. Ambrose's version, which agrees with Chrysostom's (except for the substantial novelty of Helena's presence), must also have come from eastern informants. He may have heard the story while at the court of Theodosius (this is Drijvers's theory, 97) or may have taken it from a vulgate version he had learned from some pilgrim to the Holy Land. The important role played by Macarius, the bishop of the city, in identifying the True Cross may be proof that the legend originated in Jerusalem. The insertion of Helena into the legend may have taken place between the end of the eighties and the beginning of the nineties of the fourth century. Helena's presence is in fact mentioned for the first time by Gelasius of Caesarea and by Ambrose. It is not mentioned in the diary written by the pilgrim Egeria, who visited the Holy Land between 381 and 384, although she does describe the celebrations connected with the discovery of the cross and the liturgical ceremonies of Good Friday, in which the relic of the cross plays a major role.

A Legend that Just Won't Die

Our story could now be considered to have reached its conclusion, were it not for a recently published book that once again claims that Helena discovered the cross. To discuss this theory, we must examine a few sources that show that there was special interest in the cross even before it came to be connected with the figure of Helena. Neither Eusebius of Caesarea (despite his detailed description of a chapel built on Golgotha) nor the pilgrim from Bordeaux who visited the Holy Land in 333, mention the discovery of the cross, yet we know that relics of the cross were circulating already around 350. This may be deduced from various passages written by Bishop Cyril of Jerusalem, who not only mentions these relics but also tells us that the cross was discovered in the time of Constantine. In an epistle addressed to Constantius II, dated 351, Cyril describes the miraculous appearance of a luminous cross in the sky, which he compares with the discovery of the holy cross that occurred during the reign of Constantine:

> During the reign of your father, dear to God and of saintly memory, the Wood of Salvation was discovered in Jerusalem after divine grace had allowed the discovery to him who was striving after the pious search. But in your own reign, O Lord, most pious Emperor, whose devotion to God and whose greater commitment surpass the piety of your forefathers, not from earth but from heaven miracles do come (*PG* 33, 1168B).

Cyril's claim that the cross was found during Constantine's reign is puzzling. If what he says is true (and it would be very unlikely that he would lie to Constantine's son and successor), this discovery has to have happened before Constantine died (A.D. 337) and therefore before Eusebius died (c. A.D. 340). Yet why did Eusebius, who wrote about the Holy Sepulchre, fail to mention such an important discovery? Among the many theories to explain his silence (that he did not know about it, or doubted the truth of the story, or was jealous of the prestigious role played by the Bishop of Jerusalem who occupied a position rivaling his own position in Caesarea) the least convincing is that he did not know about it, if only because of the geographic location of his episcopal residence. That his silence was not due to ignorance but was deliberate is shown by a passage from Eusebius's *Life of Constantine*. After dwelling upon the Church of the Holy Sepulchre that Constantine had built on the spot where a temple to Aphrodite previously stood, he includes the text of an epistle written by Constantine to Macarius, Bishop of Jerusalem:

> The grace dispensed by our Savior is so great, that no discourse, no matter how vast and extensive, could adequately illustrate the miracle that has occurred. In fact, that the monument (*gnorisma*) of the most Holy passion of Christ, hidden under the earth for a long time, after having concealed any mark of itself for so many years, has now returned to shine in the sight of all its servants—free at last, thanks to the elimination of the common enemy—is an event that surpasses all astonishment (*Life of Constantine* 3.30.1).

Eusebius quotes this passage while describing the building of the church of the Holy Sepulchre, but Constantine in his epistle is referring to the discovery of the cross, the true *gnorisma* or monument of Christ's passion. Comparing Eusebius's text with a passage by Jerome in which he distinguishes between the sepulchre of Christ, hidden beneath a temple to Jupiter, and Golgotha, where a temple dedicated to Venus previously stood, we may see that Eusebius has combined the two sites without mentioning the cross. Whatever the theological reasons which might have motivated Eusebius to censure the finding of the cross, the epistle written by Constantine and quoted by Eusebius testifies that the cross was discovered in the course of the 320s. We must now explain why the pilgrim of Bordeaux does not mention this important event. Some scholars have pointed out that he shows little interest in any form of relic, but perhaps it would be wiser to take his silence as an indication that the cult of the cross did not immediately become popular, but asserted itself gradually, most likely together with the cult of the Holy Sepulchre.

Now let us discuss the arguments by which the Swedish scholar Stephan Borgehammar, in a complex and documented essay written in 1991, tried to demonstrate that Helena was indeed the discoverer of the cross. He begins by stating that there is no strong evidence proving or disproving the traditional account, and that "being a person who prefers to give sources the benefit of the doubt until they are positively demonstrated to be erroneous," he intends "to present a case . . . for Helena as the one who found the Cross" (124). To prove that the legend is true he first claims that Cyril's failure to mention Helena in his epistle to Constantius II does not suggest that he was ignorant of Helena's role. First of all, there was no need for Cyril to remind Constantius of something he already knew. Secondly, Cyril was the uncle of Gelasius of Caesarea and had commissioned him to write his *Church History,* which was the only version ascribing to Macarius an active role in finding the Cross. "It does not seem at all implausible" that Cyril, "who in all probability had known Macarius personally" (128), acted as his prime source, and it is difficult to see the reason for him to completely invent Helena's participation. The weakness of this argument is evident, for it deals with unproved assumptions as if they were the truth. On one hand, it is unlikely that Cyril would have omitted to mention Helena simply because Constantius already knew the story. Cyril, eager to ingratiate himself with the emperor and well acquainted with the power of rhetoric, could only have found it to his advantage to suggest that Constantius had received a miraculous vision from the heavens, whereas Helena, his own grandmother, after much effort and a long journey, had obtained her miracle only from the earth. On the other hand, Macarius's role in the discovery of the cross promoted the interests of Jerusalem, just as Helena's role promoted the image of the imperial family: most likely in his version, Gelasius of Caesarea had blended these two converging promotional campaigns.

A further element that weakens Borgehammar's theory is the fact that the connection between the church of Santa Croce in Gerusalemme in Rome with the relics of the cross supposedly brought there by the empress is of rather late dating, because in the oldest texts the name of this basilica is given as *Hierusalem.* Borgehammar manages to glide over this difficulty thanks to an epigraph preserved in the church which explains that *Hierusalem* refers to the sacred soil of Calvary brought back by Helena from the Holy Land, but this inscription refers to Calvary, and not to the wood of the cross. Moreover, it is placed in the floor of the Gregorian Chapel, and is a copy of a late text that must have dated from the Middle Ages, as we may deduce from the use of the word *capella* and from the fact that in this inscription *ae* is constantly rendered with *e.*

Borgehammar attempts to establish the chronology of Helena's journey to the Holy Land by referring to Constantine's epistle to Macarius. He dates this epistle to the spring of 325 because it alludes to the defeat of Licinius. If the letter were dated 325, it must have been written at least one month before the Council of Nicaea, because if Macarius had already set out for the council, he could not have supervised the construction of the church. If so, another problem arises: in Eusebius's account, the description of the *martyrion* built on the Holy Sepulchre comes after his mention of the Council of Nicaea. Borgehammar finds an easy explanation for this as well: after the cross had been discovered, Constantine could have given orders to build the church, and the Holy Sepulchre could have come to light during the excavations prior to construction.

Borgehammar also uses as evidence to prove that the nails too were found at that time the fact that in the coins issued in 325 Constantine is depicted with a new crown, one that could have been made with the nails of the cross combined with his imperial helmet. Borgehammar then makes the discovery of the cross and nails coincide with Helena's journey, which is generally dated to 326–27. Since it is relatively certain that she was present at court for the celebration of the *Vicennalia* (July, 326), he suggests that her journey took place 324, immediately after the defeat of Licinius. In his opinion, Helena's gifts to the soldiers would then be better explained in the context of the celebrations of Constantine's victory at Chrysopolis (A.D. 323) than in the context of the *Vicennalia*. In conclusion, Borgehammar claims that Helena set out for her journey at the end of 324 and returned in 326, at the time of Crispus's murder. She decided to make her pilgrimage after Constantine's conquest of the East, no doubt because she realized she was getting old and had little time and energy left.

We are clearly dealing here with a succession of hypotheses the sole purpose of which is to prove that Helena discovered the cross: this claim is based on vague inferences and dates forced to fit this theory. What is even worse, if Helena did return from the East at the beginning of 326, she had three more years to live, which contradicts the only certain information we have about her life: namely, that she died shortly after her return from her pilgrimage, as Eusebius tells us. Moreover, Eusebius has omitted any mention of the discovery of the cross and speaks only of the Church of the Holy Sepulchre, and his omission of Helena's role in the building of this church would also suggest that she played no role in the discovery of the cross.

What we have said thus far seems to be sufficient to deny any historical truth to the legend that Helena participated in the finding of the True Cross even if it does not erase the link between Helena and the Cross, created by legend and strengthened over the course of centuries. Rome is now crowded with pilgrims coming to celebrate "l'Anno santo" and the basilica of Santa Croce in Gerusalemme is one of the places they have to visit. There they are reminded of Helena's legend and they worship the relics still preserved in the church. The pious homage they are invited to pay confirms once more the vitality of a tradition that has endured long beyond the *Golden Legend* and the painting cycle of Piero della Francesca.

EIGHT

HYPATIA THE INTELLECTUAL

Silvia Ronchey

Hypatia, or the Partisan Spirit of the Alexandrians

In the years of the decline of the Western Roman Empire, a century after the edict of 313 A.D. that had granted freedom of cult to the Christians, the tolerance then showed by Constantine gradually developed, under his successors, into an intolerance against the pagans. In 391 A.D. Theodosius issued a constitution that made Christianity the state religion, and in the following year a special law against all pagan cults was issued in Egypt, "cradle of all Gods" according to ancient philosophers. The policy of the Christian religious authorities of Alexandria, the main Greek cultural center of the Mediterranean *koiné* and the epicenter of this ideological seism, aimed at the annihilation of ritual paganism, the religion of the ancient temples.

> Everything happened as in the poets' myths, when the Giants held supremacy on earth: the religion of the temples in Alexandria and in the sanctuary of Serapis was dispersed to the winds; not only the ceremonies but the edifices themselves, under Theodosius, when . . . the temple of Serapis was destroyed . . . and war was waged to seize the temple's treasures.

These are the words of Eunapius, the biographer of the last Neoplatonists. The statue of Serapis, a God-demon sitting on a throne, the work of the Greek sculptor Briaxis, represented both the power of Hellenistic sovereigns and the dominion of the secrets of Hades. A mantle, covering his body, made of a bluish alloy and strewn with precious stones, represented the stars in the sky and the astrological/astronomical knowledge of the Orient. The Serapeum, with its one hundred steps in front, was the destination of pilgrims coming from all over the *oikouméne*. Its destruction, carried out by Theophilus, who very readily complied with Theodosius's edicts, was made even more appalling by its sacking. As Eunapius points out, "the only part of the Serapeum they did not steal was the floor, because the stones were too heavy to carry away."

160

The whole Church of Egypt participated in this campaign against paganism at the beginning of the fifth century. The monks came down from the mountains of Nitria to support their patriarch. "They were allowed into the holy places and were called monks whilst they, men only in appearance, lead a pig-like life and openly favored and committed a number of abominable crimes." Again the monks, five hundred of them, will come back to frighten the city at the time of bishop Cyril, Theophilus's grandchild and a future saint, who succeeded the latter in the bishopric of the main Christian metropolis of the East exactly one hundred years after Constantine's edict.

"There used to be a woman in Alexandria," Socrates, a contemporary and lawyer at the Court of Constantinople, narrates in his *Historia Ecclesiastica,*

> by the name of Hypatia. She was the daughter of Theon, a philosopher in Alexandria, and had reached such heights of wisdom that she had by far surpassed all the philosophers of her circle. She inherited from her father the teaching (*diadoché*) of the Platonic school deriving from Plotinus, and expounded all the philosophical doctrines in her addresses to a free public . . . From everywhere people would come to her to philosophize.

In *Hypatia, or the Partisan Spirit of the Alexandrians,* a long article from Suidas, a Byzantine lexicon from the tenth century, we read that Hypatia "had become such an experienced teacher, was so just and wise, but also so beautiful and attractive," that her students would fall in love with her. Suidas's information stems from two by now lost accounts from the time of Justinian: the first, whether true or fake, is by Hesychius of Miletus, and the second, of which only a few fragments have survived, is the *Vita Isidori,* the last priest of the temple of Serapis, written by the Neoplatonic Damascius, the last scholar of the Academy of Athens. Presumably it is the first that states that Hypatia,

> being more naturally gifted than her father, did not limit herself to the technical-mathematical teachings of her father, but dedicated herself to real and true philosophy, to great result. Although a woman, she would wear the *tribon* [the cape of Cynic philosophers] and would go about the city publicly, explaining to whoever felt like listening, Plato, Aristotle, or any other philosopher.

It is well known that a complex relationship tied the Roman governor to the local elites of the provincial territories in the fourth and fifth centuries of the Roman Empire. Among the various centuries-old privileges inherited by birth, there was the special "Hellenic" education, which was of strong political connotation. Influential among the aristocracy, the heiress of the intellectual dynasty that referred to the School of the Mouseion, Hypatia was mainly the teacher of the Hellenic lifestyle (*helleniké diagogé*), mostly political, that inspired the pagan aristocracy. Suidas, still probably with Hesychius's words, confirms this: she was "fluent and dialectical (*dialektiké*) in her speech, cautious and shrewd (*politiké*) in her action, so that the whole city revered her and paid homage to her."

As Socrates Scholasticus informs us, "from the Hellenic culture (*paidéia*) she had derived a self-control and a directness in her speech (*parrhesia*)" that helped her to "directly confront the powerful and to attend men's meetings without fear. All of them held a deferential attitude for her extraordinary wisdom and looked up to her, if anything, with reverential awe." Hypatia was the spokeswoman of the city aristocracy to the representative of the central Roman government, and namely with Orestes, prefect of Egypt. "The political leaders administrating in the city," Suidas tells us, "were the first to go and listen to her, as still happened in Athens. If paganism was finished, there, anyway, the name of philosophy maintained its stature and appeared worthy of consideration to those holding the most important city offices." Philosophy strongly and directly influenced the internal policy of her city. In a letter of introduction, Synesius, a pupil of hers, wrote to her: "You have always had power, may you hold it for long and may you make good use of it."

It is from this very power, however, local and based on a system of patrons, that the transformation of the ruling classes took its very first steps, having started in the provincial capitals by the political legitimization of the Church. The *polis* of late antiquity witnessed from then on the bishop, and not the philosopher, become the consultant and the "civic defender" of the imperial representative. "The Christian bishop had to have the monopoly of *parrhesia!*" wrote Peter Brown, proposing a historical, perhaps too direct syllogism on the very case of Hypatia: if during the transition from paganism to Christianity the roles of the philosopher and the bishop developed to such an extent that they coincided, what was the bishop to do if not eliminate the philosopher? "A personified *phthònos* raised arms against her," accuses Socrates. The *phthònos* of the Christians against the pagans, according to all sources, and a common opinion in ancient literature, was the cause of the violent end not only of Hypatia but together with her of the old lifestyle of the *polis,* the same one outlined in the nuanced reference to Athens on the part of Suidas.

"Because of the frequent meetings between Hypatia and Orestes," writes Socrates, "there arose among the people the suspicion that it was Hypatia's fault if Orestes did not reconcile himself with their bishop." In fact this idea is reaffirmed two centuries later in a fourth and no less important source of our study: the *Chronicle* of John of Nikiû, probably written in Coptic a few years short of the Arabic conquest of Egypt, and often neglected by scholars, as it only survived in a late Ethiopic version. In the allegiance between the prefect and the philosopher, the Coptic bishop read, in all probability rightly, "the reaction of the pagan will against the outrageous Christianity of Cyril" (Rougé).

If the Hellenic aristocracy is linked to the offices of the imperial government by means of their implicit and common adhesion to paganism as if in a sort of Freemasonry, in the political game played out in Alexandria between those forces and the emerging Christian authorities one has to take into account a fourth element: namely the Jewish community, once before Christianity the predominant party and now a rival one.

An old antagonism had opposed the Jewish mother Church to Christianity, once a simple splinter group or diverting sect in the first centuries, when it grew "in the shadow of the synagogues." On the Christian side, rivalry in proselytism was added to the theological hostility against the race "responsible for the murder of God." Bishops, from Cyril of Alexandria to Theodoret of Cyrrhus and Basil of Seleucia, preached against the Jews. The first scripts and acts of Cyril's episcopal career were characterized by a more anti-Jewish than antipagan stance: his first festal letter in 414 is an example.

In the provinces, the traditional violence between Jews and gentiles goes back to the times of the first emperors. Synesius calls the Jewish people "archenemies of the Hellenes," still bearing in mind the rebellion of the Jewish colonies in Egypt and Pentapolis in 117 under Trajan and the subsequent slaughter, according to Dio Cassius, of two hundred and twenty thousand gentiles. In the fifth century A.D., street fights were an everyday, ordinary event, like the Samaritans' riots in Palestine. Anti-Jewish rancor was as strong as ever in Alexandria, where the Jewish colony numbered one hundred thousand.

Socrates narrates, with likely impartiality, that in 414 the Jews had convinced the prefect Orestes to imprison Hierax and torture him in public. A teacher of grammar, Hierax, employed by Cyril as an agent provocateur, used to disturb and upset the citizens' assemblies in the theater. (John of Nikiû transforms him into "an educated and capable man, who had the saintly habit of reproaching the pagans as he was entirely devoted to the illustrious patriarch, and most knowledgeable in the Christian doctrine.") The Jews then ambushed Christian activists in the streets of Alexandria, at night, and according to Socrates killed "a large number" of them.

The patriarch immediately reacted with the great pogrom, a prelude to Hypatia's assassination, perpetrated by Cyril's *parabalani* against the synagogues. Stirred up by agitators, the Christian population pillaged the houses of the Jews, who were eventually banned from the city. "The Jews, who had lived in the city since the time of Alexander the Great, all had to emigrate, lost all their property, and were dispersed here and there." The patriarch's act of force was momentous: not a spontaneous and popular uprising, but rather an abuse of the Church, which once again, after the destruction of the Serapeum, made use of the violent monks as its instrument.

The development of monasticism into a mass phenomenon enhanced every political act and, as has been written, created repercussions throughout the entire history of the fifth century. At the time of Anthony of Tebaid, the desert fathers used to preach refusal of organized life, abstinence from social food rites, retreat from the world (*anachoresis*) and from nature itself. They practiced asceticism and celebrated the inner desert (*éremos*) by transferring themselves to a real one. Though a great mystic movement, Egyptian eremitism was still a limited phenomenon, in a way elitist. But its revolutionary potential, as yet unexpressed in the fourth century A.D., paved the way for currents of subversive asceticism, which in the fifth century constituted a deviance. Zealots, "beings with incandescent and fiery spirit," as Socrates calls them, these monks, often illiterate, hired by Cyril, were bands of hoodlums wandering from town to town inflamed by social hatred of the pagans, the civilized world in general, and city dwellers. As Evelyne Patlagean has written, "they pushed ascetic imperturbability over the brink of subversion. All in all, the whole monastic world was animated by the claim of their supremacy . . . and all monks had, at that time, free access to the cities."

At this precise moment the monks make their appearance in Hypatia's story. "Some monks from the mountains of Nitria, whose spirit was seething since the time of Theophilus, who had maliciously armed them . . . , and had consequently become zealots, in their fanaticism decided to fight in Cyril's name," Socrates reports. The new patriarch, who had long dwelled among them in the desert before his appointment, absorbed them in the body of the *parabalani,* "nurses/stretcher bearers," in fact clerics, who constituted his private militia in Alexandria. Suidas defines them as "abominable beings, true beasts." References to the "beastly" uncouthness of the monks, already found in Eunapius, often recur in Byzantine writers, hinting not only at the actual opinion of them, but also at a passage in Aristotle's *On Politics* saying that "the renunciation of the life in the *polis* can only make men Gods or beasts."

The attack against the prefect of Egypt's train in 415 occurred shortly before the slaughtering of Hypatia. Socrates narrates that the monks started verbally abusing Orestes, accusing him of sacrificing to the gods and of being a "Hellenic." The prefect pled innocent to these accusations of paganism, claiming to have been baptized by Atticus, bishop of Constantinople, and to be a Christian. But it is likely that it was this imprudent mention of the rival seat of Constantinople which roused the Egyptians. Someone named Ammonius seems to have thrown a stone, hitting Orestes on the head inside his own carriage. Blood spurted out, staining the toga of the representative of the Roman government. Having gone far too far, Ammonius was imprisoned and died under torture. Two reports were soon sent to Constantinople, Orestes' and Cyril's. Cyril immediately ordered a state funeral for Ammonius, and in his public eulogy not only called him a martyr but also changed his name from Ammonius to Thaumasius, "the admirable," as his gestures had been admirable: an act which openly offended the prefect.

With his behavior, however, Cyril estranged, as Socrates informs us, the more moderate wing (*hòi sophronoùntes*) of the ecclesiastical body (*laòs*), moderate at least compared to the mass (*pléthos*) of the integralists. Perhaps for this reason Cyril was advised to meet Orestes. He presented himself bearing the Gospels as a gift: the symbol of the state religion as opposed to the Old Testament of the Jews, who were in fact the actual subject matter of the discussion. With his act, Cyril was confident, Socrates writes, "that the respect for the new religion would have induced the prefect to quell his anger." But Orestes "was not softened, and an implacable war went on between them."

It is at this very moment that Suidas's sources ascribe *phthònos,* as the triggering element of the drama, to Cyril and not in general to the Christians. *Phthònos,* then, no longer as "evil will," but with the more specific and personal meaning of "envy": the bishop's rivalry against the philosopher, combined with the natural jealousy of the cleric for a woman of the world; the former and the latter belonging to two categories that, over the course of history, have nourished either great mutual love or great mutual hatred.

Suidas writes:

> One day the bishop of the opposing sect, Cyril, was passing by the house of Hypatia and noticed a number of people crowding in front of her door,
> men and horses gathering together,
> some coming, others going, others waiting outside. . . . After inquiring what they were all doing and the reason for such hustle and bustle, he was informed that it was Hypatia's day for receiving and hers was that house. Having learnt that, Cyril felt his soul bitterly bitten and for that reason he soon organized her murder, the most impious of all assassinations.

This took place "in the fourth year of Cyril's episcopate, the tenth of Honorius's consulate, the sixth of Theodosius the Second, in the month of March." Socrates writes that at the time of the aggression the monks' rage was made worse, ironically enough, "by the period of fasting." Monks and *parabalani* gathered together under Peter the Lector, also a cleric as his name tells us, and contrived "a secret plan." Both Suidas and Damascius state that a "multitude of bloodthirsty men fell upon Hypatia while she was, as usual, returning home." Theon's daughter was pulled out of her litter and dragged "to the church named after Caesar emperor," that is, in the courtyard of the Cesaraeum, recently built by Theodosius. Here, "heedless of

the revenge of gods or of humans,

these truly wicked massacred the philosopher," writes Damascius, "and while she was still faintly breathing they gouged out her eyes." "They stripped off her clothes, slaughtered her, cutting her body with sharp potsherds, and carried her remains to the so-called Cinaron and set them on fire," Socrates writes. "The pieces of her brutalized body were scattered all over the city, and all that she suffered because of the hostility (*phthònos*) against her outstanding wisdom, namely astronomical," according to this pagan source, which also defined her lynching as an "appalling crime and an immense shame to the city."

The *Historia Ecclesiastica* by Philostorgius, now lost, was written a few years after these events and has been handed down in the summary given by Photius. In Philostorgius, openly Arian and therefore hostile to the bishop of Alexandria, one reads: "The woman was slaughtered by the hand of those who profess consubstantiation." But also for Socrates of Constantinople, "what Cyril and the Church of Alexandria committed

was no small act of infamy. For murders and wars and the like are something totally alien to the spirit of Christianity."

John of Nikiû, who in a very clear, almost provocative way took Cyril's
side, gives us an almost unrecognizable version of the story. The Coptic
narration considers Hypatia's lynching almost as a legitimate execution,
something to be proud of for "the flock of believers" who committed it.
Peter is not only a lector, but also a magistrate and a perfect servant of
Christ. The encounter between the executioner and the predestined victim, guilty "of hypnotizing her students with her magic" and of exercis-
ing the "satanic" science of the stars, was neither casual nor contrived in
the secrecy of an ambush, for it happened in the very place where Hypatia taught: it is emblematic that in this version she was dragged away
from her teacher's cathedra and not from her carriage.

Then, apart from Philostorgius's brief mention, we are confronted, in
the ancient Christian sources still available to us, with a double report
of the facts. The first, the *Historia Ecclesiastica* by Socrates, a contemporary of the events, probably gives us the official version. The second,
John of Nikiû's *Chronicle,* of a slightly later time, manifestly mirrors both
the thesis and the ideology of the local Egyptian Church, which developed Cyril's doctrine in antithesis to the Constantinopolitan orthodoxy.
The chronicler concludes triumphantly: "The whole population gathered
around the patriarch Cyril and called him the new Theophilus, as he had
liberated the city from the last of its idols."

The year of Hypatia's death was 5096 from the creation of the world
for the Alexandrians, the twelfth indiction, the eighth year of the reign,
in the East, of a child emperor: Theodosius II was looked after by his
elder sister Pulcheria, who at court was called Augusta, and, although
only fifteen years old, she was the actual empress. Hostile to the pagans,
Pulcheria was so generally devoted to Christianity, and namely to the
Alexandrian orthodoxy, that she was defined by one historian as "the
purple-clad nun."

So Hypatia's murder went unpunished. The magistrate in charge filed
the case. Damascius writes: "The wrath of the emperor would have fallen
on Cyril had Edesius [probably the emperor's emissary] not corrupted
both judges and witnesses so as to avoid punishment for the murderers."
Pulcheria's devotion prevailed over the indignation of Orestes, who obtained from the government he represented, in exchange for his silence,
few measures, not enough anyway to limit the bishop's interference in
the lay administration. The number of *parabalani* was reduced and from
then on they were put under the control of, and chosen by, the prefect

of Egypt. They were also forbidden entrance in a few cities, according to the report sent to the imperial court by the city council, whose answer is contained in the *Theodosian Code.* Cyril the bishop was then acquitted and probably politically absolved too. To see him condemned by history one has to wait not until the year 451 A.D., when Monophysitism, the heresy based on Cyril's doctrine, was condemned at Chalcedon, but until the judgement of posterity, so much more appreciative of Hypatia's than of Cyril's doctrine.

The Fortune of Hypatia

Supposing Mme. Dacier was the most beautiful woman in Paris, and that in the *querelle* between the ancients and the moderns the Carmelites claimed that the poem about Mary Magdalene composed by one of them was immensely superior to Homer, and that preferring the *Iliad* to a monk's verses was an atrocious, impious act; and supposing that the archbishop of Paris had taken the side of the Carmelites against the city governor, a follower of the beautiful Mme. Dacier, and had induced the Carmelites to massacre this handsome lady in the church of Notre Dame, and to drag her naked and bleeding body to the place Maubert; well, there would have been nobody able to deny that the action of the archbishop of Paris was an evil action, one which must be repented. This, though, is precisely the story of Hypatia.

So writes Voltaire in his *Questions sur l'Encyclopédie* (1772). To Anne Dacier, the great Huguenot lady philosopher (but certainly not "la plus belle dame de Paris"), Gilles Ménage had dedicated his *Historia mulierum philosopharum* (1690): the evidence against Cyril had emerged for the first time in the absolute monarchy of France, after the mediaeval Byzantine autocracy. The complete collection of the ancient sources on the murder of Hypatia was published a few decades later, in the *Mulierum Graecarum, quae oratione prosa usae sunt, fragmenta et elogia* (1735), by the Protestant Wolf.

As a German historian has said, in the modern age "*Kulturkampf* and clericalism have placed Hypatia's case in the battlefield." On Hypatia's death and as on other episodes of early Christianity, Catholic historiography has been confronted with the Protestant, Anglican, and Jansenist schools, as well as the Enlightenment and lay schools. Voltaire spoke of Hypatia again and in more severe terms in other works, and in his *Histoire de l'établissement du Christianisme* (1777) he listed her death among the "excès du fanatisme"; via Voltaire's quotations, the characters of Hypatia's drama appeared in French eighteenth-century fiction and *en travesti* in Schiller's tragedies, and also in Vincenzo Monti's lines:

> La voce alzate, o secoli caduti,
> Gridi l'Africa all'Asia e l'innocente
> Ombra d'Ipazia il grido orrendo aiuti.

Raise your voices, fallen centuries / might Africa cry against Asia / might her cry help the shade of Hypatia.

The first of a group of three polemic poems including *Superstition* and *Danger, Fanaticism* is what prevents reason from triumphing and leaves the Church to meddle in the affairs of state.

But before France, England had already shared the posthumous case of Hypatia, in an essay dedicated to her by the Irishman John Toland, by the title of

> *Hypatia; or, The history of a most beautiful, most virtuous, most learned, and every way accomplish'd lady; who was torn to pieces by the clergy of Alexandria, to gratify the pride, emulation, and cruelty of their archbishop, commonly but undeservedly styled St. Cyril,*

which was soon contradicted, in 1721, by a pamphlet by Lewis

> *The history of Hypatia, a most impudent school-mistress of Alexandria, murder'd and torn to pieces by the populace, in defence of Saint Cyril and the Alexandrian clergy: From the aspersions of Mr. Toland.*

Hypatia enjoyed vast fame and reputation throughout the Protestant eighteenth century, as the literary production of German and English anticlericalism testify: from the *Satyres* by Henry Fielding, who imagines a very unlikely engagement between the lady philosopher and the emperor Julian the Apostate and who laments the loss of the ring in the fire of the Cinaron, to Wieland's *Moralische Briefe,* which exalts her and places her next to Socrates.

Entering into the midst of this already advanced stage of afterlife is Gibbon, who in the *Decline and Fall* certainly did not restrain himself from attacking Cyril's reputation:

> On a fatal day, in the holy season of Lent, Hypatia was torn from her chariot, stripped naked, dragged to the church, and inhumanly butchered

by the hands of Peter the reader and a troop of savage and merciless fanat-
ics: her flesh was scraped from her bones with sharp oyster shells, and her
quivering limbs were delivered to the flames. The just progress of inquiry
and punishment was stopped by seasonable gifts; but the murder of Hypatia has imprinted an indelible stain on the character and religion of Cyril
of Alexandria.

If we consider the Catholic side, from the very beginning we find
a clear resistance to even hint at the subject and in any case to put it
in correct perspective. From the time of the Counter-Reformation,
Cardinal Baronio's *Annales* try to alter the information on Cyril's politics and start to question the reliability of the sources, in particular Socrates. In the last century, it was even stated that "as Cyril was sanctified
by the Church, every good believer ought to consider him completely
justified." Still at the beginning of this century, those events were considered by religious writers as topical facts and Cyril's innocence or guilt
has been the subject of animated discussions. In 1901, after a close examination of the sources, Schaefer recriminates: "If Orestes had accepted
the offer of peace, or had with good will taken into consideration Cyril's
changed attitude, probably the bloody crime would have been averted."
Trying to defend the bishop, the historians end up accusing the mentality
of the Church, revealing that it remains similar to what it had been in
those years.

It might be surprising that in his *Mémoires pour servir à l'histoire
ecclésiastique,* Tillemont, otherwise a quite severe judge, shows a more
prudent justificative attitude towards Alexandrian Christianity. He
writes, in fact, that Hypatia's murder not only "appeared heinous to
Christian souls," but "caused great damage to the bishop." In his *Mémoires* he mentions, even if without giving them too much credit, the news
of Hypatia's belated conversion and an openly false Latin epistle stating
that the philosopheress had supposedly explained Nestorius's Christian,
though duo-physite, doctrine to Cyril on the occasion of the Council
of Ephesus, which took place a good fifteen years after her death. But
Jansenists like Tillemont, of course, defended the right of the Church to
exercise political hegemony. Proof of this is the fact that another Jansenist, Claude-Pierre Goujet, later openly celebrated Cyril's attempt in his
*Dissertation sur Hypacie où l'on justifie Saint Cyrille d'Alexandrie sur la
morte de cette savante* (1727).

The stances of the historians, in their nuances and subtlety, have had
unrestrained effects on poets. The marchioness Diodata Saluzzo Roero,

a member of the Academy of Sciences in Turin and of Arcadia under the name of Glaucilla Erotria, who besides the splendour of her high birth added "that of a soul embellished by all virtues," wrote a long poem entitled *Hypatia, or On Philosophy* (1827). She is here described as a Christian Hypatia—perhaps autobiographical—inwardly torn between her faith, the discussions of her academic entourage, and a promise to marry no one else but the Neoplatonic Isidore, the protagonist of Damascius's *Life*, probably at that time still an infant:

> Mentr'ei seguia, la vergin tra l'oscuro
> >Volgo precipitando: Io son cristiana,
> >Gridò, cristiana, né celarlo curo.
> Nulla può sul mio cor possanza umana;
> >Nulla! saria delitto or l'occultarlo,
> >E delitto appressar l'ara profana.
> Ahi lo sdegno del padre! e chi frenarlo
> >Potrìa? . . . l'allor perduto! . . . il perder quelli
> >Sì fidi amici! . . . lassa, di che parlo?
> Pera il mio nome, il volgo empia m'appelli!

While he followed the virgin running / amid the dark throng: I am a Christian, / she cried, and I do not intend to hide it. / Men have no power over my heart / None! It would be a crime to hide it, / a crime to approach the altar profane. (Alas for my father's scorn! But who could have prevented it?) / . . . The lost glory . . . the loss of such loyal friends / . . . Enough, what am I speaking of? / That my name might die, / might the crowd call me unholy!

Trembling at the thought of her father's anger, the heroine is rescued by Cyril himself, who

> Udì 'l gran fatto, venne: Io t'apparecchio
> >Tetto umil d'alga, o de la vincitrice
> >Virtù d'Iddìo (sclamò) trionfo e specchio.
> Seguimi, vieni, vergine felice!

He heard of the trouble and came to her. I will build you / a humble roof of seaweed, O / triumph and mirror (he exclaimed) / of God's conqueress virtue! / Follow me, come, happy virgin!

The story would have had a happy ending if the "impious Altiphon, a furiously passionate and unrequited lover," had not come up and stabbed her. The dying of Hypatia is presented here as a Christian martyrdom:

> Languida rosa sul reciso stelo
> Nel sangue immersa la vergine giacea
> Avvolta a mezzo nel suo bianco velo
> Soavissimamente sorridea
> Condonatrice de l'altrui delitto
> Mentre il gran segno redentor stringea.

Languishing rose on the severed stalk, / the virgin lies steeped in blood, / wrapped in a white veil, / most suavely smiling, / she forgives the crime of others / while clutching the Savior's cross.

In the Biblioteca Angelica in Rome, next to the seat of the Arcadia, there still hangs an oil portrait of Glaucilla Erotria, holding in her hand a book inscribed with the name Hypatia. A lightly conservative patriot (as "a moral purpose of her work" she was determined to prove "how ruinous are the effects of discordant opinions of the parties"), she was also the correspondent of Monti, Parini, Manzoni, Madame de Staël, and above all a reader of Tillemont, on whose description of Hypatia her poem is apparently based (or better, "hung," as she herself wrote). The Jansenist version of the story is partly responsible, then, for her total misunderstanding of history.

Another odd case of a doctrinal dispute in literary form is the novel by the Anglican Charles Kingsley, *Hypatia; or, New Foes with an Old Face*. His prose has been defined as "a pageant of sadistic eroticism" and its author "a perverted clergyman."

> On, up the nave, fresh shreds of her dress strewing the holy pavement, up the chancel steps themselves, up to the altar, right underneath the great still Christ; and there even those hell-hounds paused. She shook herself free from her tormentors, and springing back, rose for one moment to her full height, naked, snow-white against the dusky mass around, shame and indignation in those wide, clear eyes, but not a stain of fear.

However, aside from the Victorian style, we ought to consider that the Reverend Mr. Kingsley was a follower of Carlyle, a supporter of Social Reform, and yet the main literary advocate of the Christian Socialists against the contemporary Oxford movement. His *New Foes with an Old Face* actually owes much less to the aesthetic canons à la Pierre Louÿs, to whom Kingsley has been justly enough compared, and much more to the persisting controversies on heresies by which the figure of Hypatia has been able to survive in history. We could define it as an ideological-religious *Puppenspiel*. Underneath their Alexandrian garments, the targets are clearly recognizable: Tractarianism, i.e., the "heretical" claim to rebuild Anglicanism as a *via media* between Christian Roman Catholicism and Protestantism, based on proto-Christian patristic writings, and its chief exponent, Cardinal Newman, hidden behind the mask of Cyril.

But in actual terms, Hypatia's great fortune both in poetry and literature, which could never be fully retraced here, is due to the dramatic contrast between her being a woman and her being involved in two virile contexts: philosophy and a violent death, which developed into martyrdom, although lay. The reason underlying the "pure" literati's love for Hypatia was by no means her presumed conversion to Christianity but on the contrary her faithfulness to Platonism and to Hellenism, attacked by cultural barbarism from inside as well as by the ethnic barbarism from outside the empire's borders. In this fully lay predilection for Hypatia, modern poets have realized a bridge with the Alexandrians that goes beyond all other literature. As Charles Péguy wrote:

What we love and honor is this miracle of faithfulness, . . . that a soul could be so perfectly in harmony with the Platonic soul and its descendant, the Plotinian one, and generally with the Hellenic soul, with the soul of her race, of her master, of her father: in a harmony so profound, so intimate, as to reach the very sources and roots, so that in a total annihilation, when her entire world, the whole world, was losing its accord, throughout the temporal life of the world and perhaps of eternity, she alone remained in harmony until her death.

The following are the words of an epigram attributed to Palladas, whose translations, starting with the Latin one by Grotius, have shown debatable Christian allusions and only seldom have understood its definite and secretive astrological meanings:

> Quando ti vedo m'inchino e quando odo
> le tue parole guardo la casa
> astrale della vergine:
> poiché i tuoi atti si segnano in cielo,
> Ipazia venerata, perfezione
> di ogni discorso,
> stella purissima della filosofia.

I bow when I see you, and when I hear / your words I look / at the astral house of the virgin: / because your acts are traced in the heavens, / venerated Hypatia, perfection / of all speech, / purest star of philosophy.

Leconte de Lisle envisioned her as "the last chaste beam from the heavens of the Gods," gifted with "Plato's breath and Aphrodite's body," and—reversing Diodata's conclusion but still with the same freedom— imagined not Hypatia's conversion, but a return of Cyril's followers to paganism:

> Et la terre écoutait, de ton rêve charmée,
> Chanter l'abeille attique entre tes lèvres d'or. . . .
>
> Le grave enseignement des vertus éternelles
> S'épanchait de ta lèvre au fond des coeurs charmés;
> Et les Galiléens qui te rêvaient des ailes
> Oubliaient leur Dieu mort pour tes Dieux bien aimés.

And earth, enchanted by your dream, / heard the buzzing of the Attic bee between your golden lips. . . . / The grave teaching of eternal virtues / flowed from your lips down to the bottom of enchanted hearts; / and the Galileans, seeing you winged in their dreams, / forgot their dead God for your beloved Gods.

The second poem by Leconte de Lisle describes these gods of Neoplatonism in Hypatia's exchange with Cyril:

> . . . tels que les ont vus de sublimes esprits:
> Dans l'espace étoilé n'ayant point de demeures,
> Forces de l'Univers, Vertus intérieures,
> De la Terre et du Ciel concours harmonieux
> Qui charme la pensée et l'oreille et les yeux.

. . . such as they were seen by the sublime spirits: / without dwelling in the starry expanse, / Forces of the Universe, interior Virtues, / harmonious concourse of Earth and Sky, / which charms the mind, the ear and the eye.

"Black holes, invisible stars with a prodigious force of attraction," do exist also in the firmament of human memory, writes Mario Luzi in his *Libro d'Ipazia*. The word *hypáte*, etymologically connected with the concept of something acute and dominant, a feminine superlative derived from the preposition *hypér*, designates the highest note in the Greek musical scale. For Luzi the name of the daughter of Theon is a mantra-name: from which is issued "a flow, message or warning or reserve of an unexpressed power." Why Alexandria? why Hypatia? Luzi wonders, the latest one to tell her story, taking poetic license with time and space, aware of not actually being interested, as a poet, "in those people glimpsed between the summary lines of a philologist," aware of not really being "led to recognize them." History "is not finished only because it has happened"; in fact no poet speaks except in the first person of the present tense; but as a modern poet, Luzi is not afraid of poetic unfaithfulness. On the contrary, he celebrates it:

> Questo timore d'infedeltà . . . a che cosa, diciamo al preciso struggimento
> dell'attimo come fu vissuto—o come ci parve.
> Eppure quale realtà è più reale in sé
> che nella sua trasformazione in altro. . . .

> This fear of infidelity . . . to what, to the precise torment / of the moment
> as it was lived—or as we liked it. / Yet what reality is more reality in itself /
> than in its transformation into something else. . . .

The Judgment and Prejudices of the Sources

Originally, there were two versions of Hypatia's murder, the first pagan and the second Christian, and both of them existing also in two variants: a more moderate one and a more radical one. During the three centuries between the events and the formation of the properly Byzantine historical tradition after the Arab conquest, one of the narrations was lost for the West and was kept only in its oriental version: as we have already said, the *Chronicle* by John of Nikiû has survived in its Coptic edition. The two pagan accounts, one by Hesychius, the other by Damascius, have been passed down to us thanks to Suidas's lexicon; and from them flowed that line of interpretation leading to Voltaire, Gibbon, Kingsley, up to the contemporary Anglo-Saxon historians, who all believe in Cyril's responsibility.

Damascius was a pagan and therefore hostile to the bishop. Also, in the Arian (*dyssebès*) Philostorgius, the hint at the responsibility in the murder of the party of the Homoousians is evidently influenced by doctrinal rancor, by the will to damage his adversaries. It is interesting that some locutions present in Photius exactly correspond to those used in Suidas: perhaps their pagan and Arian sources, both undermining Cyril's reputation, drew upon the same literary tradition. But the most disseminated version remains nonetheless that of Socrates Scholasticus, whose *History* in this case probably complies with the point of view of the central Church, neither accusatory like Suidas or Philostorgius nor surely in favor of the bishop of Alexandria, as we have already seen. Socrates was lawyer (*scholastikòs*) at the court of Constantinople, but surely not Cyril's advocate.

Besides its diffusion in the West, starting with Cassiodorus's *Historia tripartita,* the story of Hypatia was passed down to later Byzantine historiography: to the *Chronicle* of Malala, close to the court clergy but mainly to the Church of Antioch, traditionally hostile to the Alexandrian Church; to Theophanes' *Chronicle,* during iconoclasm; to Photius in the ninth century; to Suidas in the tenth; to Nicephorus Callistus Xanthopoulos in the fourteenth. The condemnation of Cyril's politics in the ecclesiastical sources from mediaeval Byzantium certainly derives from the stories of the fifth and the sixth centuries A.D., from their influence as well as from the manuscript tradition; but the very fact they were so carefully handed down has perhaps an explanation of its own.

The fifth century was equally dominated by Christological disputes as by barbaric invasions. While the ethnic crisis in the Mediterranean Empire expanded the social turmoil, in the *poleis,* the wars between the internal factions of young Christianity were intertwined with but also prevailed over the ongoing fight against paganism. After the disputes over the Trinity in the fourth century, in which the Arian heresy had been defeated and the Alexandrian doctrine had been established as the true one by the first ecumenical council in Constantinople, the relationship between the divine and human nature of the God-Word made flesh engaged the schools of the East in a new and larger argument, in which theology was more openly transformed into politics; and the "people of the Church" became its instrument. Never as in this epoch of migrations of races and powers had the intelligentsia's theses been able to mobilize the masses to such a degree. Never before had those abstract propositions compelled tumultuous crowds out onto the streets because of one word, however full of significance, as when in Constantinople Nestorius, Cyril's adversary, changed the appellative of the Virgin Mary from *Theotókos* into *Christotókos.*

For twenty more years Cyril continued to defend with the same aggressiveness the anti-Nestorian Christological doctrine later named Monophysitism. This doctrine seemed to be accompanied everywhere by a wake of violence, perhaps because the *parabalani* always seemed to accompany their bishop. The controversy with Nestorius began in 430 A.D., and in the next year, during the first session of the Council of Ephesus, the Alexandrians, under the guide of Shenoute, a turbulent ascetic, intimidated and prevailed over the gathered fathers. Eighteen years later the same situation was repeated with the new patriarch of Constantinople, Flavian, in opposition with Dioscorus, Cyril's successor. The first two Councils of Ephesus, the one held in 431, with its street demonstrations punctuating the sessions, and the second in 449 A.D., not by chance nicknamed the "Council of Brigands" (*latrocinium*), imposed a negative mark on the political strategies and the Christological doctrine of the bishop of Alexandria. In 451 the canons of the Council of Chalcedon fully disavowed them both.

At the beginning of the century the attitude of the Church and a precise imperial order had protected the bishop of Alexandria. The Alexandrian clergy was not yet in the least suspected of heresy; on the contrary, Athanasius, the champion of Nicean orthodoxy against Arianism, was Alexandrian. Moreover, Pulcheria Augusta was a personal supporter of the Alexandrian Christianity and of Bishop Cyril. The Roman prefect Orestes in his confrontation with the bishop was opposing the most authoritative representative of the Church. Eventually, the Council of Chalcedon reversed the situation and condemned Monophysitism, if not Cyril's doctrine, perhaps only because he had died ten years before.

The orthodox Byzantine Church proclaimed the troublesome bishop of Alexandria saint, but the Monophysite Coptic Church rejected as heretical the Chalcedonian canons and went so far as to choose Cyril of Alexandria as their father and master, calling him "the judge of the ecumenical world," "Cyril the Pharaoh." They remained faithful, almost as if it were a banner, to his definition of the unique and only nature of God-Logos made flesh (*mìa physis tòu theòu lògou sesarkoméne*), fully approving the acts of violence of 415, as we have already seen in John of Nikiû. This is another reason why Cyril, although remaining within the orthodoxy and consequently present in the theological tradition and in the work of the compilers of patristic *catenae*, actually was under much discussion or at least uneasily dealt with by the official Church, in a moment when the latter was in the process of dismissing its more extremist factions, and oddly enough more tainted with Platonism.

> The Monophysites saw in him the scholar par excellence, the undisputed master to follow and obey in everything. The Nestorians, conversely, could never curse him enough. The Church sometimes held a rather difficult position between these two heresies, especially bearing in mind that the bishop of Alexandria had been appointed by Pope Celestine to proceed with the deposition and examination of Nestorius, and that he had presided at the Council of Ephesus in the name of the Pope. (Bardy)

The predominant Byzantine culture's hatred of Monophysitism is after all a sign of anti-Egyptian resentment. The condemnation of 451

A.D. brought about the extinction of Hellenism in Egypt, as the Council's sanction was followed by the decline of the Greek language and by the consequent adoption of Coptic in the liturgy. Virtually defeated at the middle of the fifth century A.D., the heretical branches of the Nestorian and Monophysite doctrine survived for centuries in the area of the empire: under different ways and different names they thrived and were disseminated from Armenia to Tibet throughout the Middle Ages. If considering them the causes of the scant resistance offered by Egypt against the Arab invasion is simply a commonplace, in any case it is evident that the doctrinal separation was the symptom of a cultural and political dissent from Byzantium. The Nestorian and Monophysite Churches settled in the Islamized territories. Their reciprocal contacts and conflicts with Constantinople's culture marked the second iconoclasm and the first Fatimid era, at the dawn of Byzantine encyclopedism. Its most typical exponent is the very Suidas who narrates Hypatia's story at length. Hence, perhaps, the survival and the revitalization of the ancient sources, even in their literary styles, where Christian and pagan perspectives converge to accuse Cyril.

It is to this redoubled perspective that we owe the posthumous transfiguration of the figure of Hypatia. If we take into account, one by one, the traits conferred on this personage by the sources, we would realize rather clearly that they are mostly imaginary. From episodes like the *aischrourgìa*, for instance, reported in Suidas's article and rightly compared to Ipparchia's *Kynogamia*, and other characteristics of her behavior, such as "to appear without false modesty among male audiences" or her "freedom of speech," *parrhesia*, which all may now wrongly appear obvious, emerges a commonplace Stoic-Cynic connotation of Hypatia, in contrast with the true elements in our possession.

In fact, the sources themselves testify that Hypatia was no longer young; moreover, both Suidas and Socrates reckoned the year of her birth to be 370 A.D.: in that era a woman of forty-five was already considered old, *palaia*. This datum is also confirmed by Malalas, who like Socrates recognizes Cyril not as the direct instigator of the murder, but as the one morally responsible. "Having received carte blanche from their bishop, the Alexandrians assaulted Hypatia and burnt her on a pyre of brushwood. She was a famous philosopher, enjoyed a great reputation, and was an old woman."

Probably the same can be said about the physical appearance of the daughter of Theon, who according to Suidas was "extraordinarily beautiful and handsome" (*sphodrà kalé te ouasa kài eueidés*). If the "perfection" and the "purity" that Palladas bestowed on her are to be understood as an astral allusion, the haughty beauty attributed to her by the fifth-century pagans had much less to do with the romantic imagery of nineteenth-century historians than with class superiority and the gift of aristocratic discretion, which together with the natural sense of social duty and of political commitment characterized the upper classes in antiquity.

Much debate has centered upon the meaning of the adverb *demosìa* used in Suidas's account, which was probably drawn from that of Damascius, to describe Hypatia's role as a teacher. Somebody translated it as "officially in charge," suggesting that Hypatia held her lectures, like her father Theon, at the Museum, or that she held in any case a teaching position subsidized either by the revenue office or directly by the local treasury. But on the basis of both classical and Byzantine usage, that meaning of the word is not necessarily apparent, and we could more correctly translate it as "publicly," in a "public" and "frequented place," that is, in the streets. This is the interpretation of the passage by all the ancient writers. Yet we can rule out that in those days an exponent of the Greek aristocracy in Alexandria would go around on foot preaching Plato: stones were flying in the air even against the prefect of Egypt into his own carriage. Hypatia's must have been tightly sealed on the way from Orestes' palace to her family residence, so much envied by the Christian bishop.

Following Praechter at the beginning of this century, some scholars have manifested a legitimate scepticism towards Suidas's information. On the basis of both the heterodox and pagan traditions, it appears that the Byzantine lexicon and its sources had purposely gathered data to discredit Cyril and to substantiate an image of Hypatia that was as close to Christianity as possible. For instance, Suidas or his sources are not concerned with describing reality as much as freeing the philosophical teaching from its aristocratic imprint and making it similar to "popular" preaching of the Cynic type. (But a dedicated pupil of hers, Synesius, asks himself: "What can ordinary people and philosophy have in common?") Suidas says she used to wear the *tribon,* not an ordinary cape as some translate it, but the uniform, as we said before, of the street philosopher. Now, during the religious persecution of pagan Hellenism, the model of Cynic philosopher was the one most easily tolerated by the Church, the last to disappear from a Christianized world, fading into the model of the Christian "holy man." The image of Hypatia given by both Suidas and his sources is actually an already hagiographical image, in accordance with the figure of a "public" saint or "civic consultant" evoked by Brown.

Synesius, Hypatia, and "Philosophia"

"Isidore was very different from Hypatia not only in the ways a man can be different from a woman, but as much as a true philosopher can be different from a woman well versed in geometry." In writing the biography of his teacher Isidore, Damascius is a well-informed witness from pagan circles and belonging moreover to the Platonic guild. Certainly the statement in the *Life of Isidore* might not convince us that Hypatia's teaching was limited to scientific initiation, which for the Platonists was the prelude to any philosophy. It might very well have been that the exponents of the metaphysical Athenian wing of Neoplatonism, rival of the Alexandrian one, fostered hostility, underestimation, or incomprehension for the members of the latter. But it is the work itself of Theon and Hypatia, or at least whatever has been preserved by direct or indirect tradition, to suggest that father and daughter did not teach the theory of Platonism but rather its technical mathematical, geometrical, and astronomical preliminaries.

According to Suidas, Hypatia wrote commentaries on classics, not on Plato or the Neoplatonists, but rather on Apollonius of Perga's *Conics* and Diophantus's *Algebra*. Hypatia's name is associated with an essay called *Astronomical Canon* by the sources (probably a commentary on the *Easy Tables* by Ptolemy). Hers is probably the "revision" (*paragnosis*) or, according to the recent hypothesis by Alan Cameron, the editing of the text of the third book of Ptolemy's *Almagestus* within Theon's commentary itself. One can in fact read, in the title passed on by the main witness of the manuscript tradition: "Edition revised by my daughter Hypatia, the philosopher." If we look closer at those pages, we can convince ourselves that Hypatia must truly have been a "master of geometry," as Damascius writes. She must have invented machines built by her disciples: a flat astrolabe, a hydroscope, and an aerometer, according to Synesius himself.

The supposed mystery of Hypatia's works and the hypothesis that other essays might have disappeared have moreover fascinated the scholars. Such a historian of sciences as Tannery has suggested "the possibility that such works still exist in a more or less cut version or under a false attribution." From various contemporary doctrines and contemporary Alexandrian philosophers it has been possible to draw the highly hypothetic conclusion that "Hypatia followed a primitive form of Neoplatonism, closer to Porphyry's than to Iamblichus's system" (Evrard in accordance with Lacombrade). On the basis of Synesius's proper type of Platonism, it has been concluded that in the Alexandrian school, "there was a neat division between the orientalizing form of Neoplatonism and its Athenian aspect: both were opposed, the former in the name of some sort of rationalism, the latter in the name of a certain neutrality towards Christianity" (Garzya). Origen's Christian Neoplatonism has also been taken into account, in as much as he, as a pupil of Ammonius, was direct witness of the middle-Platonic and non-Plotinian tradition of Alexandria. It has also been proposed that she followed the doctrine of Heracleas (Rist), to whom Christian pupils have been attributed, as they were later on to Aeneas of Gaza or John Philoponus, and eventually even to Hypatia.

But not even this is sufficient proof, as has been suggested, to speak of a "religious neutrality" (Marrou, Bregman) of the Alexandrian School. After all, if its teaching really was not straying into the realm where metaphysics and therefore religion interfere with each other, why was there so much Christian ill will (*phthònos*) for Hypatia's "astronomical knowledge," as Damascius states?

> What a marvelous subject for a poem, our journey together! It has given us the opportunity to witness what fame by itself could not prove: we have seen, we have heard the woman who is the real initiator into the mysteries and the orgies of philosophy.

So Synesius wrote, on the way back to Constantinople, after meeting Hypatia, to a scholar friend who had remained in Alexandria. The scion of an ancient family of landowners from Cyrenaica, Platonist, polygraph, politician, and eventually a Christian bishop, Synesius represents to the full the vitality, the tolerance, and at the same time the transformism characterizing the educated aristocracy in late antiquity. Trained at Hypatia's school, he left a long literary trail to posterity, unlike his teacher.

In his very many letters, almost an autobiography, connecting him to his milieu, both pagan and Christian, Synesius is the key witness of our inquiry, first as an intimate friend but second as a midway point between the protagonists of the conflict of which Hypatia remained victim. Pagan by birth, like his contemporary Augustine, converted to Christianity through the good offices of the patriarch Theophilus, the destroyer of the Serapeum, Synesius married a Christian and became a novice in that religion. As he himself said, he wanted to be initiated "into all mysteries," and Christianity was one of them. His election as bishop of Cyrene can be considered by his own admission as something of an incident, since the second canon of the Nicean Council prohibited the appointment of novices as bishops. But history later celebrated with its verdict this election, whose origin he owed to his political activism in the Pentapolis.

Synesius anyway journeyed to Egypt much earlier than these events, probably in 393 A.D., one year after Theodosius's edict and the destruction of the Serapeum. Paganism was persecuted, and Platonism was not only looked down upon by the Christians, but was also subdivided into factions, *sectae,* in competition with one another. "Today it is Egypt that keeps the seeds of wisdom alive, which it receives from Hypatia. Conversely, once the seat of wise men, Athens is now honored only by beekeepers: it is not by chance that the couple of sophists, Plutarch's students, who have remained there, draw the young to their school not with fame, not with eloquence, but with jars of Hymettos honey," writes Synesius in a letter. Hypatia is the "most venerated philosopher, cherished by God." The other pupils of the Alexandrian school are "a blessed group listening to the admirable voice" of the woman who will remain for ever "adored teacher," "benefactress," "mother, sister, teacher, patroness," "supreme judge," "blessed lady" with a "most celestial soul." Years later, in his eighty-first letter, Synesius wrote to her: "Believe me, you are the only treasure that, together with virtue, cannot be taken away from me."

Teacher and pupil are of the same age, and they were only twenty-three at the time of their first encounter. Strangely coupled in their destiny, they shall die in different places but almost at the same time. Synesius will not know about her death but shortly before it, paraphrasing the Homeric *Nostoi,* he sent her a distich that has the power of an epitaph:

> If the dead in Hades are doomed to forgetfulness
> Even down there I will remember my beloved Hypatia.

In his last letter, prostrate after the death of his young children ("Synesius should have lived only before knowing the evil of life"), he wrote these words to her: "If you do care at all about my affairs, well enough; otherwise, I do not care either."

Some activities considered "more subterranean" still within Platonism were attributed to the nearly two years of their relationship in Alexandria. Synesius might be identified with the *anèr physikòs,* inventor of a new model of alembic and the author of a contemporary treatise on alchemy bearing on the title page the dedication "to a priest of the great Serapeum." In his epistles Synesius twice repeats that "geometry is a sacred matter"; elsewhere he speaks about the virtues of *tetraktys,* symbol of Iamblichus's Neoplatonic-Pythagorean numerology. If the hints at the initiation secret in the *Epistle to Herculianus* can be evidence of some sort of esoteric teaching, in *Dion,* dedicated to Hypatia, there are certainly hidden "inviolable doctrines" (*abèbela dògmata*):

> Like those Athenian artists who in their statues had Aphrodite and the Charites embraced by Sileni and Satyrs, he who is not unable to grasp the traits of the divine even if veiled by a base aspect will not miss that my book reveals more than a few inviolable doctrines, which remain concealed to the profane thanks to my ability to dissimulate and to the great ease with which they have been placed into my speech, so that it appears as if they have been naturally fit in.

The treatise *On Dreams* "was written," Synesius writes, "all in one night, yet in that final part of the night which brought that dream that compelled me to write it, and sometimes, twice or three times, it seemed to me that I was a third person, the listener to myself." Besides Porphyry, Synesius very often quotes the Chaldean *lògia:*

> Do not tilt toward the world the Black Light
> Beneath which lies the unformed treacherous Abyss,
> Dark all round, vomiting Filth,
> Full of Images, void of Intellect.

A few years after the destruction of the Serapeum, the Chaldean oracles were put on the blacklist of the prohibited books. Anyone possessing them was liable to be charged with practicing magic and could incur the fearful sanctions issued after Constantine's edict and preceding that of Theodosius: Constantius's laws against "sorcerers and fortune tellers" and those of Theodosius himself against "haruspices" and "magicians." "Mathematics might in turbulent times be a dangerous science" (Rist). In those days the union of Neoplatonism with theurgic occultism could have been ruinous.

In all late antiquity it was very difficult to separate "positive" scientific interest from the irrational. Astronomy was inseparable from astrology. Theon, the last known member of the Mouseion in Alexandria, had published an essay on the birth of Sirius and another "on omens, the observation of birds, and the song of crows"; a third one, according to Malalas, concerned the writings of Hermes Trismegistus and of Orpheus. Hypatia, as Philostorgius tells us, "surpassed her father, especially in the art of studying the stars." Among others, Lacombrade—Synesius's main biographer—considered it evident that Hypatia had delivered to her acolytes "an esoteric doctrine at the margins of the official programs"; that the "technical astronomic teaching of Hypatia was simply a cover for the teaching of an esoteric revelation, one that was truly original."

In Synesius's *Discourse on Gifts,* dedicated to Peonius, one may read:

> Astronomy is in itself a more than worthy science, but it can serve to ascend to something higher, can be the last step, I believe, towards the mysteries of theology, a step befitting them: as the perfect body of the sky has matter beneath itself and its motion has been equated to the activity of the intellect by the most subtle philosophers. Astronomy proceeds with its demonstrations in an incontrovertible way, using geometry and arithmetic as subsidiaries; calling it the right canon of truth would not be unbecoming at all.

As proved by the contemporary blossoming of Judaic numerology and by Valens's persecution of the mathematicians, the technical nature of both Theon's and Hypatia's teaching not only does not exclude but rather substantiates the interest for esoterism and occultism. After all, these were practiced in some manner not only by the school of Proclus and Damascius or by the "last degeneration of the Sabi," but also by almost all the Neoplatonists. They remained rooted in neo-Byzantine Neoplatonism, which in turn will pass them down to our Renaissance together with the philosophy of Plato.

In seeing Hypatia outlined against the sunset of the Empire in the masculine clothes of a philosopher, almost as an Alexandrian Mlle. de Maupin, the nineteenth-century imagination was then once more mistaken, because Hypatia wore, much more likely, the robe of a priestess. The devotion and the exalted veneration expressed by Synesius in his letters, all the more peculiar as they are addressed to someone of the same age (as remarked by Rougé), can be explained only by a "sacred bond" between them, exactly as Synesius defined it, but "sacred" in its proper meaning, that is a priestly tie.

One might be surprised by the small number of true women philosophers in the history of philosophy. This circumstance has been attributed to the incapacity of female psychology to adapt to the rigors of speculation—a nineteenth-century opinion which can be confuted and which was never shared either by Pythagoreans in antiquity or by others in late antiquity or the Middle Ages, particularly the Greek Middle Ages. The stoic Apollonius wrote a large treatise, *On the Women Who Philosophized,* as we learn from Photius's *Bibliotheca.* Philochorus Grammaticus wrote on Pythagorean women, as Suidas tells us. The life and habits of women philosophizing were given a send-up by Juvenal and conversely described by Diogenes Laertius and Athenaeus.

In the seventeenth century, as we have already seen, Gilles Menage "by himself" discovered the existence of sixty-five women philosophers; in the following century Wolf published a catalogue of them including relative fragments from ancient works. The list included Platonic and Neoplatonic philosophers like Arria and Gemina, Cynics such as Hipparchia, Epicureans such as Theophila, Stoics such as Portia, Pythagoreans like Themistoclea, Theano, Myia, Arignote, Damo, Sara, Timycha, Lasthenia, Abrotelia, and Echecratia, and moreover Dialectics, Cyrenaics, Megarians, Aristotelians; or "of uncertain sect and most noble ones" like Julia Domna and Aconia Paulina, or the Byzantine Cassia and Anna Comnena. The list can continue through the centuries, up to the times of the "wise Eudocia," the wife of Constantine Palaeologus celebrated by Nicephorus Gregoras, or to Irene Panhypersebasta, daughter of Theodorus Metochites, a fourteenth-century woman philosopher under the last dynasty of the Eastern Greek Middle Ages.

However, as Lellia Cracco Ruggini has written, the wisdom and philosophy supposedly shared by so many female personalities had mainly become, especially among the last Neoplatonists and then among the Christians, knowledge of the divine. From the legendary Diotima to the Neoplatonic Sosipatra, a long succession of women alone, perhaps often gifted with extrasensory qualities, had been entrusted with the oral tradition of the secrets of Platonism, which Synesius also referred to in his *Dion,* when mentioning the relationship between Socrates and Aspasia, perhaps with a slight hint of self-reference. Women's superiority within the spiritual and supernatural realm is a legacy of the spirituality of late antiquity, received in turn by the Cabala as well as by the entire Middle Ages.

The Byzantine model of a woman philosopher is both Pythagorean and Platonic, and whereas in Psellus "the Egyptian woman" is associated with the Pythagorean *kat'exochèn* Theano, Eudocia is defined by Nicephorus Gregoras as "the new Theano and the second Hypatia." It is no coincidence that the highest frequency of women philosophers is present in this most irrational faction (*secta*), where there is an openly female monopoly on the priesthood. In many cases reported by compilers, esoteric knowledge is, after all, in a close relationship, like the two sides of a coin, with an "exoteric," strictly technical competence. Hypatia belonged to the latter category: on one side, undoubtedly a mathematician; on the other, darker but no less credible side, the figure of a priestess, largely documented and apropos to her sex, caste, political and teaching roles, the *diadoché* of the school of Alexandria.

Hypatia's Martyrdom

"You have always had power": this is, at a final analysis, the *dynastéia* that Synesius's eighty-first letter attributed to Hypatia; this is what the epithets of "mother" and "patroness" used by her pupil hint at, technical epithets for those "female protectors" of mystical religious associations that frequently combined together sacred and secular offices towards the end of the Roman Empire. A closer investigation of the sources belies the stereotype of the lady philosopher: in the history of philosophy Hypatia appears as "merely another to pass on the torch" (Rist). Her charismatic figure and her political role led her to both death and fame as a posthumous means of an initially pagan and then Christian propaganda: Hypatia, the victim of Christians, owes her renown to the ancient and modern Church because it bestowed on her the status of martyr.

Hypatia's kind of philosophy must therefore be placed first in the history of the relationship between women and the sacred in both pagan and Christian contexts and then in the history of thought; while the way she died granted her another role, that of martyr, certainly not unusual for women. Martyrdom, together with the vow of chastity, another greatly stressed quality of hers, is a regular feature of the "eminent" woman in ancient religious literature. Roman religiosity had already compiled exemplary models of sacrificial virgins. As virgin and martyr, Hypatia passed from Damascius's pagan mythology directly to the Christian mythology. Hypatia's death is described in terms of real and true sacrifice already in the ancient sources. Damascius calls her murderers *hòi sphagèis,* "the immolators"; Socrates and Philostorgius use the verb *diaspào,* the technical expression to indicate the dismemberment of the victim. The fifth century saw noble and educated female saints equally among pagans and Christians: their doctrine, especially if divulged to the public (*demosìa*), is another characteristic of the martyrs, as the trial of Socrates, alongside Christ's, is one of the two great archetypes of the Christian trial literature.

The Christian Church, the Roman government, and the Jewish community form a triangular structure underlying not only the most ancient narration of Hypatia's story, that of Socrates Scholasticus, but usually also those Christian accounts of trials called "martyrdoms," which in fact "testify" ways and modes of death sentences perceived as unjust. The roles of the accuser and of the executioner can be played by the official authorities or the masses, or by both. Literature of this kind has in fact the ultimate task of toning down, instead of enhancing, the conflict between Christianity and the Roman government. As recent scholars have pointed out, it is not by chance that the same characters keep recurring and the final verdict is always the same; that the burden of political responsibility for the murder is placed on culturally "extraneous" and religiously "impious" characters—for instance very often on the Jews—in this way avoiding having to blame the Roman authorities; and that the top representatives of the latter are usually depicted with those qualities of indecision already typical of Pilate in the Evangelic prototype. In Hypatia's case what made the stereotype of the governor-Pilate again useful was the analogous intent to lay the blame not so much or not entirely on the Jews, but on the "impious" Alexandrian clergy, the enemy of paganism on one side, and of orthodoxy itself on the other, at least for some of the Byzantine sources.

Historians have often used the term "drama" to define the contrast between Cyril and Hypatia. As has been observed, in Christian literature the genre of martyrdom is both a use of, and a sublimation into, trials of the classical dramatic genre, with preassigned roles and fixed characters: a genre that is objective and chronicle-like only in appearance, but in actual terms political and propagandistic. It is then neither improper nor casual if Hypatia's story has been written by Diodata Saluzzo or celebrated by Péguy in terms of martyrdom. As a martyr and not a philosopher, Hypatia is robbed of her leading role and of the status that the events of her life have assumed in the feminist literature, because her death and her transfiguration by the hand of historians are not an exception, but a confirmation of the fixed roles in the traditional and male perspective underlying them.

The opposition between Hypatia and Cyril has been traditionally understood as a conflict between religions and between contrasting "philosophies" or worldviews, as a confessional and ideological drama where the protagonist pays with her life for the freedom of speech, *parrhesia,* that is proper to pagan philosophy. A freedom that is a point of controversy with the Christian bishop, a male figure in opposition to her, the aggressive champion of a popular faith, whereas she represented aristocratic Hellenism, closer to the tolerant pragmatism of the Roman government and against Christian radicalism. But this view is only in part true, as the drama is more concretely and more contingently a political one. Here Orestes, representing the power of the state, plays a role that was equal to Cyril's, and the Jews are the chorus. The elements in conflict were not so much paganism against Christianity as the ruling (both local and Roman) classes, the social classes (ancient aristocracy and the new Church "bureaucracy"), and the bellicose ethnic groups, within the climate of instability that characterized the transference of power and the installation of Christianity in the life and the city structures of the late Roman Empire.

The history of philosophy has pointed out the artificiality of the opposition between pagan and Christian Platonism: "What estranged the old aristocratic literati or at least kept them away from Christianity for a certain time was not paganism in itself as much as the religion of culture, the classical ideal of *paidéia,* the *helleniké diagogé* or Greek way of living presented in Synesius's *Dion* as the most fecund and mainly effective method for cultivating one's mind" (Marrou). The opportunity to integrate Greek *paidéia* and Christian culture had already been felt and appealed to. The Christian Church persecuted ritual paganism, but from the fourth century A.D. had maintained a relative neutrality toward intellectual paganism and the teaching of philosophy. Cyril's main aim was the direct participation of the bishops in running the imperial state both in theory and practice. The target of his policy was not an ideological confrontation with pagan intellectuals, yet rather the cultic predominance in the city and the management of social disputes. The masses and not the elite—by now partly acculturated, coopted, and concordant, as Synesius's example demonstrates—were his problem. Hence Cyril's bipolar political strategies: persecutions against the concurrent Jewish ethnic group, as previously against the rival Novazianists, and the destruction of the temples, in compliance, after all, with the imperial wishes.

We have so arrived both at the core of the problem and at the end of this trial. The relevance bestowed on the history of Hypatia by the historians of the late antiquity and hence by mediaeval and modern historians is not centered on Hypatia's importance or on the essence of her character, as much as on the stature of Cyril: Hypatia is, in this drama, the false protagonist. Once the first trial is finished, should we want to start a trial against the bishop of Alexandria, we would have on the defendants' bench the whole ruling class and Platonism itself, implicated as it was in the great Arian as well as Nestorian and Monophysite controversies.

Was Cyril guilty of Hypatia's death? As with the ancient and mediae-val texts, one should also wonder about the impartiality of the modern ones. This question, posed by many historians, has developed more preg-nant meaning: could Christianity help being involved in the harshest methods of politics, in contagious violence, in fanaticism? Ecclesiasti-cal sources have put off the answer to this question until the Reforma-tion and the modern centuries. In the Protestant or Anglican literary manipulation of the figure of Hypatia, direct participation in the cam-paign against heresies, inaugurated by the Byzantines, prevailed over the poetic transformation, pre-Raphaelite and "ornate," and tinted with sadism.

On the lay side, the Damascius/Gibbon line, their judgement or preju-dice or ultimately the meaning given to Hypatia's story is simply the condemnation of the Church. According to these historians, Christianity, an all-encompassing doctrine and therefore with totalitarian tendencies, would superimpose the *polis* and would oppose the tolerance typical of the lay wise man, the philosopher. To recall Brown's image, the substi-tution of the bishop for the philosopher led to a deterioration of life in the *polis* and to a progressive decadence of politics up to contemporary times. But this interpretation is also proved false by our own discussion.

The lesson that Hypatia's story and her long historical survival can teach us is then, only or above all, methodological. In the shifting nu-ances of the various interpretations of this ancient public murder and this mysterious female character, what clearly emerges is not as much the end of paganism as the metamorphosis of Christianity, how its political thought has evolved and how the historical writer's point of view on it has equally developed critically.

(translated by Massimo Carlucci)

NINE

MELANIA THE SAINT

Andrea Giardina

Melania the Younger was a Roman noblewoman who abandoned her family, wealth, and privileges out of contempt for the world and aspired to emulate the chastity of angels in her mortal body. Many women of the Roman aristocracy had preceded her in taking such drastic steps. For over half a century, various forms of asceticism had begun to attract the mothers, wives, and daughters of Rome's rich and powerful senators. There had been a notable example even in Melania's own family. Her grandmother, Melania the Elder, niece of Antony Marcellinus, consul in A.D. 341, had devoted her life to prayer and penitence at the age of twenty-two after the deaths of her husband and of two of her three children. In 372 Melania the Elder left Rome and journeyed to Alexandria to pay a visit to the Desert Fathers. She later settled in Palestine, where she lived for twenty-seven years and founded a convent housing fifty virgins on the Mount of Olives.

By comparison, there was nothing unique about the decision of her granddaughter, Melania the Younger, to withdraw from the world and transform her life. Yet there are two reasons why she deserves an important place in this gallery of ancient Roman women.

First, and most specific, is the extraordinary mixture of radicalism and conformity with which she played her part as a holy personage. Second, there exists a detailed record of her life written by an excellent biographer. Despite its obvious stylistic weaknesses, often pointed out by modern critics, the *Life of Melania* is a consistent, richly detailed text in which explicit and oblique messages intertwine to create a complex portrait of this woman. The author has been commonly identified as Gerontius, a Monophysite monk who succeeded her as head of the convents she founded, after her death on December 31, 439.

In cases like this, it is somewhat difficult to distinguish the literary personage from the real person. Authors of saints' lives, in obedience to the rules of their genre, generally tend to reduce the more personal aspects of their character in order to stress their exemplary virtues. It is also true, however, that saints tend to create their own identities, not only by following ethical codes of behavior but by modeling themselves on accounts of lives of other saints they have read about. Thus we could say that the story of any saint's life may contain a large number of literary allusions. Yet this never succeeds in obscuring the protagonist's identity completely. Looking closely at hagiographic documents, we will see that their great charm lies in the tension they embody between the general and the particular, between the constant and the variation.

Melania's parents were Valerius Publicola, the sole surviving son of Melania the Elder, and Ceionia Albina, whose illustrious family tree included the emperor Lucius Verus. At the age of fourteen, according to the custom of the time, Melania was given in marriage to her cousin, Valerius Pinian, the seventeen-year-old son of a former prefect of Rome. The combined fortunes of this young couple represented one of the largest patrimonies of the era, although as a young bride, possession of such an enormous fortune seems to have made little impression on her. She was deeply impressed, however, by her eccentric grandmother, after whom she had been named, and who had personally received a splinter of the True Cross from the hands of the Bishop of Jerusalem. "Her parents," Palladius tells us, "forced her to marry one of the most important men in Rome, but she was continually intrigued by the stories she heard about her grandmother, and these stories ate away at her until she could no more feel bound to her marriage" (*Historia Lausiaca* 61.1).

Melania would have preferred to take the vow of virginity, remaining uncontaminated by luxury and by the flesh, but it was easier for a poor girl than for a noble maiden to hold onto her virginity. Young girls like Melania were inexorably destined, from the first cries they uttered upon coming into the world, to become the instrument of marriage strategies planned by their parents. Melania surrendered to marriage in obedience to her parents, who wished to ensure the continuity of the family line and to keep their patrimony intact. Her plans for her own life remained unchanged: she intended to follow her grandmother's example, scandalize good Roman society, and dedicate her existence to the Lord.

Birth as an Experience of Death

Melania's attitude to motherhood was instrumental in helping her obtain the freedom she desired. A few days after the wedding ceremony, she told her husband:

My lord, if you want to practice chastity together with me and live with me under a discipline of continence, I will recognize you as my lord and master. But if you cannot accept this and cannot cool the passions of your youth, I will lay all my wealth and property at your feet and allow you to do with it as you please. But release my body so that I may present it immaculate to Christ, along with my soul, on fearful Day of Judgment. This is the only way, according to the Lord, that I can satisfy my desire (*Life of Melania* 1).

From that moment, Pinian treated his wife with the indulgent and submissive devotion that was to characterize their entire marriage. He agreed to the principle of chastity, which presupposed their renunciation of the world, but only on one condition: they had to produce two children to inherit their material wealth. His wife complied and their first child, a daughter, was immediately consecrated to virginity. If Melania's first pregnancy was experienced as boring routine, the second proved harrowing. When it was nearly time, like a martyr herself, she prayed without ceasing all night long in the Church of Saint Lawrence the Martyr, never resting for a moment. Kneeling in the church at dawn, Melania begged the Lord to release her from this life "as she had desired ever since the beginning." Now that she was about to give birth to her second child, she yearned for solitude. We do not know if it was in response to her prayer or a result of the innumerable genuflections performed during her nocturnal vigil (an unintentional abortion?), or both perhaps, but the delivery was difficult and the birth premature. A boy was born but died shortly after being baptized (5).

The act of giving birth was deliverance only insofar as it was an experience of death. Her biographer describes a few miracles she performed (women saints generally perform fewer miracles than men), one of which was in connection with maternity, but in a negative sense. A woman lay in agony, wracked with the pain caused by the dead fetus in her womb. Melania intervened and helped the woman deliver her stillborn infant. This incident provided the basis of a powerful lesson for her virgin disciples, "See what sufferings the Lord has spared us!" Melania, midwife of stillborn children, plainly pointed out the misery of the female condition and extolled virginity as the only road to redemption (61).

When Salome asked the Lord, "How long will death lord it over us?" the Lord replied, "As long as you women give birth" (Clement of Alexandria *Stromata* 3.6.45). Procreation may give the illusion of continuing life but in reality it only serves to propagate death. Stifling sexual desire and defending the treasure of one's virginity was the only true way to conquer death, for it released a person from the illusion of earthly continuity.

For Whom Melania Shed No Tears

The cooling of motherly affection in favor of absolute dedication to God is a recurring theme in the stories of Christian matrons from late antiquity. Jerome poignantly portrays the scene of Paula's departure from Ostia, a journey that was to be without return: Paula is on board the ship. Her youngest son reaches out to her from the shore; her daughter, old enough to be married, begs her to put off her departure until her wedding day, but their mother gazes dry-eyed toward the horizon. "She ignored the mother in herself in order to become the handmaid of the Lord." Paula's love of God and her eagerness to see the holy places triumph over her most deeply rooted human attachments, but this repudiation of motherhood was no easy or spontaneous decision. Jerome describes Paula's choice as the outcome of a painful struggle in which a keen awareness of irreparable loss remained.

> Her whole being was in torment as if her limbs were being torn from her. She fought against her pain: far more admirable than all others was she for a greater love was overcome. In the hands of the enemy and in the hardship of prison, nothing is more cruel than parents being separated from their children. Her faith bore up under this pain against the demands of nature, and her soul found pleasure in it and desired it ... The ship sailed on across the sea, and while all her traveling companions looked back toward the shore, she gazed in the other direction, for she could not look back without torment. No one, I confess, loved her children as much as she did: before her departure, she gave them all she owned, disinheriting herself on earth to find an inheritance in heaven (Jerome *Epistles* 108.5 ff).

Many similar examples could be cited, but perhaps Paulinus of Nola best summed up this attitude describing Melania the Elder's detachment from her last surviving son. "A wholesome enlightenment" had inspired her. "She gave her child love by abandoning him and kept him with her by sending him away" (Paulinus of Nola *Epistles* 29.9).

This same detachment was also expressed on the occasion of the death of family members. In many Christian texts of the era, the death of a spouse is treated as a positive event, because it allows the survivor to live a fully "angelic" existence. Jerome describes Pammachius after the death of his wife Paulina. "Paulina will sleep so that he may awake. She has preceded her husband, leaving behind a servant of Christ." When her husband and two of her children died, Melania the Elder exclaimed, "I will serve you better now, O Lord, since you have freed me from such a heavy burden" (Jerome *Epistles* 78.10.1, 39, 5.5). Jerome also says that after the death of her beloved husband, Paula dedicated herself so intensely to the service of the Lord that it seemed she had wished for his death (108.5.1).

This attempt to view mourning as a positive experience, made more tolerable by the certainty of joining one's spouse after the end of earthly life, did not imply the denial of pain. Pain was not in question here, but rather one's way of dealing with it. To console Paula for the death of her daughter, Blesilla, Jerome wrote her a letter (*Epistles* 39) in which he gently rebukes her for her unconsolable sorrow, so unbefitting a Christian saint. The fathers of the church encouraged their disciples to assume a stoic attitude toward the death or desertion of their spouses. Weeping and wailing, tearing one's clothes, intoning dirges were all very far from the austere composure expected of the virgins, widows, and mothers who had devoted themselves to the Lord. Yet the ecclesiastical authorities also realized that "opposing reason to pain" was no easy task. Resisting the onslaughts of fear and sorrow while maintaining an unperturbed attitude of calm reflection signified elevating oneself above human nature.

Melania was deeply distressed by her mother's death: "she spent that year in deep pain" (41). And she was even more distressed by her husband's death, for she kept vigil near his tomb and fasted for nearly four years (49). If we wish to understand Melania's personality, however, it would be useful to dwell on the tears she did not shed. It is not surprising that she endured her father's agony with a "bold spirit," for although he had done his best to hinder her saintly aspirations, he repented on his deathbed and implored her forgiveness (7). Her reaction to her children's death is surprising, however. It seems she did not suffer at all when her infant son died, but seized this occasion as a pretext to put away her silk gowns forever, thereby furthering her plans to renounce luxury and break away from social conventions without causing a scandal (6). When her daughter died at the age of twelve, Melania accepted it dry-eyed and saw it as an opportunity to accelerate her withdrawal from the world. Her biographer does not even tell us the daughter's name and includes no incidents indicating Melania's feelings for her. He very clearly points out that it was not the loss of her children that caused Melania's repulsion against marriage (as was the case for other women saints). On the contrary, her moral and emotional rejection of marriage preceded the deaths of her two children, which she viewed almost as a providential liberation, free of any connotation of mourning. This radical emotional situation is confirmed by Palladius's banal attempt to explain it, for he claims that her hatred of marriage began with the death of her children (*Historia Lausiaca* 61.2). Palladius also, incidentally, mentions that Melania had a brother, about whom we know nothing.

Subversive Charity

Poverty was a prerequisite for spiritual ascent, but was not easy for the wealthy to attain, or for those who had powerful relatives. Usually when a widow or, as in our case, a young married couple, expressed the scandalous intention of giving away their patrimonies to charity, their families intervened to prevent them. In this, disapproving relatives could count on the help of the public authorities who controlled the senators' patrimonies, so as to safeguard the survival of the aristocratic families and consequently, the stability of the ruling class.

Melania and Pinian's relatives reacted violently to their plans, as did several senators. "They fought like wild beasts," Palladius reports (*Historia Lausiaca* 54.5). Among the most fervent opponents were Pinian's brother, Severus, who, according to their biographer, was under the influence of demons (10), and Melania's father, Publicola. Her father perhaps deserved a more sympathetic treatment than he received in the sources, for he had twice experienced the trauma of rejection: first, by his mother, Melania the Elder, who abandoned him after he had already lost his father and two brothers, and then by his daughter. Doubtless he deeply regretted naming his daughter after his mother, for the choice of that name had predestined the girl to follow her grandmother's example.

Aside from the obstacles posed by relatives and the authorities, there were other reasons why it was not easy for very wealthy people to dispossess themselves suddenly of everything they owned. The first problem was the actual substance of their wealth. Melania and Pinian were among the wealthiest aristocrats of their time. The estate owned by one of them alone provided them with an income sufficient to feed 29,000 people for a year. In Rome they owned a palace so sumptuous no one else could afford to buy it, and it was eventually burned down when the city was sacked by Alaric. They also had a villa in an outlying area of

Rome, where "thousands" of slaves worked, and many lands and estates scattered about the empire, in Campania, Sicily, Spain, Numidia, Mauretania, Africa, Brittany, and Gaul (*Life of Melania* and Palladius, 61.5).

The dismantling of this huge amount of property was made even more difficult by its extremely widespread and varied geographical distribution. Another obstacle was the almost natural tendency of wealth to increase in late antiquity. A passage from the *Life of Macrina* (20) by Gregory of Nyssa best illustrates this point: when Macrina's parents died, their property was divided among nine children, but after a few years the individual portion of each of the heirs had increased so greatly that it surpassed the original gross amount. Although this may be an exaggeration, Gregory's statement is indicative of a general tendency created by the enormous social imbalances of the era.

The last obstacle was perhaps the great seductive power that this immense wealth had over Melania, despite her determination to become a saint. It appears that gold gave her hallucinations. One day after she and her husband had brought some "forty-five thousand pounds" of gold into the house, to distribute to the poor and the holy, she had a vision in which she saw the house filled with flickering flames and heard the devil whisper, "What is this kingdom of heaven that may be bought with such riches?" (17). Sometimes the devil would bring back old memories to Melania, reminding her of a beloved villa she once owned, probably situated in Sicily:

> "We used to have an estate that everyone admired," Melania recalled. "The splendor of its baths was unequaled anywhere else in the world. On one side lay the sea and on the other a wood rich with varied kinds of trees, teeming with boar, deer, and other woodland animals. From the swimming pool, bathers could view the boats running before the wind, then look to the other side and observe the animals at the edge of the wood. Here too the devil found opportunities for mischief, for he would cause me to rest my eyes on its varied and beautiful marbles and would bring to my mind the enormous income received from that villa. Located round the baths there were, in fact, sixty-two dwellings" (18).

Christian authors did not believe that it was necessary for a person to give away all his property at once in order to lead a saintly life. There were, in fact, more reasonable and socially useful ways of making the transition from extreme wealth to extreme poverty. Jerome praised Paula because she did not completely disinherit her children: "She loved her children so much that before leaving, she gave them all her property, disinheriting herself on earth to find her inheritance in heaven" (*Epistles* 108.6.5). We must interpret the phrase "all her property" to mean everything that she had not yet given to the poor (see 5.1). Marcella had wanted to give everything she owned to the poor, but she gave her jewels and all her personal property to her brother's children, so as not to upset her mother. "She did not want to disappoint her relatives," Jerome comments with obvious approval (127.4). Those who gave with *timiditas* deserved blame (130.14); those who gave with *prudentia* were worthy of praise (108.16.2; see also 15.6).

Neither timid nor prudent, Melania "gave without restraint" (20) creating great panic in her family and alarming the Senate. In 408, when Alaric attacked Rome and demanded an enormous ransom, the city prefect, Gabinius Barbarus Pompeianus, suggested that the Senate make use of the property of Melania and Pinian in order to comply with the ultimatum of the Visigoths (19). At first glance it is hard to see why the young couple should have objected to this proposal: its purpose was humanitarian, to save Rome and spare the population suffering. Actually, Melania and her husband were deeply offended by the prefect's proposal. The prefect, a pagan, was acting according to the traditional mentality of the ancient city: pagan gifts concerned the city, the people, i.e. the collective body of all citizens, and were thought of as a civic duty. Christian gifts, on the other hand, were charity to the poor, and thought of as a social and moral duty, not a civic one. The opposition both of the young couple's relatives and of the political authorities is easy to understand. It is surprising to learn, however, that the beneficiaries of Melania and Pinian's charity also expressed perplexity and put up a firm resistance. One clamorous reaction came from a group of "eight thousand" slaves belonging to their estate outside Rome. When they discovered that their masters intended to liberate them en masse, they rebelled, claiming, "We absolutely do not want to be sold." This resistance upset Melania and Pinian, "If the slaves of suburbia who are under our direct governance have dared oppose us, Melania asked, what will those in distant lands do?" (10 ff.). Obviously, being the slave of a rich and powerful master was considered preferable to being a poor freedman with no point of reference: thus this gift of freedom was cause for dismay rather than rejoicing.

Charity became subversive if given without any consideration of the delicate social equilibrium or of the productive system. The ecclesiastical authorities were also deeply worried by Melania and Pinian's actions. When the couple reached Africa, they continued to frenetically dispense their riches. They sold their lands, giving the proceeds to the poor and holy and destined other funds for the release of prisoners. The concerned African bishops, Augustine, Alypius, and Aurelius, made an appeal: "What you give to the monasteries," they claimed, "is quickly consumed. If you wish to win eternal merit, give the houses together with their incomes" (20). For an idea of the kind of properties Melania and her husband donated to the church, the estate they gave to the church of Tagaste may serve as an example: a genuine *latifundium* of late antiquity, an estate even larger than the city itself, with a villa and numerous craftsmen, including expert gold-, silver-, and coppersmiths, and even with two bishops, one Catholic, the other heretical (21.16 ff. L). In the age of Augustine, estates like this one were not easily built up, and the money gained from the sale of the property, for which no adequate opportunities for reinvestment could be found, was quickly frittered away.

Melania and Pinian welcomed the African bishops' suggestion and donated sources of income to the African monasteries (22). This was a more reasonable practice, and other high-ranking aristocrats in this era made their contributions to the church in similar ways. For example, in 432 Anicia Faltona Proba bequeathed to the church, the poor, and the monasteries a large sum from the income of her estates in Asia, which was to be paid out yearly (*Acta Conc. Oec.* 1.2, p. 90, 2–5 Schwartz). Again, Olympias displayed "prudence" in Jerome's meaning of the word when she donated land and flourishing estates (aside from great sums of gold and silver) scattered throughout the provinces of Thrace, Galatia, Cappadocia Prima, and Bithynia, as well as a number of properties in Constantinople (*Life of Olympias* 5.20 ff, 13.9 ff). Melania the Elder managed to assist churches, monasteries, foreigners, and prisoners, drawing on her own financial resources for an exceptionally long period of time—nearly forty years—because she adopted a tactic quite the opposite of her granddaughter's. The means through which Melania the Elder's works of charity were financed were paid to her periodically "by relatives, by her son in person, and by her administrators." This betokens a family situation quite different from the crude and violent reaction of Melania and Pinian's relatives to the young couple's drastic initiatives, initiatives that were however made slightly easier by their lack of children.

Such radical charity and such an abrupt transition from the highest to the humblest condition could at times make people wonder whether pride and vanity were not the real motives underlying their extreme behavior. To this question Melania replied:

If the enemy tried to make me feel proud of my poverty, then I, trusting in God's power, would respond to his outrageous act of wickedness by saying, "How many men fallen into barbarian's hands have been deprived of their freedom? How many victims of the ire of kings have lost all their property and even their lives? How many have been left destitute by their parents, how many rich men have suddenly become poor because of sycophants and bandits?" (62)

Melania's reply is revealing because it is so unsatisfactory. To counteract the vanity that might easily have accompanied her exceptional spiritual ascent, she evokes the image of universal poverty and bases her argument on relativism. In doing this, she is forced to ignore the difference inexorably separating those who choose to be poor from those who have no choice. She doesn't seem to realize that there is a difference between a fasting ascetic and a starving man, between a scantily clad saint braving the elements, warmed from within by the flame of faith, and a naked pauper suffering from exposure.

Melania's attitude toward clothing deserves brief mention here, for her whole biography is punctuated by her relationship to clothing. Clothes, fabric, the adopting of unusual materials for her garments, all served to mark important events, transitions, in her life. As a child, Melania was so used to wearing only soft, delicate fabrics that even contact with the precious embroidery decorating her garments would irritate her skin (31). Once she found her vocation, though still a young girl, she began to wear a rough wool under her silk gown, unbeknownst to her parents (4). We have already noted that she used her son's death as a pretext to put away her silk gowns forever. When she and her husband had sworn themselves to an angelic lifestyle but were not yet able to achieve complete mystical fulfillment because of their youth, they reorganized their wardrobe. Melania chose for herself a secondhand robe of modest value. Her husband, as could be expected, was a bit more attached to the habits and fashions of the times. He exchanged the elegant robes suited to his rank for the humbler "garments of Cilicia," and later, maliciously prompted by his wife, adopted "garments of Antioch," which were less expensive (8). When Melania dedicated herself completely to an ascetic life, she made herself a mantle, shawl, and hooded cloak of horsehair, a more suitable fabric for monastic living (31). To describe the importance of fasting in beautifying the soul, Melania often used a bizarre metaphor, comparing it to the importance of shoes in a bride's attire (43). Her eccentric mode of dress became quite inappropriate on at least two occasions when meeting ladies of royal lineage (11, 58). Even on the triumphant occasion of her death, clothing played a noteworthy role. Her burial clothes were "worthy of her saintliness," for the various pieces of her burial clothes made up an extraordinary collage of relics: a tunic that had once belonged to a saint, a veil once worn by a servant of God, a piece of another saint's robe, a cincture, a hood, and a second hood of horsehair folded under her head as a pillow, all of which had previously belonged to people renowned as holy personages. Gerontius informs us that no linen was used except for the winding sheet wrapped around her body laid out as we have described above (69).

In the Holy Land

For a Roman noblewoman, rejection of the world meant above all rejection of Rome. Melania found the city so oppressive that she had nightmares of being surrounded by walls with no way out: a distressing paradox of an urban aporia (16). Just seeing the walls of Rome could make some women, such as Fabiola, feel that they were entrapped. Despite these and other anxieties that marked her ascetic transformation, Melania's abandonment of Rome occurred gradually. First, she and her husband moved to their villa outside Rome, then together with her mother, Albina, they moved to Campania, later to Sicily, Africa, and finally to their so yearned-for destination, Palestine.

In the fourth century it was firmly believed that the "heights of virtue" could not be attained except after having worshipped Christ in the very places where he taught the Gospel and had been crucified. Everyone who wanted to be counted among the foremost Christians of the world gathered together in Palestine, as Jerome informs us:

> The most precious gem among the jewels of the Church is the chorus of monks and virgins. The champions of faith in Gaul hasten to come here. Out of our universe altogether, the Breton, if he has made progress in devotion, abandons the land where the sun sets and takes off to visit this land that he knows only through its fame and through the Holy Scripture. And what should we say of the Armenians and Persians, the peoples of India, Ethiopia, and nearby Egypt, teeming with monks; the peoples of Pontus and Cappadocia, of Syria Coele, of Mesopotamia, and all those swarms of people from farther East? Their voices are dissonant but their piety is one" (*Epistles* 46.10).

We have already mentioned the names of some of the aristocratic Roman women who moved to the Holy Land. Melania the Elder and Paula were only two of many protagonists who participated in this mystical and select exodus. The representations of pilgrimages to the Holy Land dating from this period display recurring motifs that show us what values (aside from the strictly religious ones) figured in such a choice. The withdrawal to the Holy Land could for instance represent the ideal contrast between the city and the country. Paula, who, Jerome tells us, "exchanged splendid palaces of gold for the poverty of rough clay," scorned being first among Roman aristocrats and went to live in Bethlehem, a "rustic land." The allure of Palestine also contributed to a shift away from the civic values from an earthly realm to the more spiritual values represented by the Holy Land and city of the Lord. This shift is evident in the words used by some of these saints and pilgrims to describe their experiences. When Paula reached Palestine, she had no doubts: "Here is my resting place, because this is the land of my Lord. Here will I live, because the Savior chose this land as his own" (Jerome *Epistles* 108.10.7). Thus Paula became a fellow citizen (*civis*) with Christ.

The oppressive specter of the city could also manifest itself in the Holy Land. To sensitive souls Jerusalem sometimes showed a negative side, tainted with the evils of the ancient Greco-Roman city. In a letter to Paulinus of Nola written in 395 (*Epistles* 54.4), Jerome, who called himself an *amator* of the Lord's manger and of the stall in Bethlehem, harshly criticized the city so "full of people, where there is a curia, a barracks, where there are prostitutes, mimes, buffoons, in other words, everything you find in other cities," a promiscuous place that ought to be inhabited only by monks, but where the two sexes mingled indecently. Even Melania felt that life in Jerusalem was not conducive to mystical perfection and preferred to withdraw to a dark cell and later to a convent on the Mount of Olives (41).

These religious communities of saintly women, however, both in the city and in the country, were constantly under the scrutiny of the entire Christian world: under the eyes of the local people, of pilgrims, of the faithful who flocked to Palestine from all over the earth, and to whom wonderful tales were told of aristocratic ladies who had abandoned their gilded palaces for humble convents in the Holy Land. These women who withdrew to convents in Palestine were by no means seeking to imitate the reclusive Macrina, who shut herself away in a monastery in Pontus in the hope of achieving complete anonymity (Gregory of Nyssa, *Life of*

Macrina 11). The zealous noblewomen praying near the monuments of Christ's earthly presence in Palestine were anything but anonymous, for they were considered living monuments themselves, "precious jewels of the Church." They occupied a place at the center of the world, and the attention of all Christendom was focused on them. Jerome writes:

> She who scorned the glory of a single city is celebrated in the judgment of the entire world; she who while living in Rome was known to no one outside Rome, now, hidden away in Bethlehem, is celebrated both in Roman and in barbarian lands. Which country does not send people to the holy places? Who in the holy places has found anything more admirable than Paula? (*Epistles* 108.3.3)

A person's decision to retire to the Holy Land must also be considered within the more general context of the concept of burial and death in late antiquity. It has been remarked that by examining the layout of burials near the tombs of saints, one may trace "the pattern of power distribution within the Christian community." This was equally true of burial in holy places. If it was important to live in Palestine, it was even more important to die there. Paula was lucky and worthy enough to be buried in Palestine, in the very grotto of our Lord. Jerome dedicated an inscription to her that was placed over the entrance of the grotto.

> Do you see this narrow sepulcher carved in the rock? It is the resting place of Paula, who dwells in the kingdom of heaven. Leaving behind her brother, her relatives, Rome, her country, her riches, and her children, she was buried in the grotto of Bethlehem. Here is your manger, Lord, here the Magi brought mystic gifts to man and God (*Epistles* 108.33).

Melania buried her mother and her husband on the Mount of Olives, in a chapel she had built in honor of the apostles. Gerontius does not tell us where Melania herself was buried, but we can assume that she is buried in the same holy place.

Perhaps for no other female saint of this period did retirement to the Holy Land represent such an excellent opportunity to capture public attention. Melania's sincere and ardent love for Christ was combined with an ill-concealed narcissism. Unlike Macrina, she did not want to be forgotten by her fellow human beings. In her apparent seclusion in the monasteries of the Mount of Olives, the city remained for her—apart from everything else—her only mirror, the only way to verify her identity, the only actual way to measure her progress in sanctity. The city conceived as the capital of the world, as the seat of the imperial palace and its court, as the arena where war against the heresies was waged.

After a few years Melania interrupted her sojourn in the Holy Land to visit Constantinople, but not without first asking advice as to the advisability of this journey. Her pretext was a visit to her uncle Volusian, former prefect of Rome and prefect of the praetorium, whom she intended to convert. This seems curious for a woman who did not rank family ties very high on her scale of values. Her journey to Constantinople was a crescendo of confirmation of her self-image. In every city, in every region she traversed, bishops and other clerics rendered her high honors, monks and virgins rushed to meet her and despaired when it was time for her to leave (51). In Tripoli an employee of the imperial post prostrated himself at the feet of the "great lady" and begged to be forgiven for not recognizing her. Her entry into Constantinople is described in her biography with the solemn simplicity befitting an imperial arrival: "She entered Constantinople" (53). During her stay in the city, Melania was literally assaulted by women of senatorial rank and men of high culture who wished to consult her on questions of orthodoxy (the Nestorian heresy was the burning question of the day). She even became the spiritual teacher of the emperor Theodosius II, the empress, and their daughter (54–56). The epilogue of this story was even more uplifting for her. The empress Eudocia chose Melania as her "spiritual mother" and later joined her in Palestine, where she visited Melania's convent and treated the virgins "as her own sisters" (58).

By the Book

The great Christian ladies of late antiquity were often renowned for their learning. In the era of the republic, it was already customary to praise a politician's culture and erudition by saying that he was equally fluent in Latin and Greek. This intellectual legacy of the Roman upper classes was passed down to late antiquity and became part of the ethical model of the Christian lady, who was expected not only to have perfect knowledge of Greek and Latin, but also to be well versed in Hebrew. Jerome tells us that Blesilla mastered this language in a few days and rivaled the learning of the famous scholar Origen (*Epistles* 39.1). Under Jerome's guidance, Paula studied Hebrew and learned to intone the psalms without any Latin inflections. Her daughter, Eustochio, followed her example (108.26.3). This plurilingualism was no mere ornament, because it paved the way for scriptural interpretation and inquiry. In an era still brimming over with heresies, knowledge of these languages served above all to help in distinguishing true scripture from false.

The cultural achievements of these women had another important characteristic: the women were all associated with the idea of virginity, even in the case of widows or chaste mothers. Women, unlike men, were expected to acquire their knowledge of sacred things without being contaminated by pagan culture.

Melania spent several hours each day poring over religious books and collections of sermons, carefully transcribing in her elegant handwriting the texts she believed were necessary for her own edification. When this demanding task was done, she sought recreation by reading the lives of the Fathers (23). Three or four times a year, she read through the Old and New Testaments and distributed copies of excerpts transcribed by her own hand. During religious services she recited the psalms from memory. Like all good scholars of antiquity, Melania was also a collector of manuscripts, and she bought or borrowed as many as she could. Her biographer tells us that she read her books with such concentration that no nuance of expression or concept escaped her. She was also perfectly bilingual: when she read Latin it seemed she knew no Greek and when she read Greek it seemed she knew no Latin (26). She preferred the select company of bishops who were both holy and famous, but above all, erudite scholars with whom she could discuss matters of divinity (36). She stayed a while in Tagaste to enjoy the company of Bishop Alypius, the renowned interpreter of the Holy Scriptures (21). We have already seen the extraordinary welcome she received in Constantinople as an expert in divinity.

For people like Melania, the acquisition of this cultural identity and the decision to move to the Holy Land were closely linked. Even in the first pilgrimages to that region, great interest had been shown in the study of sacred texts. Toward the middle of the second century, Melito, Bishop of Sardis, journeyed to the Holy Land to see the places where the word of God had been preached and realized. His main purpose was "to gain a thorough knowledge of the books of the Old Testament" and make a list of them in their proper order. Around 212, another bishop, Alexander of Caesarea in Cappadocia, went to Jerusalem to pray and to obtain direct knowledge of the places where the biblical events had occurred. These men were motivated primarily by a religious quest to verify the biblical past and to research the traditions of the Old Testament. In other travelers this quest was accompanied by an intellectual curiosity to see the places they had studied and read about. The desire to verify one's knowledge through direct experience, to see with one's own eyes, was a legacy of classical culture and the antique roots of this attitude were obvious even to the Fathers of the Church. Jerome compared Christians visiting the Holy Land to students of ancient Greece visiting Athens, or to lovers of Virgil following Aeneas's traces through the Mediterranean. For all cultivated Christians, Melania included, Jerusalem became "our Athens."

Melania's cultural aspirations went beyond a search for personal enrichment or spiritual fulfillment of a soul totally devoted to the Lord. They became the hub around which she built her new identity and reorganized her place in her family.

Women could become saints as virgins, widows, or mothers. After the deaths of her children and before that of her husband (he died in fact only eight years before she did), Melania did not fit into any of these three categories. This is why her renunciation of the world seemed so much more radical. To create a new identity, certain bonds had to be untied, and others reformulated, beginning with her marriage. The first thing Melania did was to impose sexual abstinence on her husband. The practice of chastity made him her "brother," a brother in the spirit (37 and 40), the term generally used to describe such relationships. The rule of chastity between spouses was only a preliminary condition, not enough to ensure to a woman in search of sanctity full moral autonomy. That goal could be attained only through a sort of self-chosen widowhood, a voluntary *viduitas* that removed the husband from his role of *paterfamilias.* Pinian, in fact, assumed the role of a son, as he was aware, "Ever since we gave our word to God and began to live a pure life, you have become for me like your holy mother, Albina" (8). In the Roman tradition, when the marriage reached the perfection of a harmonious imbalance, the husband would often declare that he loved his wife as a daughter. This was not necessarily an allusion to an age difference between spouses. Basically, the husband was viewed as an authoritative father, governing his wife as an eternal child in need of reassurance and guidance from him, the dispenser of wisdom and governor of their life together. Pinian did not play this role in his marriage to Melania; rather, it was the reverse. We have already noted that Melania did not feel for her father, Publicola, the affection a daughter normally feels. Here we must add an important detail: Melania openly declared that she was not his heir but her grandmother's.

Melania rebelled against marriage: "If you want me to recognize you as the lord and master of my life, renounce my body" (1). The moment his wife pronounced these words, Pinian discovered that he was neither lord nor master, and, therefore, not even a husband. Once he accepted the idea of chastity, their roles were reversed: The wife imparted instruction to her husband and led him by the hand. Pinian was the weak one needing support, persuasion, and enlightenment while Melania held the power of cultural authority and transmitted all her learning to him. From that moment on, Pinian made no decisions or suggestions of his own. He became a woman, while she became a man: a virile woman—*mulier virilis*, in Greek *gynè andréia*—according to a commonplace of the time, in which the pagan and philosophical matrix is evident. Melania's virility is emphasized repeatedly by her biographer, beginning with the prologue where her deeds are defined as *andragathèmata,* manly undertakings. This virility is celebrated with due ceremony in the scene of her encounter with the "queen" Serena:

> [The queen] was deeply moved by the sight of the blessed Melania dressed in humble clothes. She welcomed her, seated her on a golden throne and then called together all the people in the palace saying, "Come and see the woman whom we admired four years ago, splendid in her worldly dignity. Now she has grown old in heavenly wisdom. Let us learn from her how reason, guided by piety, triumphs over the pleasures of the flesh. Here is a woman who after abandoning her refined upbringing, her great riches, the prestige of her rank, indeed, all that it is pleasurable in this life, fears neither the weakness of the flesh nor self-chosen poverty, nor any of those other things that make us tremble. Instead she has restrained nature and dedicated herself to dying each day, and has demonstrated to the world through her own deeds that the female sex is in no way inferior to the male sex in the practice of virtue if one's intention is firm." (12)

Later Melania received even more important recognition. "Like a man" she was welcomed by the holy fathers in the desert of Nitria, who had previously welcomed and honored her grandmother, Melania the Elder (39).

Melania's biography reemploys this *topos* with a significant addition. Her transformation did not end with her acquisition of a masculine temperament and intellect. Becoming manly (almost because of the very impetus generated by such an undertaking), Melania also acquired celestial attributes (39). In such a definition we may grasp just how far the Christian revaluation of female identity could go, and at the same time, test the intrinsic limits of that revaluation. It went very far in acknowledging that the female soul could not only equal the male soul, but even surpass it and acquire a divine nature. Yet this triumph of the female condition could not occur directly, but only via the previous attainment of a virile identity. In other words, the limit lay in the difficulty of answering the question, "What is a woman?"

Behind many noble women saints of late antiquity, we may glimpse the figures of important men, such as Jerome, Paula's spiritual guide. Melania instead was her own creation. Gerontius, her biographer, was a timid and subordinate figure, a devoted admirer, an attentive servant who lived in the light she reflected. He too seems to have played the role of a son and approached the task of recording her story with reverential awe, for she was "the holy mother who lives among the angels," as we learn from his prologue.

A daughter's transfiguration into the mother of her own mother was not an unusual theme in the "lives" of women saints in this epoch. This transformation was easier for virgins to achieve. Thanks to their unique condition and to the exclusive virtues deriving from this status, virgins could become the spiritual mothers of their own mothers and the spiritual teachers of anyone who appreciates the beauty of their example. Melania respected her mother, both for her venerable age and for her piety, but she also dominated her, as an episode in her biography illustrates. One day, Albina, prompted by loving intentions, timidly entered the cell where her daughter was busy with her studies. Melania did not look up from her books or even speak to her mother until she had finished and only then allowed Albina to speak briefly with her, just for "the amount of time strictly necessary." Melania's mother was deeply touched by her daughter's display of intense moral strength and her sense of duty. This episode implies another reversal of traditional roles, and it is significant that this reversal is described in terms of Melania's privileged relationship to reading and writing. Books and book learning conferred a special authority upon women, the authority of the *paterfamilias*. Melania's story is not only the story of a noble maiden who becomes a saint, but the story of a wife who becomes a *paterfamilias*.

On some sarcophagi dating from the second and third centuries A.D., married couples are sometimes portrayed in the following fashion: the husband holds his right hand raised, and in his left he holds a scroll, symbol of his learning and authority; his wife stands or sits beside him in the obsequious pose of a pupil under discipline. If we wished to portray Melania and Pinian in a similar manner, we would have to show Melania with the book, and Pinian, devoted servant of both wife and book, sitting beside her.

Bibliographic Notes

Introduction

1. *Inscriptiones Latinae liberae reipublicae* 1193 (Rome); *Corpus inscriptionum Latinarum* 9.193 (Brindisi); *CIL* 3.2118 (Salona).

2. For a description of the life and daily chores of a *vilica* see Cato, *De agricultura* 143 and Columella, *De re rustica* 12.1–3.

3. The epitaph of the anonymous matron dating from the republican era is collected in the *CIL* 6.1527, 31670, and 37053 (= *Inscriptiones Latinae selectae* 8393). See especially M. Durry, ed. and trans., *Eloge funèbre d'une matrone romaine (Eloge dit de Turia)* (Paris, 1950); E. Wiestrand, *The So-called "Laudatio Turiae": Introduction, Text, Translation and Commentary* (Lund, 1976). Aconia Fabia Paulina's epitaph is collected in the *CIL* 6.1779 (= *Inscriptiones Latinae selectae* 1779; *Carmina Latina epigraphica* 111). For a study of this inscription, see G. Polara, "Le inscrizioni sul cippo tombale di Vezzio Agorio Pretestato," *Vichiana* 4 (1967): 264.

4. On this subject, see J. Beauchamp, "Le vocabulaire de la faiblesse féminine dans les textes juridiques romains du troisième et quatrième siècle," *Revue historique du droit français et étranger* 54 (1976): 485–508; S. Dixon, "'Infirmitas sexus': Womanly Weakness in Roman Law," *Tijdscrif voor Rechtsgeschiedenis* 52 (1984): 343–71.

5. Concerning the different treatment of newborn sons and daughters by their fathers, see Y. Thomas, "Tollere liberos," *Conférences de l'Institut de Droit romain de Paris,* 1984; Y. Thomas, "Le ventre: Corps maternel, droit paternel," *Le gendre humain* 14 (1986): 211. On female infanticide see D. Engels, "The Problem of Female Infanticide in the Greco-Roman World," *Classical Philology* 75 (1980): 112–20. See also comments by W. V. Harris, "The Theoretical Possibility of Extensive Infanticide in the Greco-Roman World," *Classical Quarterly* 32 (1982): 114–15. Concerning marriage strategies in the upper echelons of the Roman nobility, see J. Andreau and H. Bruhns, eds., *Parenté et stratégies familiales dans l'antiquité romaine* (Rome, 1990).

6. On the subject of *patria potestas,* see J. A. Crook, "Patria potestas," *Classical Quarterly* 17 (1967): 113. More recent studies may be found in Y. Thomas, "Droit domestique et droit politique à Rome: Remarques sur le pécule et les 'honorés' des fils de famille," Mélange de l'Ecole française de Rome, *Antiquité* 94 (1982): 527. Y. Thomas, "'Vitae necisque potestas': Le père, la cité, la mort,"

in *Du châtiment dans la cité: Supplices corporels et peine de mort dans le monde antique* (Rome, 1984), 499; W. K. Lasey, "Patria potestas," in B. Rawson, ed., *The Family in Ancient Rome: New Perspectives* (London and Sydney, 1986), 121; W. V. Harris, "The Roman Father's Power of Life and Death," in *Studies in Roman Law, in Memory of A. A. Schiller* (Leiden, 1986), 81–95.

7. On the education of sons and daughters, see B. Rawson, "The Roman Children," in B. Rawson, ed., *The Family,* 170; P. Veyne, "L'impero romano," in Ph. Aries and G. Duby, eds., *La vita privata dall'impero romano all'anno mille* (Rome and Bari), 12.

8. G. Matringe, "La puissance paternelle et le mariage des fils et des filles de famille en droit romain (sous l'empire et en Occident)," in *Studi in onore di Edoardo Volterra,* 5 (Milan, 1971), 191–237; Y. Thomas, "Mariages endogamiques à Rome: Patrimoine, pouvoir, et parenté depuis l'époque archaïque," *Revue d'histoire du droit français et étranger* 58 (1980): 345–82; and Y. Thomas, "The Division of the Sexes in Roman Law," in G. Duby and M. Perrot, eds., A. Goldhammer, trans., *A History of Women in the West,* vol. 1, *From Ancient Goddesses to Christian Saints* (Cambridge: Belknap Press, Harvard, 1992).

9. On this specific case, see S. Dickson, "Family Finances: Tullia and Terentia," in B. Rawson, ed., *The Family,* 93–120. For a more general discussion, see J. A. Crook, "'His' and 'Hers': What Degree of Financial Responsibility Did Husband and Wife Have for the Matrimonial Home and Their Life in Common, in a Roman Marriage?" in J. Andreau and H. Bruhns, eds., *Parenté et stratégies,* 153–72.

10. Concerning Marcia's marriages, see E. Malcovati, "Clodia, Fulvia, Marzia, Terenzia," *Quaderni di Studi romani. Donne di Roma antica,* 2d ed. (Rome, 1946); M. Humbert, *Le remarriage à Rome: Etude d'histoire juridique et sociale* (Milan, 1972), 98; R. Flacelière, "Caton d'Utique et les femmes," in *L'Italie préromaine et la Rome républicaine. Mélanges offerts à Jacques Heurgon,* vol. 1 (Rome, 1976), 298; Y. Thomas, "Le ventre," 218; M. Salvadore, *Due donne romane: Immagini del matrimonio antico* (Palermo, 1990), 13; E. Cantarella, "Marzia e la 'locatio ventris,'" in R. Raffaelli, ed., *Vicende e figure femminili in Grecia e a Roma. Atti del Convegno Pesaro 28–30 apr. 1994* (Ancona, 1995), 251.

11. On Hortensia's activities in 42 B.C. and on her speech defending women, see L. Peppe, *Posizione giuridica e ruolo sociale della donna romana in età repubblicana* (Milan, 1974), 16.

12. On Marcia's remarriage to her first husband, see Plutarch, *Life of Cato* 52.5.

13. In this sense, see P. Grimal, *L'amour à Rome* (Paris, 1963), 263; D. Babut, *Plutarque et le stoïcisme* (Paris, 1969), 173.

14. The circumstances surrounding Drusus's birth are discussed in the present volume in Fraschetti, "Livia the Politician."

15. On P. Quintilius Varus's family ties with Agrippa as documented in *Kölner Papyri* 7.6, ed. M. Gronewald (Opladen, 1976), no. 35, see Rheinold, "Marcus Agrippa's Son-in-Law, P. Quintilius Varus," *Classical Quarterly* 67 (1972): 119. Tiberius married Julia when Agrippa died. He had previously been married to Vipsania, the daughter of Agrippa, Augustus's colleague. For a study of Vipsania,

see M. Th. Raepsaet-Charlier, *Prosopographie des femmes de l'ordre sénatorial (Iᵉ–IIᵉ s.)* (Louvain, 1987), 362, 811. In similar fashion, in this same period, P. Quintilius Varus, through his marriage to Claudia Pulchra, daughter of Messalla Barbatus Appianus cos. or. 10 d.c. and of Claudia Marcella (Stein, *PIR* 2d ed., 265–66 n. 1103), also became directly related to the prince's family, given that Claudia Pulchra was the daughter of Augustus Marcella Minor's nephew (Groag, *PIR* 2d ed., 265 n. 1103).

16. R. Syme, *The Augustan Aristocracy* (Oxford, 1986), 302.

17. On the figure of Antonia, a "woman whose praise surpassed the splendor of the men in her family," and whose behavior after her husband's death was universally considered exemplary, see Valerius Maximus 4.3, 3. *Univirae* women are discussed in J. Straub, "Calpurnia univiria," in Bonner, *Historia Augusta Colloquium 1966–67* (Bonn, 1968), 101–18 (= J. Straub, *Regeneratio imperii* [Darmstad, 1972], 351). See also M. Lightman and W. Feisel, "'Univira': An Example of Continuity and Change in Roman Society," *Church History* 46 (1977): 19–32.

18. In this regard, see S. Treggiari and S. Dorken, "Women Living with Two Husbands in *CIL* 6,"*Liverpool Classical Monthly* 6 (1981): 269. See also B. Rawson, "Roman Concubinate and Other 'De Facto' Marriages," *Transactions of the American Philological Society* 104 (1974): 279.

19. See Y. Thomas, "La divisione dei sessi," 158.

20. This was Caesar's opinion, as reported in Plutarch, *Life of Cato,* 52.6–7. "This is why Caesar scorned Cato, charging him with avarice and with trafficking in marriage. 'For why,' demanded Caesar, 'should Cato give up his wife if he wanted her, or why, if he did not want her, should he take her back again? Unless he had set her as a bait for Hortensius when she was young so that he might take her back when she was rich.'"

21. See in detail P. Zannini, *Studi sulla "tutela mulierum"* (Turin, 1976). Cases of women being guardians are examined in T. Masiello, *La donna tutrice: Modelli culturali e prassi giuridica fra gli Antonini e i Severi* (Naples, 1979).

22. Ovid, *Ars amatoria* 3.611–66.

23. Y. Thomas, "Le ventre," 211–36.

24. Cato's speech was recorded by Livy, 34.2–4. See in particular 34.2.6: "I do not know, I say, whether this madness is more shameful for you, tribunes, or for the consuls: for you, if you have brought these women here to support the sedition of the tribunes; or for us, if we must accept laws dictated by a secession of women, as formerly by a secession of plebeians."

25. On Tanaquil's role in passing the power on to Servius Tullius, see P. M. Martin, "Tanaquil, la 'faiseuse de rois,'" *Latomus* 44 (1985): 5–15, also J. Hall, "Livy's Tanaquil and the Image of Asseverative Etruscan Women in Latin Historical Literature of the Early Empire," *Augustan Age* 4 (1985): 31–38. This article suggests that Livy's portrait of Tanaquil was modeled on Urgulania, Livia's famous friend.

26. See A. Pontrandolfo and A. Rouveret, *Le tombe dipinte di Paestum* (Modena, 1992). See more particularly A. Bottini and A. Greco, "Tomba a camera

nel territorio pestano: Alcune considerazioni sulla posizione della donna," *Dialoghi d'archeologia* 7 (1974–75): 231–74.

27. P. Veyne, *L'impero romano,* 30.

28. Concerning Seneca and his views on women, see A. L. Motto, "Seneca on Women's Liberation," *Classical World* 65 (1972): 155–57. See also C. E. Manning, "Seneca and the Stoics on Equality of the Sexes,"*Mnemosyne* 26 (1973): 170–77.

29. On this subject see E. Pagels, *Adam, Eve, and the Serpent* (New York, 1988).

30. On the episode concerning Lucretia, see A. Guarino, "Il 'dossier' di Lucrezia," in *Le origini quiritarie. Raccolta di scritti romanistici* (Naples, 1973), 121–28; G. Piccaluga, "Lucrezia: Creazione, uso e consumo del cliché femminile nella cultura romana," in J. Vibaek, ed., *Donne e società. Atti del 60 Congresso di Studi antropologici, Palermo, 25–27 nov. 1982* (Palermo, 1987), 99–113; R. A. Bauman, "The Rape of Lucretia: 'Quod metus causa' and the Criminal Law," *Latomus* 52 (1993): 550–66.

31. The funerals of Clodius and of Caesar are discussed by A. Fraschetti in *Roma e il principe* (Rome and Bari, 1990), 46.

32. For a study of Marcus Fabius Ambustus's daughter, wife of Licinius Stolon, see C. S. Kraus, "'Initium turbandi omnia a femina ortum est': Fabia Minor and the Elections of 367 B.C.," *Phoenix* 45 (1991): 314–25; S. Lanciotti, "Questioni di famiglia: Le due figlie di M. Fabio Ambusto," in R. Raffaelli, ed., *Vicende e figure femminili,* 283.

33. The figures of Verginia and Lucretia are discussed in S. R. Joshel, "The Body Female and the Body Politic," in R. Amy, ed., *Pornography and Representation in Greece and Rome* (Oxford, 1991), 112–30.

34. This has been noted by M. Beard in "The Sexual Status of Vestal Virgins," *Journal of Roman Studies* 70 (1980): 149–65. See also J. Scheid, "Le Flamine de Jupiter, les vestales et le général triomphant," *Le temps de la réflexion* 7 (1986): 213–30.

35. Jerome, *Commentarium in Sophaniam prophetam, Prol.,* in *PL* 25.1137C: "he did not blush to discuss philosophy in a private house while a matron listened."

CHAPTER ONE

Sources

The most important sources concerning the myth of Claudia are: Cicero *De haruspicium responsis* 12.26; Diodorus 34.33,1–3; Livy 29.11.1–8; 14.5–14; Ovid *Fasti* 4.179–372; Propertius 4.11.45–54; Valerius Maximus 1.8.11; Seneca *Frag.* 80 (Haase.3.1886.433); Statius *Silvae* 1.245–46; Pliny the Elder *Natural History* 7.120. 35; Tacitus *Annals* 4.64; Appian *Punic Wars* 56; Herodian 1.11; Julian *Orationes* 5.159c–161b (= *On the Great Mother* 1).

On the story of Claudia protecting her father (or brother) in triumph, see Cicero, *Pro Caelio* 34; Valerius Maximus 5.4.6. For documentation concerning the coins, see M. Crawford, *Roman Republican Coinage* (London, 1974), n. 512.

Studies

F. Bömer, "Kybele in Rom: Die Geschichte ihres Kultes als politisches Phäno-men," in *Mitteilungen des deutschen archäologischen Instituts: Rom* 71 (1964): 130–51.

Ph. Borgeaud, "Quelques remarques sur la mythologie divine à Rome, à pro-pos de Denys d'Halicarnasse" (*Ant. Rom.* 2: 18–20), in F. Graf, ed., *Mythos in mythenloser Gesellschaft* (Stuttgart and Leipzig, 1993), 175–87.

I. Bremmer, in I. Bremmer and N. Horsfall, *Roman Myth and Mythography* (London, 1987), 105–12.

J. Gérard, "Légende et politique autour de la mère des dieux, *Revue des études latines* (1963): 153–75.

E. S. Gruen, *Studies in Greek Culture and Roman Policy* (Leiden, 1990), 5–33.

Th. Köves, "Zum Empfang des Magna Mater in Rom," Historia 12 (1963) 321–47.

D. Porte, "Claudia Quinta et le problème de la lauatio de Cybele en 204 av. J.C.," *Klio* 66 (1984): 93–103.

CHAPTER TWO
Sources

For a quick review of source materials concerning Cornelia, F. Münzer's study published in 1900 is still worth a look. See *R.E.* 4.1 n. 407, coll.1592–95 (to be completed by the additions found in Supplb. 3 [1918], col. 261).

To Livy's account of her marriage, we must make the following addition to 38.57.7, proposed by C. F. Konrad (*Philologus* 133 [1989]: 155–57, included by Briscoe in the recent Teubnerian edition [Stuttgart, 1991], 602): "*cum illa [Anti-stia] . . . adiecisset non (ni)si Ti. Graccho daret, expertem consilii debuisse matrem esse,*" which is intended to justify Scipio's great relief at the agreement (laetum tam concordi iudicio) that followed Antistia's protest.

Concerning Jerome *Comm. in Sophoniam prophetam,* we refer to the edition by M. Adriaen, *Corp. Christ.* 76a (Turnhout, 1970).

For mention of the Gracchi in Diodorus, see the anthology edited by P. Bot-teri, *Les fragments de l'histoire des Gracques dans la "Bibliothèque" de Diodore de Sicile* (Geneva, 1992).

Studies

On Cornelia. S. Barnard, "Cornelia and the Women of her Family," *Latomus* 49 (1990): 383–92; L. Burckhardt–J. von Ungern-Sternberg, "Cornelia, Mutter der Gracchen," in *Reine Männersache? Frauen in Männerdomänen der antiken Welt,* ed. M. H. Dettenhofer (Köln-Weimar-Wien, 1994), 97–132; G. Corradi, "Cornelia e Sempronia," *Donne di Roma antica* 8 (Rome, 1946); A Guarino, "Minima de Gracchis," in *Studi in onore di A. Biscardi,* vol. 1 (Milan, 1982), 53–56; L. M. Günther, "Cornelia und Ptolemaios VIII: Zur Historizität des Heir-atsantrages (Plut. TG 1.3)," *Historia* 39 (1990): 124–28; C. F. Konrad, "Livy on the Betrothal of Cornelia Gracchi (38.57.7)" *Philologus* 133 (1989): 155–57; M. Maxey, *Cornelia* (Chicago, 1933); K. M. Moir, "Pliny *H. N.* 7.57 and the Marriage of Tiberius Gracchus," *CQ* 33 (1933): 136–45; D. Tudor, *Donne celebri del mondo antico* (Italian translation, Milan, 1980); J. E. Phillips, "Roman Mothers and the Life of their Adult Daughters," *Helios* 6 (1978): 69–80.

On the fragments of her letters. Aside from Cugusi's commentary in *Epistolographi Latini minores* 124.1.2 (Turin, 1970), 65–73, other reliable sources containing critical overviews of previous opinions may be found in P. Cugusi, "Studi sull'epistolografia latina I. L'età preciceroniana," *Ann. Fac. Lett. Fil. Mag. Cagliari* 33 (1970): 54–65 (very useful for its analysis of Carisio's contested quotation, 130.19 Barwick = 1.102.20 Keil); H. U. Instinsky, "Zur Echtheitsfrage der Brieffragmente der Cornelia, Mutter der Gracchen," *Chiron* 1 (1971): 177–89; N. Horsfall, "The 'Letter of Cornelia': Yet More Problems," *Athenaeum* 65 (1987): 23–34; and lastly, A. López López, "Cornelia, madre de la epistolografia latina," in *Mnemosynum C. Codoñer a discipulis oblatum,* ed. A. Ramos Guerreira, *Acta Salmanticensia* 247 (Salamanca, 1991), 161–73.

Concerning the statue and the inscription on its base. F. Coarelli, "La statue de Cornélie, mère des Gracques, et la crise politique à Rome au temps de Saturninus," in *Le dernier siècle de la République romaine et l'époque augustéenne* (Strasbourg, 15–16 fevr. 1978), 13–28; R. G. Lewis, "Some Mothers ..." *Athenaeum* 66 (1988): 198–200; M. Kajava, "Cornelia Africani f. Gracchorum," *Arctos* 23 (1989): 119–31.

The following are works not specifically dedicated to Cornelia but which discuss major aspects of her biography: G. Bandelli, "I figli dell'Africano," *Index* 5 (1974–75): 127–39; R. A. Bauman, *Women and Politics in Ancient Rome* (London and New York, 1992), see pp. 41–59 on Cornelia and women in the age of the Gracchi; A. H. Bernstein, *Tiberius Sempronius Gracchus: Tradition and Apostasis* (Ithaca, 1978), 42–55; M. Bettini, *Nascere: Storie di donne, donnole, madri ed eroi* (Turin, 1998), 109–12 and nn. 28–44; H. C. Boren, *The Gracchi* (New York, 1968); M. van den Bruwaene, "L'opposition à Scipion Emilien après la morte de Tibérius Gracchus," *Phoibos* 5 (1950–51): 229–38; J. Carcopino, *Autour des Gracques,* 2d ed., with appendix, ed. C. Nicolet (Paris, 1967), see pp. 47–83 on the subject of Cornelia's marriage and 103–11 on the subject of Aemilianus's death; S. Dixon, "Polybius on Roman Women and Property," *AJPh* 106 (1985): 143–70; S. Dixon, *The Roman Mother* (London and Sydney, 1988); D.C. Earl, "Tiberius Gracchus: A Study in Politics," *Coll. Latomus* 66 (Brussels, 1963), see esp. pp. 50–58; B. Foertsch, *Die politische Rolle der Frau in der römischen Republik* (Stuttgart, 1935), 56–72; I. J. García Pinilla, "Los Gracos considerados a través de los textos latinos no históricos," *Habis* 21 (1990): 93–99; J. P. Hallet, *Fathers and Daughters in Roman Society: Women and the Elite Family* (Princeton, 1984); C. Hermann, "Le rôle judiciare et politique des femmes sous la République romaine," *Coll. Latomus* 67 (Brussels, 1964): 86–89; B. von Hesberg-Tonn, "Coniunx Carissima: Untersuchungen zum Normcharakter in Erscheinungsbild der römischen Frau," (diss., Stuttgart, 1983), 654–70; Th. Mommsen, "Die Scipionenprozesse," *Hermes* 1 (1866): 161–216, later published as *Römische*

Forschungen II (Berlin, 1879, reprinted Hildesheim, 1962), 417–510; W. Schuller, *Frauen in der römischen Geschichte* (Konstanz, 1987), 34–46; D. Stockton, *The Gracchi* (Oxford, 1979), 22–26.

General studies. The following is a partial list of texts dealing with some of the topics, either more general or more specific, touched upon in this essay: L. Archer, S. Fischler, M. Wyke, eds., *Women in Ancient Societies: An Illusion of the Night* (New York, 1994); A. E. Astin, *Scipio Aemilianus* (Oxford, 1967); J. Béranger, "Les jugements de Cicéron sur les Gracques," *ANRW* 1.3 (1973): 732–63; E. E. Best, "Cicero, Livy, and Educated Roman Women" *CJ* 65 (1970): 199–204; M. Bettini, *Il ritratto dell'amante* (Turin, 1992); L. Canfora, "L'educazione," in *Storia di Roma* (dir. A. Schiavone), 4, *Caratteri e morfologie* (Turin, 1989), 735–70; E. Cantarella, *L'ambiguo malanno,* 2d ed. (Rome, 1985; translated as *Pandora's Daughters* [Baltimore and London, 1987]); E. Cantarella, "La vita delle donne," in *Storia di Roma,* 557–608; E. Cantarella, *Passato prossimo: Donne romane da Tacita a Sulpicia* (Milan, 1996); G. Cardinali, *Studi graccani* (Genoa 1912, reprinted 1965); S. Dixon, *The Roman Family* (Baltimore and London, 1992); F. Dupont, *La vita quotidiana nella Roma repubblicana* (Rome and Bari, 1990 [Italian translation of Dupont's work pub. Paris, 1989]); D. F. Epstein, *Personal Enmity in Roman Politics 218–43* B.C. (London, New York, and Sydney, 1987); J. K. Evans, *War, Women, and Children in Ancient Rome* (London, 1991); L. Ferrero Raditsa, "Augustus' Legislation Concerning Marriage, Procreation, Love Affairs, and Adultery," *ANRW* 2.13 (1980): 278–339; P. Fraccaro, *Studi sull'età dei Gracchi* (Città di Castello, 1914, reprinted 1967); A. Fraschetti, "La sepoltura delle Vestali e la città," in *Du châtiment dans la cité. Coll. Ec. Fr. Rome* 79 (Rome, 1984), 97–128; E. Gabba, *Appiano e la storia delle guerre civili* (Florence, 1956); A. Fraschetti, "Il tentativo dei Gracchi," in *Storia di Roma,* 2.1 (Turin, 1990), 671–89; G. Garbarino, *Roma e la filosofia greca dalle origini alla fine del II secolo a.C.* (Turin, 1973); J. F. Gardner, *Women in Roman Law and Society* (London and Sydney, 1986); P. Grimal, *Il secolo degli Scipioni* (Brescia, 1981 [Italian translation of Grimal's work pub. Paris, 1975]); P. Grimal, "Matrona: Les lois, les moeurs, le langage," *AFL Nice* 50 (1985): 195–203; T. Hillard, "'Materna Auctoritas': The Political Influence of Roman 'Matronae'," *Classicum* 9 (1983): 10–13, 28; B. Kreck, "Untersuchungen zur politischen und sozialen Rolle der Frau in der späten römischen Republik" (diss., Marburg, 1975); G. Lahusen, *Untersuchungen zur Ehrenstatue in Rom: Literarische und epigraphische Zeugnisse* (Rome, 1983); F. Le Corsu, *Plutarque et les femmes dans les "Vies parallèles"* (Paris, 1981); C. E. Manning, "Seneca and the Stoics on the Equality of the Sexes," *Mnemosyne* 26 (1973): 170–77; J. McIntosh Snyder, *The Woman and the Lyre: Women Writers in Classical Greece and Rome* (Carbondale and Edwardsville, Ill., 1989); F. Münzer, *Römische Adelsparteien und Adelsfamilien* (Stuttgart, 1920); C. Nicolet, *Les Gracques* (Paris, 1967); J. M. Pailler, "Les matrones romaines et les empoisonnements criminels sous la République," *CRAI,* 1987: 111–28; T. G. Parkin, *Demography and Roman Society* (Baltimore, 1992); L. Peppe, *Posizione giuridica e ruolo sociale della donna in età repubblicana* (Milan, 1984); L. Perelli, *I Gracchi* (Rome, 1993); C. Petrocelli, *La stola e il silenzio:*

Sulla condizione femminile nel mondo romano (Palermo, 1989, 1990); S. B. Pomeroy, *Donne in Atene e Roma* (Turin, 1978 [Italian translation of Pomeroy's work pub. New York, 1975]); S. B. Pomeroy, "The Relationship of the Married Woman to her Blood Relatives in Rome," *AncSoc* 7 (1976): 215–27; S. B. Pomeroy, ed., *Women's History and Ancient History* (Chapel Hill and London, 1991); B. Rawson, ed., *The Family in Ancient Rome: New Perspectives* (Ithaca, N.Y., 1986); B. Rawson, ed., *Marriage, Divorce, and Children in Ancient Rome* (Oxford and Canberra, 1991); A. Rousselle "La politica dei corpi: Tra procreazione e continenza a Roma," in M. Duby and M. Perrot, *Storia delle donne*, I, *L'Antichità*, ed. P. Schmitt Pantel (Rome and Bari, 1990), 317–72; L. Salvioni, "Le madri dell'ira nelle 'Vite' di Plutarco," *GFF* 5 (1982): 83–92; J. Scheid, "Indispensabili 'straniere': I ruoli religiosi delle donne a Roma," in *Storia delle donne*, 424–64; Y. Thomas, "La divisione dei sessi nel diritto romano," in *Storia delle donne*, 103–76; S. Treggiari, "'Digna Condicio' Betrothals in the Roman Upper Class," *ECI Views*, n. s., 3 (1984): 419–51. S. Treggiari, *Roman Marriage* (Oxford, 1991); G. Viden, *Women in Roman Literature* (Goteborg, 1993); M. E. Waithe, *A History of Women Philosophers*, vol. 1, *Ancient Women Philosophers, 600 B.C.–A.D. 500* (Dordrecht, Boston, and Lancaster, 1987); P. Walcot, "On Widows and Their Reputation in Antiquity," *SO* 66 (1991): 5–26; I. Worthington, "The Death of Scipio Aemilianus," *Hermes* 117 (1989) 253–56.

Chapter Three

Sources

Principal sources are as follows. Appian, *The Civil War* (especially books 4 and 5); Dio Cassius, *Histories* (especially books 45–48). Other information may be found in Cicero, *To Atticus, To his Family, On His Home, Philippicae* (second and third especially), *Pro Milone* (with Asconius's comment) *CIL* 11.6721; Martial, *Epigrams* 11; Pliny the Elder, *Natural History;* Plutarch, *Life of Antony;* Suetonius, *Life of Augustus;* Valerius Maximus, *Memorable Deeds and Facts;* Varro, *The Country Estate;* Velleius Paterculus, *History of Rome.*

Studies

C. L. Babcock, "The Early Career of Fulvia," *AJP 86*, 1 (1985): 1–32; J. P. V.D. Balsdon, *Roman Women: Their History and Habits* (London, 1962); T. R. S. Broughton, *The Magistrates of the Roman Republic* (Atlanta, 1951); F. Chamoux, *Marc-Antoine, dernier prince de l'Orient grec* (Paris, 1986); G. Clark, "Roman Women," *Greece and Rome* 28, 2 (1981): 193–212; S. Dixon, "A Family Business: Women's Role in Patronage and Politics, 80–44 B.C.," *Classica et Mediaevalis* 34 (1983): 91–112; S. Dixon, "The Marriage Alliance in the Roman Elite," *Journal of Family History* 10 (1985): 353–78; G. Fau, *L'émancipation féminine à Rome* (Paris, 1978); V. Gardthausen, *Augustus und seine Zeit* (Leipzig, 1891); W. Helbig, "Osservazioni sopra i ritratti di Fulvia e di Ottavia," *Monumenti Antichi* 1: 572–90; F. Hinard, *Les proscriptions de la Rome républicaine* (Rome, 1985); E. Malcovati, "Clodia, Fulvia, Marzia, Terentia," in *Donne di Roma antica.*

Quaderni di Studi Romani (Rome, 1945), 1–30; H. Mattingly, *Roman Coins* (London, 1960–62); F. Münzer, *RE* n. 113, coll 281–84; A. Piganiol, *La conquête romaine* (Paris, 1966); L. Ross Taylor, "Caesar's Colleagues in the Pontifical College," *AJP* 63 (1942): 396; C. Virlouvet, *Famines et émeutes à Rome des origines de la République à la mort de Néron* (Rome, 1985).

CHAPTER FOUR
Lycoris

The basic study of the historic figure of Lycoris/Cytheris is the article by S. Mazzarino, "Contributo alla lettura del nuovo Gallo e alla storia della mima Lycoris," *Helikon* 20–21 (1980–81): 3–26. See also Mazzarino, "Un nuovo epigramma di Gallo e l'antica lettura epigrafica (un problema di datazione)," *Quaderni catanesi* 2 (1980): 7–50; "L'iscrizione latina nella trilingue di Philae e i carmi di Gallo scoperti a Qaṣr Ibrīm," *Rheinisches Museum für Philologie*, n.s. 125 (1982): 313–37. See also P. Grimal, "La femme à Rome et dans la civilisation romaine," in Grimal, ed., *Histoire mondiale de la femme: Préhistoire et Antiquité* (Paris: Nouvelle librairie de France, 1965), 377–485, see esp. 440; Ch. Garton, *Personal Aspects of the Roman Theatre* (Toronto: Hakkert, 1972), 141–67; S. B. Pomeroy, *Goddesses, Whores, Wives, and Slaves: Women in Classical Antiquity* (New York: Shocken Books, reprint, 1995); M. Bonaria, in *Enciclopedia virgiliana*, vol.3 (Rome: Istituto dell'Enciclopedia italiana, 1987), *s.v.* "Licoride" (not updated).

The name Lycoris not only has refined undertones, but also calls to mind the Greek *lykos,* or "wolf," with its erotic connotations. In his *Satire* 6.123, on women, Juvenal reveals the pseudonym used by Messalina during her outings in disguise to brothels: Lycisca, "wolf cub." The same name is used for another *puella* in Martial (4.17.1). Concerning Greek *cognomina* see H. Solin, *Die griechischen Personennamen in Rom: Ein Namenbuch,* 3 vols. (Berlin and New York: De Gruyter, 1982). Brief mention of Lycoris is made in P. Veyne, *Love, Poetry, and the West* (Chicago, 1984).

Concerning Eutrapelus, see C. Nicolet, *L'ordre équestre à l'époque républicaine (312–43 av J.C.),* 2 vols. (Paris: Boccard, 1974–76), 1082; M. Malavolta, in *Enciclopedia oraziana,* vol. 1 (Rome: Istituto dell'Enciclopedia italiana, 1994), *s.v.* "Eutrapelo, Publio Volumnio." Her Greek *cognomen* does not imply libertine origins and was probably only a nickname. Doubts have been raised concerning the identity of Eutrapelus and other Volumnii connected to Antony. D. R. Shackleton Bailey, in *Two Studies in Roman Nomenclature* (New York: American Philological Association, 1976), 77, suggests that Lycoris was the "Volumnia" mentioned by Cicero in *Letters to His Friends* 14.16. Mazzarino, "Contributo," p. 5 n. 3, has developed this same theory, reaching some very convincing conclusions.

Concerning Eutrapelus's banquet held in the year 46 B.C., see Veyne, *Love, Poetry, and the West,* 114 and 173 (the two passages cited provide conflicting interpretations). Doubts concerning Lycoris's relationship with Brutus have been voiced by E. Rawson, *Cassius and Brutus: The Memory of the Liberators* (1986), reprint. in *Roman Culture and Society* (Oxford: Clarendon Press, 1991), 488–507. See esp. p. 496. On the performance given in Posillipo, see R. Syme, "Who was Vedius Pollio?" in *Roman Papers*, vol. 2 (Oxford, 1979), 518–29, and R. Syme, *History in Ovid* (Oxford, 1978), 200 ff.; M. Bonaria, in *Enciclopedia virgiliana*, vol. 1, *s.v.* "Bucoliche 15. La recitazione." The *Bucolics* were probably composed between 42 and 39 B.C. Cicero died at the end of 43 B.C., but this is no reason to doubt this testimony, as the sixth eclogue could have been composed apart from the other *Bucolics*.

For Gallus's biography, see L. Winniczuk, "Cornelius Gallus, Poet and Statesman," *Eos* 56 (1951–66): 127–45. (There are a few flaws in this article; for example, Eutrapelus is described as a senator.) See also J.-P. Boucher, *Caius Cornelius Gallus* (Paris, 1966). See also Mazzarino, "Contributo."

Gallus's papyrus may be dated between the last quarter of the first century B.C. and the first quarter of the first century A.D. The date coincides with the Roman occupation of the site, which was conquered in 25 B.C. This citadel, located just beyond the border, probably served later as an outpost. The *editio princeps* of the papyrus, which came to light during excavations by the Egypt Exploration Society, was edited by R. D. Anderson, P. J. Parsons and R. G. M. Nisbet, in "Elegiacs by Gallus from Qaṣr Ibrīm," *Journal of Roman Studies* 69 (1979): 125–55. For more detailed studies, see A. Barchiesi, "Notizie sul 'nuovo Gallo'," *Atene e Roma*, n.s., 26 (1981): 53–66; A. M. Morelli, "Rassegna sul nuovo Gallo," in V. Tandoi, ed., *Disiecti membra poetae: Studi di poesia latina in frammenti*, vol. 2 (Foggia: Atlantica, 1985), 140–83; and A. M. Morelli, "Sulla genuinità del papiro di Gallo," ibid., vol. 3 (1988), 104–19. Aside from various articles and notes, there is also an interesting monograph by L. Nicastri in *Cornelio Gallo e l'elegia ellenistico-romana: Studio dei nuovi frammenti* (Naples: M. D'Auria, 1984). On the elegiac genre, see Veyne, *Love, Poetry, and the West;* J. C. Hallet, "The Role of Women in Roman Elegy: Counter-cultural Feminism," in J. Peradotto and J. P. Sullivan, eds., *Women in the Ancient World: The Arethusa Papers* (Albany: New York State University Press, 1984), 251–62. The verse concerning Lycoris reads "tristia ṇequit[ia . . .] Lycori tua" "Sad, Lycoris, because of your bad behavior." The part concerning Cato, quite illegible, has been reconstructed by Nicastri (*Cornelio Gallo*, 95), as follows: "And if she bears witness to the same for me (or rather if my verses are worthy of her) before you, O Viscus, I will not withdraw. Nothing do I fear, O Cato, if you are the judge." On the identity of Cato, see the above-mentioned bibliographical references. The only scholar to suggest that the figure of Cato may not be identified as Valerius Cato is A. S. Hollis (who, however, identifies the figure as the censor or as Cato's father), in "The New Gallus, 8–9," *Classical Quarterly*, n.s. 30 (1980): 541. This problem remains without a solution if we base our study only on the Qaṣr Ibrīm fragments. In my opinion the issue must be reexamined by historians. See the bibliography in G. Cresci Marrone's *Ecumene augustea: Una politica per il consenso* (Rome: "L'Erma" di Bretschneider, 1993), 141 ff. There is a problem of interpretation concerning the tenth *Bucolic,* line 44 ("Nunc insanus amor duris te Martis in armis"), which contains an old conjecture now rejected by many modern editors. Many manuscripts read *"me"* in the place of *"te."* According to this hypothesis, it would not have been Gallus who fought (against Lucius Antonius) while Lycoris was far from her homeland, but rather her soldier. Servius (*Commentary on the Bucolics* 10.1) tells us "This Gallus loved his meretrix Cytheris, freedwoman of Volumnius, who after having spurned him, followed Antony to Gaul." The Antony in question could not be Mark, but rather his brother Lucius, who indeed, in 41 had won a victory beyond the Alps. On the other hand, the "me" of the conjecture sounds rather like a *lectio facilior.* It is more likely that in Servius's comment, the mention of Antony is generic, thus misleading (according to another commentator, Philargyrius, Lycoris followed Caesar!). Servius's mistake might not have been that far off the mark. After all, it is certain that Lycoris accompanied an "Antonian," one of Antony's men, to the north. Aside from these reconstructions, we must keep in mind the fictional literary context of the tenth *Bucolic.* On this point, see the classic essay by G. B. Conte in *Virgilio: Il genere e i suoi confini* (Milan: Garzanti, 1984), 9–42; available in English in G. B. Conte, *The Rhetoric of Imitation: Genre and Poetic Memory in Virgil and Other Latin Poets* (Ithaca, N.Y., 1986).

Mimes and Mime

The classic text for the study of the evolution of Roman theater is *The Roman Stage* by W. Beare, 3d ed. (London: Methuen, 1964; reprint, 1977). However, Beare has decidedly diminished the role of mime, making a sharp distinction between cultivated theater and those other forms of scenic representations, such as mime, that to his refined taste seem rather remote from the theater proper. See G. Chiarini's introduction to the Italian translation of this work ("W. Beare e il teatro latino," in W. Beare, *I Romani a teatro* [Rome and Bari: Laterza, 1982], v–xxvi). Some of these positions now have now been reexamined in an evocative work by F. Dupont, *L'acteur roi* (Paris: Les Belles Lettres, 1985).

The main study of mime is H. Reich, *Der Mimus,* 2 vols. (Berlin, 1903). This work, and a large part of the later bibliography (see E. Wurst, in *RE* 15.2 coll. 1727–64, *s.v.* "Mimos") considers mime as a universal Mediterranean genre. M. Bonaria's study, *Romani mimi,* 2d ed. (Rome: Edizioni dell'Ateneo, 1965) is also very useful. It gathers together fragments and testimonies concerning mime in Rome (with rather prudish translations). See also R. Rieches, "Mimus und Atellana," in E. Lefèvre, ed., *Das römische Drama* (Darmstadt: Wissenshaftliche Buchgesellschaft, 1978), 348–77, esp. p. 348 and the recent synthesis in L. Cicu, "Problemi e strutture del mimo a Roma," *Quaderni di Sandalion* 3 (Sassari: Gallizzi, 1988; includes bibliography). Another bibliography is found in AA.VV., *Lo spazio letterario di Roma antica, V, Cronologia e bibliografia della letteratura latina* (Rome: Salerno, 1991), 275. On the social position of actors, see J. E. Spruit, *De Juridische en Sociale positie van de Romeinse Acteurs* (Assen: Van Gorcum and Prakke, 1966); M. Ducos, "La condition des acteurs à Rome: Données juridiques et sociales," in J. Blänsdorf, ed., *Theater und Gesellschaft in Imperium Romanum* (Tübingen: Francke, 1990), 19–33; H. Leppin, *Histrionen, Untersu-*

chungen zur sozialen Stellung von Bühnenkünstmalern im Westen des römischen Reiches zur Zeit der Republik und des Principats (Bonn: Habelt, 1992). Concerning freedmen artists see S. Treggiari, *Roman Freedmen during the Late Republic* (Oxford: Clarendon Press, 1969), 140, 224. See also "Libertine Ladies," *Classical World* 64 (1970–71), 196–98; G. Fabre, *Libertus: Recherches sur les rapports patron-affranchi à la fin de la République romaine* (Paris, 1981), 184, 354–57. (On p.354 it is erroneously stated that Antony's affair with Lycoris occurred after Gallus's affair with her.) General information may be found in A. Wallace-Hadrill, *Patronage in Ancient Society* (London and New York: Routledge, 1990), 63–87.

On women's cultural role in the Republican era, see E. Rawson, *Intellectual Life in the Late Roman Republic* (London: Duckworth, 1985), 46–48; C. Petrocelli, *La stola e il silenzio: Sulla condizione femminile nel mondo romano* (Palermo: Sellerio, 1989), 308–21; and W. V. Harris, *Ancient Literacy* (Cambridge: Harvard University Press, 1989).

CHAPTER FIVE

All the ancient sources on Livia not specifically cited in the text may be found in L. Ollendorff, *RE* 13.1 (1926), coll. 900 ff; See also *PIR*, 5.1 (1970), 73 ff.

Her important role in Roman politics has been discussed by R. Syme in *The Roman Revolution* (Oxford, 1939).

Concerning the Perusian War, see Gabba, "Le colonie triumvirali di Antonio in Italia," *Parola del passato* 8 (1953): 101 (= *Esercito e società nella tarda repubblica romana* [Florence, 1973], 459), and Gabba, "The Perusin War and Triumviral Italy," *Harvard Studies in Classical Philology* 76 (1971): 139. See also J. M. Roddaz, "Lucius Antonius," Historia 37 (1988): 317. See also the essay by C. Virlouvet in this same volume.

Concerning the date of Livia's marriage to Augustus, see J. Gage, "Le calendrier d'Auguste," in *Res gestae divi Augusti*, 3d ed. (Paris, 1977), 166. See also J. Carcopino, "Le mariage de Octave et de Livia et la naissance de Germanicus," *Revue historique* 161 (1929): 215, and G. V. Sumner, "Germanicus and Drusus Caesar," *Latomus* 26 (1967): 424–25, n. 1. See also S. Priuli, "Osservazioni sul feriale di Spello," *Tituli* 2 (Rome, 1980), 68; A.Vassileiou, "Sur les dates de naissances de Drusus, de Gaius et Lucius Caesar," *Revue de philologie* 58 (1984): 44. On Marcia and her marriage see M. Salvadore, *Due donne romane* (Palermo 1990), 13, and bibliography. For a discussion of marriage strategies in the Roman upper classes, see J. Andreau and H. Bruhns, eds., *Parenté et stratégies familiales dans l'antiquité romaine* (Rome, 1990). On the subject of Augustus's policy of reconciliation adopted after the end of the civil wars, see A. Fraschetti, *Roma e il principe* (Rome and Bari, 1990), 79.

Concerning the honors conferred upon Livia and Octavia in A.D. 35, see C. R. A. Bauman, "Tribunician Sacrosanctity in 44, 36, 35 B.C.," *Rheinisches Museum* 124 (1981): 167. On Augustus's "moralistic" legislation, with which Livia seems to have totally agreed, see L. Ferrero Raditsa, "Augustus' Legislation Concerning Marriage, Procreation, Love Affairs, and Adultery," *ANRW* 2.13: 278.

On the *domus Augusta* and its annual celebrations, see Fraschetti, *Roma e il principe,* 5. For a study of Augustus's house on the Palatine, where Livia also lived, see G. Carrettoni, *Das Haus des Augustus auf dem Palatin* (Mainz, 1983). For a discussion of Agrippa's role and on his relationship with Livia in general, see J. Rodaz, *Marcus Agrippa* (Rome, 1984).

The subject of mourning in the *domus Augusta* has been treated by Fraschetti in *Roma e il principe,* 81; see also H. von Hesberg and S. Panciera, "Das Mausoleum des Augustus: Der Bau und seine Inschriften," *Bayerische Akademie der Wissenschaften* 108 (1994): 72. Concerning Varro Murena's plot and Livia's role, see Syme, *The Roman Revolution.* Concerning the differing attitudes shown by Octavia and Livia on the occasion of the deaths of their sons Marcellus and Germanicus, see J. Maurin, "'Funus' et rites de separation," *Annali dell'Istituto universitario orientale. Sez. Archeologia e Storia antica* 6 (1984): 207–8. Concerning the dedication of the *porticus Liviae,* see S. B. Platner and Th. Ashby, A *Topographical Dictionary of Ancient Rome* (Oxford, 1929), 423. For a study of Tiberius's retirement to Rhodes, see B. Lewick, "Tiberius' Retirement to Rhodes in 6 B.C.," *Latomus* 31 (1972): 799. On the scandal involving Julia see A. Ferrill, "Augustus and His Daughter: A Modern Myth," in *Studies in Latin Literature and Roman History,* vol. 2 (Brussels, 1980), 345–46. (It is not easy to share his hypercritical views on some issues.) See also E. Meise, *Untersuchungen zur Geschichte der Julisch-Claudischen Dynastie* (Munich, 1969). On Livia's role after the death of Augustus, see A. Fraschetti, "Osservazioni sulla 'tabula Siarensis' ('Frag.I' 11.6–8)," *Epigraphica* 50 (1988): 56. On the Palatine games organized by Livia, see M. A. Cavallaro, *Spese e spettacoli: Aspetti economico-strutturali degli spettacoli nella Roma giulio-claudia* (Bonn, 1984), 43, 47.

Concerning Livia and Tiberius's complex relationship, see B. Lewick, *Tiberius the Politician* (London, 1976); M. Pani, *Tendenze politiche della successione al principato di Augusto* (Bari, 1979). On Germanicus's death, see Fraschetti, *Roma e il principe,* 88.

Chapter Six

The story of Perpetua and her companions may be found in the *Passio Perpetuae,* which exists in two versions, Latin and Greek, and in the *Acta,* also in two versions, A and B, the latter being the briefer version. The critical edition of the *Passio Perpetuae* has been edited by C. I. M. I. van Beek, *Passio Sanctarum Perpetuae et Felicitatis: Textum Graecum et Latinum ad fidem codicum mss.* (Nijmegen, 1936). This also includes both the A and the B versions of the *Acta minora.* Van Beek has also published a briefer version of this material in *Florilegium Patristicum* 43 (Bonn, 1938), without the *Acta.* Now see J. Amat, ed., *Passion de Perpétue et de Félicité; suivi des Actes,* Sources Chrétiennes, no. 417 (Paris, 1996).

The available critical bibliography is vast. All the best-known scholars in the field of hagiography (to name one: Pio Franchi de' Cavalieri) have written about the *Passio Perpetuae,* as have many important scholars of comparative literature, such as E. Auerbach. My intention here is only to furnish a guide to the analysis of a few aspects of the critical debate with particular reference to studies in Italian. For an important overview of the question, I refer the reader to *Atti e passioni dei martiri,* ed. A. A. R. Bastiaensen et al. (Milan, 1987), 109–11.

There is not a single aspect of the *Passio Perpetuae* left untouched by critics, often with contradictory results, as is often the case for the great writings of the past that have deep emotive resonance. Beginning with the figure of Perpetua herself, even the most obvious details, such as her age, given by the compiler as "twenty-two years," have been subject to debate. Some critics have wished to underline her extreme youth (M. Fumagalli Beonio Brocchieri in P. Dronke, *Donne e cultura nel Medioevo: Scrittrici medievali dal II al XIV secolo* [Milan, 1986], viii). Others tend to stress her maturity, in relation to the average age of marriage in the ancient world. She is generally portrayed as a very sensitive person, but W. Frend, in "Blandina and Perpetua: Two Early Christian Heroines," in J. Rougé and W. R. Turcan, eds., *Les martyrs de Lyons (177)* (Paris, 1978), 168–86, describes her attitude as almost fanatical. An in-depth examination of Perpetua's personality may be found in A. Valerio, "Le figure femminili negli Atti dei Martiri del II secolo," *Rassegna di Teologia* 22 (1981): 28–44. See also P. A. Gramaglia, "Personificazioni e modelli del femminile nella transizione dalla cultura classica a quella cristiana," in G. Galli, ed., *Interpretazione e personificazione: Personificazioni e modelli del femminile* (Genoa, 1988), 101–15, and, especially, C. Mazzucco, *"E fui fatta maschio": La donna nel cristianesimo primitivo (secoli I–III)* (Turin, 1989), 119. My own essay owes much to the very balanced analysis of this study.

The main questions concerning the *Passio Perpetuae* may be summed up as follows. From the moment the Greek text of the *Passio Perpetuae* was discovered by F. Rendel Harris and Seth K. Gifford in 1890, the problem arose as to which text came first, with a wide range of possible solutions. Sometimes the Latin and sometimes the Greek text have been considered the earlier version, while a number of intermediary solutions have also been proposed: for example, that Perpetua's text was written originally in Greek, while that of Saturus was originally in Latin, or vice versa, that the story of Perpetua and the compiler's own narrative were originally in Latin, and the Saturus text in Greek. This last solution, proposed by A. Fridh, *Le problème de la Passion des Saintes Perpétue et Félicité* (Göteborg, 1968), is still held to by some. Currently the tendency is to consider the Latin text the earlier one, but in some cases priority is still given to the Greek text. See L. Robert, "Une vision de Perpétue martyre à Carthage," *Comptes rendus de l'Académie des Inscriptions et Belles Lettres* (1982): 228–76, a text that influenced R. Lane Fox in his wide-ranging work, *Pagans and Christians* (Italian translation, Rome and Bari, 1991), 430, 818. Another problematic issue has been the attempt to identify Tertullian as the compiler, owing to linguistic similarities to his style, which are pointed out by P. de Labriolle, *La crise montaniste* (Paris, 1913), 345–51. For a discussion of the issues in question, see R. Braun, "Nouvelles observations linguistiques sur le rédacteur de la *Passio Perpetuae,*" *Vigiliae Christianae* 33 (1979): 105–17. This theory has currently been abandoned. The authenticity of the sections regarding Perpetua and Saturus has also been lengthily discussed and it has been suggested that these figures were literary creations of the compiler. It is in this context that we find the most curious discrepancies. E. Corsini, in "Proposte per una lettura della *Passio Perpetuae*," in *Forma futuri: Studi in onore del card. Michele Pellegrino* (Turin, 1975), 492, justifiably takes a critical attitude toward J. Fontaine's position, contained in another important stylistic study of the *Passio:* "Tendances et difficultés d'une prose chrétienne naissante: l'Esthétique composite de la *Passio Perpetuae*," in Fontaine, *Aspects et problèmes de la prose d'art latine au IIIe siècle* (Turin, 1968), 69–97. Fontaine claims to maintain an intermediate position between two extreme theories, i.e. acceptance or denial of Perpetua's visions as authentic experiences. He suggests that the text was compiled in three distinct phases, in which the last phase was done either by Perpetua's catechumen brother or by another member of the community, who was perhaps a priest (p. 87). It is not clear why this would be an intermediate position, denying the compiler's assertion (that Perpetua wrote the text herself) in order to substitute for this a complex hypothesis that cannot be proved. The only valid methodological position, given the compiler's explicit affirmation, is to ask oneself if that claim, so solemnly set forth, conflicts with any known external data or with any internal incongruities. In the absence of negative results, the diversity of styles pointed out by critics during the course of numerous studies must be considered sufficient proof to affirm the authenticity of these documents. The current tendency is to accept the authenticity of the writings of Perpetua and Saturus and to emphasize the value of the Perpetua text. For example, M. Alexandre uses it in the conclusion to the first volume (edited by P. Schmitt Pantel) of the *Storia delle donne in Occidente,* ed. G. Duby and M. Perrot (Rome and Bari, 1990), 549–53.

Two tendencies prevail in interpreting Perpetua's visions. The first views them as a manifestation of the subconscious, the second as a literary creation. For a Jungian interpretation see M. L. von Franz, "Die *Passio Perpetuae:* Versuch einer psychologischen Deutung," in C. G. Jung, *Aion: Untersuchungen zu Symbolgeschichte* (Zurich, 1951), 389–496. Concerning the recent translation into Italian (Como, 1994) see the observations of C. Mazzucco in *Rivista di Storia e Letteratura Religiosa* 30 (1994): 644–46. D. Devoti has given a Freudian interpretation of the visions in "Sogno e conversione nei Padri: Considerazioni preliminari," *Augustinianum* 27 (1987): 101–36; D. Devoti, "La passion de Perpétue: Un nœud familial," in E. Livingstone, ed., *Studia Patristica,* vol. 26 (Leuven, 1991): 66–72. A few to-the-point comments by E. Zocca (influenced by the ideas of Matteblanco) concerning the need to keep the primitive polysemy in Perpetua's language appear in "Un passo controverso della *Passio Perpetuae*, IV, 9: 'de caseo quod mulgebat dedit mihi quasi buccellam'," *Studi e Materiali di Storia delle Religioni* 50 (1984): 147–54. Generally critics who interpret her visions as manifestations of the subconscious underline the presence of pagan vestiges in them. Other interesting issues are raised by E. R. Dodds in *Pagans and Christians in an Age of Anxiety* (Italian translation, Florence, 1970) and in Dronke, *Donne e cultura,* 11–29. The most cogent arguments opposing a psychoanalytical interpretation are found in Corsini, "Proposte," 481–541: "We believe that these visions, rather than being an almost spontaneous record of an authentic experience, are actually rational literary creations meant to convey a message and that they are presented in a form that may be identified as a form of catechism, influenced by a long Biblio-Christian tradition" (495–96). Corsini's article is full of many insightful observations, but ultimately his approach is overly rigid in its attempt to impose consistency upon the contents of these visions and to identify all the symbols appearing in them, denying the intrusion of pagan vestiges. See Gramaglia's remarks on this method in *Rivista di Storia e Letteratura Religiosa* 26 (1990): 180–86.

Many studies have been done of specific aspects of the visions. F. J. Dölger has written two studies, one concerning the Dinocrates visions, the other concerning the Egyptian one in *Antike und Christentum* 2 (1930): 1–40. Robert, "Une vision de Perpétue," sees in Perpetua's battle with the Egyptian a retelling of *Pythia Carthaginis,* an opinion confuted by J. Aronen, "Pythia Carthaginis o immagini cristiane nella visione di Perpetua?" in A. Mastino, ed., *L'Africa romana: Atti del VI Convegno di studio* (Sassari, 1989), 643–48. The Dinocrates visions, which pose notable problems in the light of later orthodox doctrines, became a subject of debate as early as the time of Augustine (*De an. et eius origine* 1.10). Augustine, unable to solve some doctrinal problems raised by the text, revoked its authenticity. The shadowy place where Perpetua sees her dead brother has been interpreted as hell (Dölger, 1930) or as purgatory in embryonic form. See J. Le Goff, *La naissance du Purgatoire* (Paris, 1981), 30; M. P. Ciccarese, "Le più antiche rappresentazioni del purgatorio, dalla *Passio Perpetuae* alla fine del IX sec.," *Romanobarbarica* 7 (1982–83): 33–76. An overall view is given by J. Amat in *Songes et visions: L'au-delà dans la littérature latine tardive* (Paris, 1985), 66–86, 118–31. Amat has also written an analysis of the psychological differences between Perpetua and Saturus, "L'autenticité des songes de la passion de Perpétue et de Félicité," *Augustinianum* 29 (1989): 177–91. On the vision of Perpetua's Egyptian opponent, see Habermehl, *Perpetua und Ägypter oder bielder der bösen in frühen Afrikanischen Christentum: Ein Versuch zur Passio Sanctarum Perpetuae et Felicitatis* (Berlin, 1992). For a study of the sections written by the compiler, see C. Mazzucco, "Il significato cristiano della 'libertas' proclamata dai martiri della *Passio Perpetuae et Felicitatis,*" *Vigiliae Christianae* 34 (1980): 105–19. Now see G. Lanata, "Sogni di donne nel primo cristianesimo," in *Donne sante sante donne: Esperienza religiosa e storia del genere* (Torino, 1996): 61–98.

On the question of Montanist influence on the *Passio Perpetuae* or on the martyrs themselves (a question which for many years has been linked to the attempt to identify Tertullian as the compiler), P. de Labriolle's study (*La crise montaniste*) still today offers a valid starting point for inquiry. His presentation of the facts is exhaustive, deeply marked by his conviction that Tertullian was indeed the compiler. He concludes that "we meet not a single statement that may be clearly and openly considered Montanist" (353), and his ideological concerns (aside from his conviction that Tertullian was the compiler) are clearly indicated in his discussion of the prologue: "What is most disturbing is that the compiler (let us say Tertullian) intends to allow recent visions and new prophecies to become part of the instrumentum Ecclesiae." Corsini is far more blunt than Labriolle in denying the compiler's Montanism ("Proposte," 485). By contrast,

P. Monceaux (*Histoire littéraire de l'Afrique chrétienne* [Paris, 1901], 78), finds a connection between the *Passion of Perpetua* and the sect of the Artotyrites, "the cheese-eaters," who were considered Montanists. L. Gatti, in "La Passio SS. Perpetuae et Felicitatis," *Didaskaleion* 1 (1923): 31–43, provides a synthesis of the arguments suggesting that the compiler was influenced by Montanism. T. D. Barnes, in *Tertullian: A Historical and Literary Study* (Oxford, 1971), 77–89, considers Perpetua a Montanist. Concerning the marginalization of women that followed the struggle against Montanism, see the classic study by P. de Labriolle, "'Mulieres in ecclesia taceant': Un aspect de la lutte antimontaniste," *Bulletin d'ancienne littérature e d'archéologie chrétienne* 1 (1911): 3–24, 103–22. Now see Ch. Trevett, *Montanism: Gender, Authority, and the New Prophecy* (Cambridge, 1996); A. Wypusterk, "Magic Montanism, Perpetua, and the Severan Persecution," *Vigiliae Christianae* 51 (1997): 276–97.

Concerning the African communities and persecution in general, see W. H. C. Frend, *Martyrdom and Persecution in the Early Church* (Oxford, 1965), 363 ff. On anti-Christian legislation in the times of Perpetua and on the presumed existence of an edict issued by Septimius Severus, see E. dal Covolo, *I Severi e il cristianesimo* (Rome, 1989). On the connection between the charisma of martyrdom and prophecy, see M. Lods, *Confesseurs et martyrs successeurs des prophètes dans l'église des trois premiers siècles* (Neuchatel and Paris, 1958); W. Rordorf, "L'espérance des martyrs chrétiens" in *Forma futuri*, 445–61. For a discussion of female martyrs, see C. Mazzucco, "Una figura di donna cristiana: La martire," in *Atti del II Convegno nazionale di Studi su "La donna nel mondo antico,"* ed. R. Uglione (Turin, 1989), 167–95. For an opposite point of view, see F. E. Consolino, "La donna negli *Acta Martyrum*," in *La donna nel pensiero cristiano antico*, ed. U. Mattioli (Genoa, 1992), 95–117. See also the remarks by M. Simonetti in the same volume, 7–10.

On the structure of the *Passio Perpetuae:* T. Sardella, "Strutture temporali e modelli di cultura: Rapporti tra antitradizionalismo storico e modello martiriale nella *Passio Perpetuae et Felicitatis*," *Augustinianum* 30 (1990): 259–78; and S. Boesch Gajano, "Le metamorfosi del racconto," in *Lo spazio letterario di Roma antica*, vol. 3 (Rome, 1990), 224–30; Brent D. Shaw, "The Passion of Perpetua," *Past and Present* 139 (1993): 3–45.

Concerning the authenticity of the *Acta Minora*, see the van Beek edition of 1936, 98–103 (Introduction). For a more recent discussion of the *Acta*, see J. W. Halporn, "Literary History and Generic Expectations," *Vigiliae Christianae* 45 (1991): 223–41, although this study is somewhat oversimplistic in its attempt to show that the differences between the *Acta* and the *Passio Perpetuae* derive from differences in literary genres.

CHAPTER SEVEN

Biography

General sources concerning Helena: *PLRE* 1, *Fl. Iulia Helena* 3, 410; R. Klein, "Helena II (Kaiserin)" *RAC* 14 (1987): 355 ff.; O. Seeck, "Helena 2," *RE* 7: 2, 2820–23; H. Leclercq, "Hélène, impératrice," *DACL* 6. 2: 2126 ff.; *Bibl.*

Sanct. 4: 98 ff. A very well documented and well balanced monograph on Helena by Jan Willem Drijvers has recently been published: *Helena Augusta, the Mother of Constantine the Great and the Legend of Her Finding of the True Cross* (Leiden and New York, 1992). On the following points, see especially pages indicated (sources and bibliography are provided): city of birth (9); humble origins (17); issuing of coins (40); inscriptions (45); Eusebius's silence concerning the discovery of the Cross (83); comparison of antique versions of the *inventio* (95); Helena as leading figure in the discovery (131). The biography of Helena written by Almann of Hautvillers may be read in *AA.SS.* Aug. 3. Antwerp, 1738, 580 ff. Concerning this biography see F. E. Consolino, "L'invenzione di una biografia: Almanno di Hautvillers e la vita di Sant'Elena," *Hagiographica* 1 (1994): 81 ff.

Helena's role in the exiling of Theodora's sons (an idea held by J. Bidez, *La vie de l'empereur Julien* [Paris, 1930], 7, and by O. Seeck, *RE* 7.2: 2821) has recently been reproposed by Klein, *RAC* 14: 356. Aside from the sources I have cited, further evidence on their exile may be found in Ausonius, *Prof.* 16.11 ff (*dum Constantini fratres opulenta Tolosa / exilii specie sepositos cohibet*) and 17.9 (which cites Narbona as the residence for the sons of Dalmatius, half-brother of Constantine); Ammianus 14.11,27 (Gallus, son of Constantius, also half-brother of Constantine, was born in Massa in Etruria). These texts all confirm the fact that Constantine's half-brothers were exiled, but do not mention Helena.

Epigraphy

Inscriptions mentioning Helena: *CIL* 6.1136 of Rome (commemorates the rebuilding of the baths near the Palatium Sessoranium) and *CIL* 9.2446 of Saepinum (dedicated to her before she became Augusta); *CIL* 6.1134 = *ILS* 709 (found in the garden of the convent contiguous to the church of Santa Croce in Gerusalemme); *CIL* 6.1135 (now lost—had been found behind the Lateran basilica); *CIL* 678 (originally for Fausta, located in Sorrento); *CIL* 8.1633 (found in Africa in Sicca Veneria); *CIL* 10.517 = *ILS* 708 of the *corrector* of Bruttius and Lucania; *CIL* 10.1483 of Naples.

The True Cross

On her discovery of the Cross, aside from the references in the bibliography on Helena mentioned above, see *DACL* 3.2 s.v. *Croix (invention et exaltation de la vraie)*, 3131–39, and the book by S. Borgehammar, *How the Holy Cross Was Found: From Event to Medieval Legend* (Stockholm, 1991). For mention of the Cross in Cyril, see *Cathechesis* 4.10, *PG* 33, 470A "the world is full of pieces of wood from the cross"; 10.19, *PG* 33, 685B–687A "The holy wood of the cross that we may see in our midst, thanks to the efforts of those who, in faith, took pieces of it with them, has by now filled the entire world." Similar considerations may be found in 13.4, *PG* 33, 776 B. On the original version of the legend (Syriac, Greek, or Latin?), J. Straubinger, "Die Kreuzauffindungslegende: Untersuchungen über ihre altchristliche Fassungen mit besonderer Berucksichtigung der syrischen Texte" (diss., Paderborn, 1912), proposed that it was of Syriac origin, written in Odessa in the first half of the fifth century. M. Pardyová Vodová remains the only scholar who still believes that it was Latin in origin, but offers no valid evidence to prove this: "L'impératrice Hélène et l'invention de la Sainte Croix," *Sborník prací filos. fak archeol. klas.* 25 (1980): 235. On the three different Latin versions in circulation during the Middle Ages, see the critical edition by Borgehammar, *The Holy Cross,* 201 ff. He proposes that the legend was of Palestinian origin and claims that the original text must have been in Greek. The Syriac version would thus have been derived from a Latin translation of the Greek original. The text of the inscription in the church of Santa Croce in Gerusalemme mentioned by Borgehammar (129) reads "Hic tellus sancta Calvarie Solime ab beata Helena in inferiorem fornicem demissa servata est atque inde nomen Hierusalem capelle inditum" (a text which he has drawn from a guide to the basilica by D. B. Bedini, "Le reliquie della Passione del Signore" [3d ed., Rome, 1987], p. 30).

Chapter Eight
Hypatia, or the Partisan Spirit of the Alexandrians

The laws by Constantius against sorcerers and fortune tellers (356–357) and those by Theodosius against haruspices and magicians (385) are collected in the *Codex Theodosianus;* see also Socrates Scholasticus, *Ecclesiastica historia,* ed. R. Hussey (Oxford, 1853), 5, 16 (*PG* 67, coll. 604); on Valens's persecution of the "mathematicians" (*mathematici*), see. A. Piganiol, *L'empire chrétien (325–395),* vol. 4, pt. 2, *Histoire romaine* (Paris, 1972), 160–61. For a general discussion of Theodosius's antipagan policies, see the classic study by H. Bloch, "The Pagan Revival in the West at the End of the Fourth Century," in *The Conflict between Paganism and Christianity in the Fourth Century,* ed. A. Momigliano (Oxford, 1963). For a study of Theodosian legislation and a juridical discussion of the concept of intolerance, see *Atti dell'Accademia Romanistica Costantiniana. VI Convegno Internazionale (Spello, October 12–15, 1983),* ed. G. Crifò (Perugia, 1986), in particular pp. 1–22 (J. Gaudemet) and 363–417 (O. Bucci). Eunapius's account of the destruction of the Serapeum may be found in Eunapius, *Lives of the Philosophers,* Loeb Classical Library 134 (Cambridge and London, 1921), 422–23; see also Sozomen's account in *Storia ecclesiastica* 7.15, in *PG* 67, coll. 1452. The description of the temple and statue of Serapis may be found in Clement of Alexandria, *Protrepticus* 4, 28: *The Exhortation to the Greeks . . .* ed. G. W. Butterworth, Loeb Classical Library 92 (Cambridge and London, 1968), 106–10; see also W. Hornbostel, *Sarapis* (Amsterdam, 1973); W. Amelung, "Le Sarapis de Briaxis," *Revue Archéologique* (1903): 177–204. Concerning the economic and social setting of Alexandria, see P. Fraser, *Ptolemaic Alexandria* (Oxford, 1972), 43–51.

The story of Hypatia's murder and of the events preceding it are recounted in book 7 of the *Ecclesiastica historia* of Socrates Scholasticus, chap. 15, source of the quotes used in this essay, 760–62 (*PG* 67, coll. 768 ff.). For Suidas's article on Hypatia (Y 166), see *Suidae Lexicon,* vol. 4, ed. A. Adler (Stuttgart, 1971), 644–46; see also P. Tannery, "L'article de Suidas sur Hypatie," in *Annales de la*

Faculté des Lettres de Bordeaux, II (1880), 199; a German translation and commentary appear in R. Asmus, *Das Leben des Philosophen Isidoros von Damaskios aus Damaskos* (Leipzig, 1911), 31–33. The fragments of Damascius's *Life of Isidore,* drawn from Suidas and from Photius's *Bibliotheca,* are collected in Damascius's *Vitae Isidori reliquiae,* ed. C. Zintzen, Bibliotheca Graeca et Latina Suppletoria 1 (Hildesheim, 1967); on Hypatia, see specifically pp. 76–81 and 218–21. For a study of Hesychius of Miletus's *Onomatologos,* a collection of biographies of pagan men of letters composed in the sixth century (the text is now lost, but fragments are preserved in Photius and in Suidas), see H. Hunger, *Die hochsprachliche profane Literatur der Byzantiner,* vol. 1, 250. The quotations from Synesius were taken from *Ep.* 81 = Sinesio, *Opere di Sinesio di Cirene: Epistole, operette, inni,* ed. A. Garzya (Turin, 1989), 230. The essay by P. Brown, "Il filosofo e il monaco: Due scelte tardoantiche," appeared in *Storia di Roma* 3/1 (Turin, 1993), 877–94. On *parrhesia* and the holy man, see also L. Cracco Ruggini, "Potere e carismi in età imperiale," *Studi Storici* (July–September, 1979): 585–607. The relationship between the provincial Roman government and the local ruling classes are discussed in P. Desideri, *Dione di Prusa: Un intellettuale greco nell'Impero romano* (Messina and Florence, 1978). The chronicle of John of Nikiû may be found in H. Zotenberg, *Chronique de Jean, évêque de Nikiou, texte éthiopien* (Paris, 1883)—but see also the English translation by R. H. Charles, *The Chronicle of John, Bishop of Nikiu* (London and Oxford, 1916). The rediscovery of this important source for research on Hypatia was made by J. Rougé, "La politique de Cyrille d'Alexandrie et le meurtre d'Hypatie," *Cristianesimo nella Storia* 11/3 (1990): 485–504.

Concerning the relations between pagans, Jews, and Christians in the fifth century, see L. Cracco Ruggini, "Pagani, ebrei e cristiani: Odio sociologico e odio teologico nel mondo antico," in *Gli Ebrei nell'alto Medioevo,* Settimane di Studio del Centro Italiano di Studi sull'Alto Medioevo 26 (Spoleto, 1980). The Jewish revolt of A.D. 115–17 is described by Dio Cassius in his *Roman History,* 59, 32; see Dio Cassius, *Roman History,* Loeb Classical Library, 9 vols., ed. E. Cary and B. Foster, vol.7, 360–65. The pogrom of 414 in Alexandria and the events leading up to it are discussed in Socrates, *Ecclesiastica historia* 7.13, 14 (Hussey, 753–60).

The evolution of Egyptian monasticism as a mass phenomenon in the fifth century is discussed in E. Patlagean, "Lingue e confessioni religiose fra Oriente e Occidente," *Storia di Roma* 3/1: 979 ff. On Cyril's visit to the desert of Nitria, see *Synaxarium Alexandrinum,* ed. I. B. Chabot, I. Forget, I. Guidi, and H. Hyvernat, Latin translation by I. Forget, *CSCO* 78 (Rome, 1922), 72. The fact that the Alexandrian *parabalani* were also clerics is demonstrated by the law regulating their order, which appears in the *Codex Theodosianus* 16.2.42 (September 416), ed. Mommsen, vol. 1, 850: *de clericis.* The quoted passage concerning them was taken from Suidas, Adler 4, 645, 13–14 (θηριώδεις ἄνθρωποι, ὡς ἀληθῶς σχέτλιοι). Aristotle's comment is taken from *On Politics* 1253 A 29, ed. J. Aubonnet, *Les Belles Lettres* (Paris, 1960), 14; the first person to quote it in relationship to Christian *anachoresis* was Julian the Apostate. In describing the crowd outside

Hypatia's house, the Suidas source refers to Homer (*Iliad* 21.26). Damascius uses another Homeric reference later in describing the monks' violence when they killed Hypatia (*Iliad* 16.388 and *Odyssey* 22.40). Concerning the scene of the crime, the Caesareum of Alexandria, see A. Martin, "Les premiers siècles du christianisme à Alexandrie: Essai de topographie religieuse (IIIᵉ–Vᵉ siècles)," *Revue des Etudes Augustiniennes* 30 (1984): 211–25. A summary of events concerning the court and the empire in the year of Hypatia's death may be found in E. de Muralt, *Essai de chronographie byzantine* (Amsterdam, 1963), 25–26. The definition of Pulcheria as "purple-clad nun" is taken from an essay by G. Bigoni, "Ipazia Alessandrina," *Atti del Regio Istituto Veneto di Scienze, Lettere ed Arti*, t. 5, ser. 6 (1886–87): 397–437, 495–526, 681–710. The imperial reply to the envoy sent from Alexandria to the court of Constantinople is preserved in the *Codex Theodosianus* 12.12.15 and 12.2.42 (October 416), ed. Mommsen, vol. 1, 729–30.

The Fortune of Hypatia

The passage from Voltaire is taken from *Questions sur l'Encyclopédie*, pt. 9 (1772), XIX, 392; the allusion refers to the quarrel between Madame Dacier and La Motte. In 1714 Anne Dacier defended the "purity" of Homer in her *Traité des causes de la corruption du goût* (see V. Fournel, *Nouvelle biographie générale*, vol. 11 [Paris, 1855], s.v. "Dacier, Anne Lefèvre," coll. 757–64). The dedication "ad Annam Fabram Daceriam, feminarum quot sunt, quot fuere, doctissima," appears on pp. 4–5 of *Historia mulierum philosopharum* by G. Ménage (Lyons, 1690). The following quotation is taken from the entry "Hypatia" by K. Praechter in *Paulys Real-Encyclopädie*, vol. 9 (Stuttgart, 1916), col. 248 (242–50). The *Histoire de l'établissement du Christianisme* appears in *Oeuvres complètes de Voltaire*, vol. 6, *Philosophie: Dialogues* (Paris, 1876), 582–616; the Alexandrian episode is discussed in chapter 24 ("Excès du fanatisme"), p. 613. Hypatia is mentioned by Fielding in *A Journey from this World to the Next* (1743). The passage that follows is taken from C. M. Wieland, *Sämtliche Werke*, vol. 13 (Leipzig, 1798). The passage from Gibbon is taken from chapter 47 of the *Decline and Fall of the Roman Empire*.

Baronius discusses Cyril's policies and the death of Hypatia in the fifth volume of *Annales ecclesiastici* (Rome, 1602), 350–51, 379–80. For the following quotation, see E. Rensi's introduction to the unusual book by A. Agabiti, *Ipazia: La prima martire della libertà di pensiero* (Catania, 1979; 1st ed., Rome, 1914), 9. Father F. Schaefer's comments are drawn from his article "St. Cyril of Alexandria and the Murder of Hypatia," in *Catholic University Bulletin* 8 (1902): 441–53. Mention of Hypatia's Latin epistle to Cyril may be found in L. S. Le Nain de Tillemont, *Mémoires pour servir à l'histoire ecclésiastique des six premiers siècles*, vol. 14 (Venice, 1732), 274–76 (Art. 3., "Hypacie philosophe payenne est massacrée l'an de Jésus-Christ 415"), and 606. C.-P. Goujet's dissertation is discussed in Desmolets, *Continuation des Mémoires de littérature et d'histoire*, vol. 5, 139–91.

The notes on Diodata Saluzzo Roero were taken from the review of *Poema d'Ipazia ossia delle Filosofie* (Turin, 1827 and 1834), written for the "Arcadian Journal" by her friend Enrichetta Dionigi Orfei: "Del poema d'Ipazia, ossia delle Filosofie, mandato alla luce dalla Marchesa Diodata Saluzzo Roero," *Giornale Arcadico di Scienze, Lettere ed Arti* 83 (April, May, and June, 1840): 286–95, and from "Biografia di Diodata Saluzzo, scritta da se medesima," published years earlier in the same journal, vol. 36 (October, November, and December, 1827). On the sources and origin of the poem, see L. Berardo, "Ipazia o delle ideologie," in *Il romanticismo in Piemonte, Diodata Saluzzo. Atti del Convegno di Studi, Saluzzo, 29 settembre 1990,* ed. M. Guglielminetti and P. Trivero (Florence, 1992), 143–54.

The most accessible edition of Kingsley's novel (1853) is that in Everyman's Library (London and New York, 1968). A critique of the author and his prose appear in J. M. Rist, "Hypatia," *Phoenix* 29/1 (1965): 215. A comparison with Pierre Louÿs appears in H. I. Marrou, "Sinesio di Cirene e il neoplatonismo alessandrino," in *Il conflitto tra paganesimo e cristianesimo,* 139–64. Other references to Hypatia's fate in nineteenth-century literature may be found in R. Asmus, "Hypatia in Tradition und Dichtung," *Studien zur vergleichenden Literaturgeschichte* 7 (1907): 11–44; see also H. von Schubert, "Hypatia von Alexandrien in Wahrheit und Dichtung," *Preussischer Jahrbuch* 124 (1906): 42–60.

The passage from C. Péguy was taken from *Onzième cahier de la Quinzaine de la huitième série,* reprinted in *Oeuvres en prose 1898–1908* (Paris, 1959), 1110–11. Palladas's epigram may be found in the *Anthologia Palatina* 9, 400 (*Anthologie greque, première partie: Anthologie palatine,* vol. 8, ed. P. Waltz [Paris, 1974], 25). Grotius's Latin translation appears as an addendum to Philostorgius's *editio princeps.* On the erroneous Christian interpretation of the poem, compare G. Luck, "Palladas: Christian or Pagan?" *Harvard Studies in Classical Philology* 63 (1958): 455–71; and A. Bowra, "Palladas and the Converted Olympias," *Byzantinische Zeitschrift* 53 (1960): 1–17; to J. Irmscher, "Pallas und Hypatia (Zu *Anthologia Palatina* 9, 40)," in *Actes de la VIème Conférence Internationale des Etudes Classiques des Pays Socialistes: Plovdiv, Bulgaria, 24–28 aprile 1962,* ed. B. Gerov, V. Velkov, and K. Tapkova-Zamova (Sofia, 1963), 313–18. The problem has now been treated in a book that was just coming out as the original edition of this volume was going to press, G. Beretta, *Ipazia d'Alessandria* (Rome, 1993), 89–90, 139–40, 187–233, 250–51. The two poems by Leconte de Lisle are found in *Oeuvres de Leconte de Lisle,* a critical edition by E. Pich, vol. 1, *Poèmes antiques* (Paris: Les Belles Lettres, 1977), 63–66, 272–87. The lines from M. Luzi are taken from *Libro di Ipazia,* introduction by G. Pampaloni, with a note by G. Quiriconi (Milan: Biblioteca Universale Rizzoli, 1980).

The Judgment and Prejudices of the Sources

Concerning references to Hypatia in late source materials, see Cassiodorus, *Historia ecclesiastica tripartita,* ed. W. Jacob and R. Hanslik, *CSEL* 71 (Vienna, 1952), 643–44; Philostorgius, *Kirchengeschichte,* ed. J. Bidez (Leipzig, 1913), 2d ed., ed. F. Winkelmann (Berlin, 1972), 111, 3–8 and 28–31; Malalas, *Chrono-*

graphia, ed. L. Dindorf (Bonn, 1831), 14, 5, 22–23, 359. See also "The *Chronicle of John Malalas,*" trans. E. Jeffreys, M. Jeffreys, and R. Scott, *Byzantina Australiensia* 4 (Melbourne, 1986), 195–96; *Theophanis Chronographia,* ed. C. de Boor, vol. 1 (Leipzig, 1883), 82, 16. Mention of Xanthopoulos appears in Migne *PG* 146, coll. 1105–8; concerning the relationship of Xanthopoulos to the *Ecclesiastica Historia* of Socrates Scholasticus, see G. Gentz, *Die Kirchengeschichte des Nicephorus Callistus Xanthopoulos und ihre Quellen* (Berlin, 1966). For the ecclesiastical history of the African church in the fifth century in general, see L. Duchesne, *Histoire ancienne de l'église,* vol. 3 (Paris, 1910), 287–518; concerning religious controversies and their social repercussions, see also J. Gouillard, "L'hérésie dans l'empire byzantin des origines au XIIᵉ siècle," *Travaux et Mémoires* 1 (1965): 299–324. The passage from G. Bardy is taken from his article "Cyrille d'Alexandrie," in *Dictionnaire d'histoire et de théologie ecclésiastique,* vol. 13 (Paris, 1956), col. 1176. Among the more recent studies of Cyril of Alexandria, see F. Gebremedhin, "Life-giving Blessing: An Inquiry into the Eucharistic Doctrine of Cyril of Alexandria," *Acta Universitatis Upsaliensis: Studia Doctrinae Christianae Upsaliensia* 17 (Uppsala, 1977), see bibliography at 112–19. Concerning Cyril's fortune with the commentators, see J. Reuss, *Matthäus-, Markus-, und Johannes-Katenen nach den handschriftlichen Quellen untersucht* (Münster, 1941). For a discussion of the decline of Hellenism in Egypt, the development of the nationalistic Coptic church, and the role played by Cyril in it, see W. H. C. Frend, *The Rise of the Monophysite Movement: Chapters in the History of the Church in the Fifth and Sixth Centuries* (Cambridge, 1972); M. Roncaglia, *Histoire de l'Eglise copte,* vol. 1 (Beirut, 1966); J. Maspéro, *Histoire des patriarches d'Alexandrie depuis la mort de l'empereur Anastase jusqu'à la réconciliation des Eglise jacobites (518–613),* posthumous edition, ed. A. Fortescue and G. Wiet (Paris, 1923). Concerning ecclesiastic culture in the Islamized territories in the ninth century, see S. Griffith, *Arabic Christianity in the Monasteries of Ninth-Century Palestine* (Brookfield, Vt.: Variorum, 1992).

On the Stoic-Cynic vision of Hypatia appearing in some of the ancient sources, see Rist, *Hypatia,* 220–21. On her *aischrourgìa,* see D. Shanzer, "Merely a Cynic Gesture?" *Rivista di Filologia e di Istruzione Classica* 113 (1985): 61–66. For a discussion of her public lecturing, see E. Evrard, "A quel titre Hypatie enseigna-t-elle la philosophie?" *Revue des Etudes Grecques* 90 (1977): 69–74; this same opinion has recently been expressed by M. O. Goulet-Cazé, "L'arrière-plan scolaire de *La vie de Plotin,*" in L. Brisson, M. O. Goulet-Cazé, and D. O'Brien, *Porphyre: La vie de Plotin* (Paris, 1982), 245–46; see also C. Lacombrade, *Synésios de Cyrène: Hellène et chrétien* (Paris, 1951), 44; Rist, *Hypatia,* 220–21; Marrou, "Sinesio di Cirene," 148. Skepticism concerning the account of Suidas has been expressed in Praechter, "Hypatia," col. 243. The quotation from Synesius (Δήμῳ γὰρ δὴ φιλοσοφίᾳ τί πρὸς ἄλληλα?) is taken from *Ep.* 105, 92–93 = p. 276 Garzya. For a study of the church's relationship with the last Cynic speakers, see P. de Labriolle, *La réaction païenne: Etude sur la polémique antichrétienne du Iᵉʳ au VIIᵉ siècle* (Paris, 1934), 83–87.

Concerning the image of Hypatia in nineteenth-century historiography, see R. Hoche, "Hypatia, die Tochter Theons," *Philologus* 15 (1860): 435–74. See also H. Ligier, "De Hypatia philosopha et eclectismi alexandrini fine" (diss., Dijon, 1879); W. A. Meyer, *Hypatia von Alexandria: Ein Beitrag zur Geschichte des Neuplatonismus* (Heidelberg, 1886). See also J. C. Wernsdorf, "Dissertationes academicae 1–4 de Hypatia philosopha Alexandrina" (Wittenberg, 1747–48), and S. Wolf, "Hypatia die Philosophin von Alexandrien" (Program, Vienna [Czernowitz], 1879). On the saint's role as civic consultant, see P. Brown, "The Rise and Function of the Holy Man in Late Antiquity," in his book *Society and the Holy in Late Antiquity* (Berkeley, 1982); J. Seiber, "Early Byzantine Urban Saints," *British Archaeological Reports: Supplementary Series* 37 (London, 1977).

Synesius, Hypatia, and "Philosophia"

The quotation from Damascius is taken from *Vita Isidori*, fr. 164 (p. 218 Zintzen) = Photius, *Bibliothèque*, vol. 6, ed. R. Henry, 38, 14. Mention of Theon's inscription (Ἐκδόσεως παραγνωσθείσης τῇ φιλοσόφῳ θυγατρί μου Ὑπατίᾳ) may be found in *Commentaires de Pappus et de Théon d'Alexandrie sur l'Almageste*, vol. 3, ed. A. Rome (Vatican City, 1943), 807, 4–5.

For a discussion of Hypatia's role as editor of the *Almagest* (but not of the comment itself as previously suggested), see Al. Cameron, "Isidore of Myletus and Hypatia: On the Editing of Mathematical Texts," *Greek, Roman, and Byzantine Studies* 31 (1990): 103–87. This article rejects and rectifies the theories expressed by Rome, *Commentaires*, cxvii–cxxi; by A. Tihon, in *Le "Grand commentaire" de Théon d'Alexandrie aux Tables faciles de Ptolémée*, Studi e Testi no. 315, vol. 1, ed. T. Mogenet and A. Tihon (Vatican City, 1985), in part. p. 221; and by W. Knorr, *Textual Studies in Ancient and Mediaeval Geometry* (Boston, 1989), 756. For a study of Hypatia's other works and a partial discussion of the interpretation of the passage in Suidas (taken from Hesychius of Miletus) mentioned in the *Astronomical Canon*, see Tannery, "L'article de Suidas sur Hypatie," 199. For a rather far-fetched theory, see Beretta, *Ipazia d'Alessandria*. The author considers the "ἀστρονομικὸς κανών" mentioned in the sources as an original work by Hypatia in which she made "accessible to men and women of her time" a "new scientific knowledge," originating from her supposed "inspired intuition" in "combining the study and methods discussed in Apollonius's *Conics* with the studies and methods of Diophantine arithmetic." Thanks to this idea, Hypatia supposedly anticipated Descartes by a thousand years. Knowledge of this work did not survive to modern times because she was murdered, which led to the "dispersion of the school associated with her."

Synesius discusses the machines invented by Hypatia in *Ep.* 15 = pp. 100–102 Garzya and in *Discourse on Gifts* 4 = p. 544 Garzya; see also Lacombrade, *Synésios de Cyrène*, 42–43. The quotations which follow are taken from P. Tannery, "Sur la religion des derniers mathématiciens de l'Antiquité," *Annales de Philosophie Chrétienne* 34 (1896), reprinted as *Mémoires scientifiques*, vol. 2, *Sciences exactes dans l'antiquité: 1883–1898* (Paris, 1912), 527–38; from Evrard, "A quel titre," 69 (see Lacombrade, *Synésios de Cyrène*, 49–50); from Synesius, *Works*, Introduction, 32. An interesting comparison of Hypatia's school with those of Origen and Heracleas appears in Rist, *Hypatia*, 218. Concerning Hypatia's intellectual circle, see the article by M. Dzielska in *Paganism in the Later Roman Empire and in Byzantium* (Kraków, 1991), 45–60; and in Dzielska, *Hypatia z Aleksandrii* (Kraków, 1993), which appeared just as the original edition of this book was going to press. Concerning the "religious neutrality" of Hypatia's teachings, see Marrou, "Sinesio di Cirene," 151; and J. Bregman, *Synesius of Cyrene: Philosopher-Bishop* (Berkeley, Los Angeles, and London, 1982), 38.

Concerning Synesius's election as bishop, see J. H. W. G. Liebeschütz, "Why Did Synesius Become Bishop of Ptolemais?" *Byzantion* 56 (1986): 180–95. The quotations are taken from *Ep.* 137, 7–8 (to Herculianus) = p. 330 Garzya; from *Ep.* 136, 15–20 (to his brother) = p. 330 Garzya; from *Ep.* 5, 262–64 (to his brother) = p. 90 Garzya; from *Discourse on Gifts* (to Peonius), par. 4 = p. 546 Garzya; from *Ep.* 16, 2–3 (to Hypatia) = p. 102 Garzya; from *Ep.* 154, 86 (to Hypatia) = p. 374 Garzya; from *Ep.* 10, 1 and 11 (to Hypatia) = pp. 94–96 Garzya; and from *Ep.* 81, 13–14 (to Hypatia) = p. 230 Garzya; from *Ep.*124, 1–2 (to Hypatia) = p.302 Garzya (Εἰ δὲ θανόντων περ καταλήθοντ᾽ εἰν ἀίδαο, / αὐτὰρ ἐγὼ κἀκεῖ τῆς φίλης Ὑπατίας μεμνήσομαι: *Nostoi*, fr. 6 Allen); from *Ep.* 16, 14–15 (to Hypatia) = p. 102 Garzya. For an interpretation of several passages from these epistles, see J. Vogt, "Das unverletzliche Gut: Synesios und Hypatia" in Vogt, *Begegnung mit Synesios, dem Philosophen, Priester und Feldherrn: Gesammelte Beiträge* (Darmstadt, 1985), 84–91.

The alchemy tract πρὸς Διόσκορον was first attributed to Synesius of Cyrene at the end of the nineteenth century: see M. Berthelot and C. E. Ruelle, *Collection des anciens alchimistes grecs*, vol. 2 (Paris, 1887), 56–69; for specific mention of the manuscript, see vol. 1, p. 199. Synesius discusses sacred geometry in *Epp.* 93 and 131; the *tetraktys* is discussed in *Epp.* 143 and 154; references to esoteric initiation may be found in *Epp.* 143 and 157. The statements concerning *Dion* and *On Dreams* are taken from *Ep.* 154, 68–75 and 95–99 = pp. 374–76 Garzya, which Synesius sent to Hypatia before publishing these two works. The quotation from the Chaldean oracles, taken from the latter (par. 7 = p. 570 Garzya), corresponds to fr. 163 of the Des Places edition (*Oracles chaldaïques* [Paris: Les Belles Lettres, 1971], 106). The following quotation is taken from Rist, *Hypatia*, 216.

The ancient sources referring to Theon of Alexandria's works include Suidas Θ 205 (vol.2, p. 702 Adler), and Malalas, *Chronographia* 13.5.15, in Hussey p. 343. For a study of the Commentaries on Ptolemy, see Rome, *Commentaires de Pappus et de Théon*, vol. 2, lxxxii–lxxxvi; Mogenet and Tihon, *Le "Grand commentaire";* A. Tihon, ed. and trans., *Le "Petit commentaire" de Théon d'Alexandrie aux Tables faciles de Ptolémée*, Studi e Testi, no. 282 (Vatican City, 1978). Concerning the dubious attribution to Theon of an astrological poem included as part of the hermetic writings collected in the *Greek Anthology,* see G. Fowden, *The Egyptian Hermes* (Cambridge, 1986), 178 n. It is also very unlikely that

Theon was the author of a commentary on Aratus's *Phenomena* (see E. Maass, ed., *Commentariorum in Aratum reliquiae* [Berlin, 1898; reprint, 1958], 146–51).

Philostorgius's comments may be found in *Ecclesiastica historia* 8.9, p. 111, 3–5 Bidez (here Photius concurs in several points with the passage in Suidas we have already mentioned). For a discussion of the reasons that might have led the fifth-century historian to describe the philosopher in the terms he uses, see Bidez, *Einleitung,* cix–cx. Lacombrade suggests that Hypatia's teachings may have leaned toward the esoteric in *Synésios de Cyrène,* 49ff; concerning the relationship that may have existed between Synesius and Hypatia, see also Bregman, *Synesius of Cyrene,* 28; the theory that astrology and divination were still being taught in the school of mathematics in Alexandria in Hypatia's time has been suggested by M. Kline, among others, in his book on the history of mathematical thought, *Mathematical Thought from Ancient to Modern Times,* vol. 1 (New York, 1990). The passage from Synesius dealing with astronomy was taken from *Discourse on Gifts,* par. 4 = p. 544 Garzya. Rougé's remark is taken from "La politique de Cyrille d'Alexandrie," 495.

References to women philosophers mentioned in ancient sources were catalogued by J. C. Wolf, *Mulierum Graecarum, quae oratione prosa usae sunt, fragmenta et elogia Graece et Latine.... Catalogus foeminarum sapientia artibus scriptisve apud Graecos Romanos aliasque gentes olim illustrium* (London, 1739). The quotation from L. Cracco Ruggini is from "La donna e il sacro tra paganesimo e cristianesimo," in *La donna nel mondo antico: Atti del II Convegno Nazionale di Studi, Turin, 18, 19, 20 Aprile 1988,* ed. R. Uglione (Turin, 1989), 275. On the subject of theurgic *diadoché* transmitted only by women, see Marino in *Vita Procli* (ed. J. F. Boissonade) in the appendix of the Cobet edition of Diogene Laerzio (Paris, 1862), 165: Proclus supposedly received his initiation into the Chaldean rites from Asclepigenia, Plutarch's daughter. Theano's and Hypatia's names are linked in Psellus's "Epitaph for his mother": K. N. Sathas, *Mesaionike Bibliotheke,* vol. 5 (Venice and Paris, 1876; reprint, Athens, 1972), 59ff. (καὶ ὁπόσα καὶ τὸ θῆλυ ἦσαν Σιβύλλαι, τε καὶ Σαπφὼ ἡ μουσοποιός, Θεανώ τε καὶ ἡ Αἰγυπτία σοφή) Concerning Eudoxia, see Nicephorus Gregoras, *Byzantina Historia,* vol. 1, ed. L. Schopen (Bonn, 1824) 8.3.2–3, p. 294.

Hypatia's Martyrdom

For a study of Hypatia's charismatic role, her idealized image, and its political-social implications in the late Roman empire, see Cracco Ruggini, *La donna e il sacro,* 255–56 et al.; and Ruggini, "Juridical Status and Historical Role of Women in Roman Patriarchal Society," *Klio* 71, no. 2 (1989): 604–19; for a discussion of the characteristics of the late-antique *virgo,* see F. E. Consolino, "Dagli 'exempla' ad un esempio di comportamento cristiano: Il 'De exhortatione virginitatis' di Ambrogio," *Rivista Storica Italiana* 94/2 (1982): 462–63. On the Acts of Martyrs as a genre, see G. Lanata, *Gli atti dei martiri come documenti processuali* (Milan: Giuffrè, 1973); the stereotypes appearing in texts on martyrs and their political intentions have been treated by S. Ronchey, "Gli atti dei martiri tra politica e letteratura," in *Storia di Roma* 3/2 (Turin: Einaudi, 1993), 781–

825; and in *Indagine sul martirio di San Policarpo* (Rome: Istituto Storico Italiano per il Medio Evo, 1990).

For a feminist reading of Hypatia's story, see M. Alic, *Hypatia's Heritage: A History of Women in Science from Antiquity through the Nineteenth Century* (Boston: Beacon Press, 1986); see also Beretta, *Ipazia d'Alessandria,* which seems more a *rêverie* than a scientific essay. Hypatia has also inspired I. Morici, in *Conversazioni con Ipazia* (Milan: Nuove Edizioni, 1985). See also Hypatia, ed., *Quattro giovedì e un venerdì per la filosofia* (Milan, 1988); and *Autorità scientifica autorità femminile* (Rome, 1992).

The passage from Marrou was taken from "Sinesio di Cirene," 155–57. For the most recent and authoritative discussion of Cyril's politics, see "La politique de Cyrille d'Alexandrie," especially pp. 489–90 and 502–3.

Chapter Nine

N. B. The *Life of Melania* has been preserved in both a Greek and a Latin version. Today scholars generally agree that the original version was in Greek. Except for a few references flagged by the letter L, the passages quoted in the text are all taken from the Greek version.

The references listed below are limited to studies necessary for a first approach and to the sources that were used in the preparation of this essay.

Editions and translations of the *Life of Melania:* Edition of the Greek and Latin text, Italian translation of the Greek text with commentary by M. Rampolla Del Tindaro, *Santa Melania Giuniore senatrice romana* (Rome, 1905). Edition of the Greek text with French translation and commentary by D. Gorce, "Vie de Sainte Melanie," *Sources Chrétiennes* 90 (Paris, 1962). Edition of the Greek text with English translation, commentary by Elizabeth A. Clark, *Life of Melania the Younger* (New York, 1984); concerning the earlier dating of the Greek version compared to the Latin one, see pp. 10 ff. On the manuscript tradition in general see J. E. Salisbury and R. Wojtowicz, "The Life of Melania the Younger: A Partial Reevaluation of the Manuscript Tradition," *Manuscripta* 33 (1989): 137–44.

For hagiography and biography, see Sofia Boesch Gajano, "Le metamorfosi del racconto," in G. Cavallo, P. Fedeli, and A. Giardina, eds., *Lo spazio letterario di Roma antica,* vol. 3 (Rome, 1990), 217–43.

Concerning women mystics, marriage, and sexuality in late antiquity, see Elena Giannarelli, *La tipologia femminile nella biografia e nella autobiografia cristiana del IV secolo* (Rome, 1980); Aline Rousselle, *Porneia: De la maitrîse du corps à la privation sensorielle, IIIe–IVe siècles de l'ère chrétienne* (Paris, 1983); Franca Ela Consolino, "Modelli di comportamento e modi di santificazione per l'aristocrazia femminile d'Occidente," in A. Giardina, ed., *Società romana e impero tardoantico,* vol. 1 (Rome and Bari, 1986), 273–306, 684–99; Elizabeth A. Clark, *Jerome, Chrysostom, and Friends* (New York and Toronto, 1979); Elizabeth A. Clark, *Ascetic Piety and Women's Faith: Essays on Late Ancient Chris-*

tianity (Lewiston and Toronto, 1986); Elizabeth A. Clark, "Ideology, History, and the Construction of 'Woman' in Late Ancient Christianity" Journal of Early Christian Studies 2 (1994): 155–84; Rita Lizzi, "Una società esortata all'ascetismo: Misure legislative e motivazioni economiche nel IV–V secolo d. C., *Studi storici* 30 (1989): 129–53; P. Brown, *The Body and Society: Men, Women, and Sexual Renunciation in Early Christianity* (New York, 1988). See also Angeliki E. Laiou, ed., *Consent and Coercion to Sex and Marriage in Ancient and Medieval Societies* (Washington, 1993).

For biographical information concerning Melania and her *gens,* see A. H. M. Jones, J. R. Martindale, and J. Morris, *The Prosopography of the Later Roman Empire,* vol. 1 (Cambridge, 1971), 592f.

On Melania the Elder see: F. X. Murphy, "Melania the Elder. A Biographical Note," *Traditio* 5 (1947): 59–77.

On the aristocracy of the West during the fourth and fifth centuries, see S. Mazzarino, *Antico, tardoantico ed èra costantiniana,* vol. 1 (Bari, 1974).

Concerning aristocratic families and their patrimonies in late antiquity see D. Vera, "Forme e funzioni della rendita fondiaria nella tarda antichità," in *Società romana e impero tardoantico,* vol. 1, 367–447, 723–60.

For a discussion of Melania's and Pinian's fortune, see P. Allard, "Une grande fortune romaine au Vᵉ siècle," *Revue des questions historiques* 81 (1907): 5–30.

On their style of charity, see A. Giardina, "Carità eversiva: Le donazioni di Melania la Giovane e gli equilibri della società tardoromana," *Studi storici* 29 (1988): 127–42. See also G. A. Cecconi, "Un evergete mancato: Piniano a Ippona," *Athenaeum* 66 (1988): 371–89.

On the subject of slaves refusing their freedom, see A. Giardina, "Lavoro e storia sociale: Antagonismi e alleanze dall'ellenismo al tardoantico," *Opus* 1 (1982): 5.

Concerning journeys to the Holy Land, see F. Parente, "La conoscenza della Terra Santa come esperienza religiosa dell'Occidente cristiano dal IV secolo alle Crociate," in *Popoli e paesi nella cultura altomedievale. Settimane di Studio del Centro italiano di Studi sull'Alto Medioevo, XXIX* (Spoleto, 1983), 231–316; E. D. Hunt, *Holy Land Pilgrimage in the Later Roman Empire, A.D. 312–460* (Oxford, 1984); "Gaul and the Holy Land in the Early Fifth Century," in J. Drinkwater and H. Elton, eds., *Fifth-Century Gaul: A Crisis of Identity* (Cambridge, 1992), 264–74; P. Maraval, *Lieux Saints et pèlerinages d'Orient: Histoire et géographie des origines à la conquête arabe* (Paris, 1985).

For a discussion of burial in holy places, see P. Brown, *The Cult of the Saints* (Chicago, 1981).

Concerning the other women of later antiquity discussed in this essay, see, for Melania the Elder: Paulinus of Nola *Epistulae* 29, in *Corpus Scriptorum Ecclesiasticorum Latinorum* 28; Palladius, *Historia Lausiaca,* introduction by Christine Mohrmann, critical text and commentary by G. J. M. Bartelink, trans. M. Barchiesi (Milan: Fondazione Lorenzo Valla, 1974). For Paula, see Jerome, *Epistle* 108 (the so-called *Epitaphium sanctae Paulae*). This text may now be found in *Vita di Martino, Vita di Ilarione, In memoria di Paola,* introduction by

Christine Mohrmann, critical text and commentary by A. A. R. Bastiaensen and J. W. Smit, trans. L. Canali and C. Moreschini (Milan: Fondazione Lorenzo Valla, 1975). For Macrina, see Gregory of Nyssa, "Vie de Sainte Macrine," ed. P. Maraval, *Sources Chrétiennes* 178 (Paris, 1971). For Olympias, see John Chrysostom, "Lettres à Olympias," 2d ed., also including the "Vie anonyme d'Olympias," ed. Anne-Marie Malingrey, *Sources Chrétiennes,* 13 bis (Paris, 1968).

Index